D0893324

THE NEW INTERNATIONAL
ECONOMIC ORDER:
A U.S. RESPONSE

UNA-USA Policy Studies Book Series

The United Nations Association of the USA is a private, nonprofit organization dedicated to broadening public understanding of the activities of the United Nations and other multilateral institutions. Through its nationwide membership and network of affiliated national organizations, UNA-USA conducts a broad range of programs to inform and involve the public in foreign affairs issues.

The UNA-USA Policy Studies Program conducts projects involving research and analysis of a wide spectrum of policy issues of concern to the international community. The Program brings together panels of interested and knowledgeable Americans to study and make recommendations on specific problems of US foreign policy and multilateral activities. As part of this process, a number of papers are commissioned from leading specialists.

The UNA-USA Policy Studies Book Series contains books based on rewritten and edited collections of some of these papers. UNA-USA is responsible for the choice of the subject areas and the decision to publish the volumes, but the responsibility for the content of the papers and for opinions expressed in them rests with the individual authors and editors.

Already published:
Disaster Assistance: Appraisal, Reform and New Approaches, edited by Lynn H. Stephens and Stephen Green.

THE NEW INTERNATIONAL ECONOMIC ORDER: A U.S. RESPONSE

Edited by
David B. H. Denoon

New York · New York University Press · 1979

WILLIAM MADISON RANDALL LIBRARY UNC AT WILMINGTON

Copyright © 1979 by UNA-USA

Library of Congress Cataloging in Publication Data
Main entry under title:

The New international economic order.

  (UNA-USA policy studies book series)
  Includes biographical references.
  1. International economic relations—Addresses,
essays, lectures. 2. United States—Foreign economic
relations—Addresses, essays, lectures. I. Denoon,
David. II. Series: United Nations Association of the
United States of America. UNA-USA policy studies book
series.
HF1411.N429   382.1'0973   79-1997
ISBN 0-8147-1769-1
     0-8147-1770-5 pbk.

Manufactured in the United States of America

HF1411
.N429

FOREWORD

This volume is a response to the turmoil created in U.S. economic policy during the early 1970s by the increases in Organization of Petroleum Exporting Country (OPEC) oil prices and the Less Developed Country (LDC) demands for a reshaping of the entire international economic system. The unanimity and vehemence of the LDC claims took the U.S. Government by surprise. Although ultimately the United States responded with some interesting counter-proposals, there had been no long-run planning for alternative means of dealing with the "North-South" issues. More importantly, the American public and its opinion leaders had insufficient background on these issues to provide an appropriate political setting from which a balanced assessment of U.S. policy choices could be made.

This left the U.S. Government in a difficult position because the public was besieged with a rash of hasty and, in many cases, counter-productive ideas—making it hard to form a coalition of support for a constructive approach to the new circumstances. By 1976, the Sixth and Seventh Special Sessions of the U.N. General Assembly had taken place and the Economic Charter of the Rights and Duties of States had been passed; and yet, there was still little public understanding of the issues in the North-South negotiations. At this time, the United Nations Association of the U.S.A. (UNA-USA) approached me with an intriguing idea. They asked if I would be willing to chair a group of labor, business, agricultural, and academic leaders in a study of North-South economic questions. The intent, as we initially discussed

201718

it, was for the group to evaluate a broad range of competing claims raised by the LDCs and to make policy recommendations to both the U.S. Government and the international community on particularly promising proposals. As we refined the concept, our informal working group (Cyrus Vance, I. W. Abel, Robert Roosa, and Leonard Woodcock) became the Steering Committee; and we named the enterprise: the UNA Economic Policy Council. We decided on two central objectives:

a) focusing on those proposals for restructuring the international economic system which yield adequate joint gains for both the Developed and Developing countries, and

b) formulating a package of recommendations which would respond to the essential challenges to the present system, and yet be sufficiently pragmatic to be of use to the U.S. Congress and Executive Branch.

The development of the Economic Policy Council (EPC) proceeded in several stages. With the help of Robert Ratner, now President of UNA-USA, and Jacob Clayman, now President of the Industrial Union Department of the AFL-CIO, we contacted a broad range of outstanding individuals who could effectively represent the divergent views in the American business, labor, research, and farm communities. We received a very strong response, making it possible for us to form three separate panels to address distinct parts of the North-South debates.

To start the analytic work we asked David Denoon, who had been teaching a graduate course on the New International Economic Order, at New York University, to identify a list of feasible and lively policy topics for the EPC to consider. We assembled the entire Economic Policy Council for our first plenary session in September 1976. At that time, we discussed the potential capabilities of the EPC and reaffirmed the hopes of the Steering Committee that the group could play a unique role in intermediating between the international community and U.S. policymakers. From the agenda of proposed topics, we agreed to concentrate on three policy areas: Trade, Commodity Management, and Capital Flow questions. We also decided to operate in a relatively decentralized manner by having each topic area covered by a panel which met independently until it had results to report to a Council Plenary session.

Chairman were chosen for each panel, and we were very fortunate in those who agreed to serve. Sol Chaikin, President of the International Ladies Garment Workers Union, led the Trade group; Jack Parker, Vice Chairman of General Electric, headed up the Commodity Management review; and Gaylord Freeman, Honorary Chairman of The First National Bank of Chicago, chaired the Capital Flow panel. As the panels met during the fall of 1976 and winter of 1977, the members decided on the questions they felt were most important to research. At this point, we added support staff by choosing a coordinator for each panel.

It was in the numerous discussions between the Council members, the Panel Coordinators, and the Steering Committee that the more detailed plans for each group evolved. We agreed that the EPC should first publish its policy recommendations, but that it would be useful as well for the public to see the best of the technical papers which provided background for our discussions.

We, then, asked David Denoon to plan the overall research for the project and write the scope of work for each paper in a way that would assist our policy review process and ultimately lead to papers that could be chapters in an integrated volume. Although individual EPC members may not necessarily agree with all the conclusions in these chapters, we were quite pleased with the overall results. The first chapter gives some historical background on the New International Economic Order and sets the geo-political context for U.S. policy-making. Then, by having the studies done in a parallel fashion, each chapter states the significance of the topic area for the U.S. economy, outlines the major proposals under consideration in international fora, and evaluates the impact inside the United States of the preferable

---

* For a list of the Council members through 1978, please see Annex I to this volume.

options. We, therefore, have a cohesive set of studies that allows the reader to scan very divergent sectors and assess alternative responses.

We, thus, see this volume as the technical sequel to the policy recommendations published last June by the UNA-USA titled, *The Global Economic Challenge: Volume I.* Since that time, the EPC has taken on three new panel topics (Trade Rules in the 1980s, Technology Transfer, and Energy & Jobs); and we hope to continue to contribute to the international economic policy debates in this manner.

Although, at the time of this writing, there is once again considerable turmoil in the Mideast and great concern about the world economic system, the American public is likely to take only a vacillating interest in North-South affairs until the full significance of our economic links to the LDCs is appreciated. We hope this UNA effort will not only lead to a more consistent U.S. strategy toward the LDCs, but that the joint labor/business/agriculture/academic format that we have employed will be tried by other groups as well.

Finally, in addition to thanking all of those individuals mentioned above, I would like to extend my appreciation to each member of the Economic Policy Council and the UNA staff for their splendid effort and cooperation.

> Robert O. Anderson
> Chairman, ARCO, Inc.
> Chairman, UNA Economic Policy Council

March 1979

PREFACE

This book is an attempt to look at the issues raised by the New International Economic Order debates. The approach taken is to present the findings in a manner that would be of use to an American policy-maker who needs a balanced, quantitative assessment of alternative strategies for dealing with the post-1973 economic challenges.

In the *Foreword* above, Robert O. Anderson covers the genesis of the United Nation's Association Economic Policy Council (EPC) and discusses the basic objectives agreed upon for the group. The EPC goal of providing a forum where representatives from a broad range of American institutions could analyze the North-South dialogue is a unique and very valuable one.

The rationale for this book is straight-forward. Most of the literature on the New International Economic Order (NIEO) is either predominantly ideological or overly technical. The ideological approach (either pro or con) is useful in that it heightens awareness of the issues involved, but it rarely provides feasible policy choices, and often tends to polarize views on the topic. Many of the technical studies have focused on particular, narrow Less Developed Country (LDC) needs; though this research is essential for the development of an informed dialogue, it does not provide a pragmatic framework for Americans to use in approaching the NIEO issues. Despite the technical detail presented in these chapters, each is clearly written and should be accessible to policy-makers, the interested public, as well as scholars and graduate students.

These studies do not present any single schema for addressing the world's development and international economic reorganization needs. However, the structure of the book follows the format of the Economic Policy Council project in dividing the topics into Trade, Commodity Management, and Capital Flow issues. Moreover, there are several basic themes which cut across all the chapters:

1) the recognition that substantial joint gains are available to both the Developed and Developing countries through agreements and accommodations which will permit greater trade and specialization;

2) economists have been preoccupied during the last three decades with bringing about transformation in the LDC economies, but they now must increasingly look at means for accelerating change and adjustment in the Developed countries if continuing gains from trade are to be achieved;

3) the world economic system needs stability and predictability if investors are to continue providing the resources for greater specialization;

4) the integration of the world economy has made each country's domestic performance increasingly linked to the performance of other nations; this means that there are rising tangible rewards for cooperation, not just on individual commodities or trade agreements, but in the measurably more difficult area of synchronizing macroeconomic policy.

A quick look at these four themes shows that they exhibit neither the certainty nor the unilateral "concessionary" character which is the hallmark of the NIEO demands. The "joint gains" and "linked performance" arguments reflect more than just an American perspective, however. The NIEO proposals have a fundamental flaw, though. If accepted, they might well lead to a major redistribution of world income, but they are relatively static in nature and do not provide the incentives necessary for the continuing evolution of an increasingly integrated world economy.

In the chapters on TRADE, *Baldwin, Richardson, and Mutti* identify adjustment within the Developed countries and world income redistribution as the two problems most critical for the United States in the 1980s. Their overview of trade policy questions is relatively optimistic about useful modifications to the mechanics of the present trading system (through exchange rate movements and reductions in non-tariff barriers), but cautions that the rate of future growth in trade depends upon finding politically acceptable means for easing adjustment to trade-induced change. *Stern, Deardorff, and Greene* use their elaborate general equilibrium model to estimate the price, income, and employment effects of various tariff reduction and harmonization proposals that might have been tried in the Tokyo Round trade negotiations. Although there are very minor net job losses in the United States from the tariff reductions, the most interesting results are: the price reductions which occur in both importing and exporting industries, and the employment and income shifts which favor the growth of traded-goods sectors. *Neumann* takes the Stern, Deardorff and Greene estimates of employment shifts, and calculates the cost of differing adjustment assistance programs which might be devised to deal with those workers who don't find new jobs. The most significant conclusion from all three trade studies, however, is that benefits from reduced tariffs and increased trade far outweigh the costs and could easily be handled with effective government programs. Additionally, it is important to note that the job displacement from trade-related reasons is a small percentage of the total annual U.S. job changes which result from other processes like technological change and shifts in consumer demand.

The case studies on COMMODITY MANAGEMENT were specifically chosen to illustrate the variety in market characteristics of internationally traded commodities. *Cochrane* analyzes the peculiarities of the grains markets and shows what large, random elements are introduced by weather variations and political decisions on "adequate stocks." Although there is no universally perceived right to have access to minerals, there is a growing consensus that the world community should not countenance starvation. As four countries (the United States, Canada, Australia, and Argentina) are the globe's major grain exporters, they face particular pressures during times of shortages. The solution is clearly to have both exporters and importers share in the cost of storing adequate supplies. *Smith* reviews the history of the International Tin Agreement, and explains why it has had only the most minimal effect on moderating fluctuations in tin prices. Here, unlike grains, the major exporters (Malaysia, Bolivia, and Indonesia) are all LDCs and the financial resources necessary to run an effective Tin Agreement are not staggering; what is lacking is sufficient concern to mobilize the effort. *Woods* surveys the bauxite market and shows, not withstanding some poorly researched claims to the contrary, that there is very little likelihood the bauxite exporters will be able to drastically raise their prices again (in real terms) as they did in 1974. There are simply too many alternative sources for aluminum, and these sources are widely distributed on the earth's surface—so a more intransigent International Bauxite Association seems implausible. These commodity studies, thus, document how ill-advised it may be to make sweeping claims about "commodity power."

The CAPITAL FLOW chapters deal with another area which appeared to be in crisis in the post-1973 era. *Long and Venerosa* have put together a remarkable data series by going substantially beyond any previously published sources to estimate LDC debt. Their figures include not only public and publically guaranteed debt, but private short and medium-term obligations as well. It is the soaring growth of the private debt in the 1970s which has raised spectres of a "debt catastrophe." Interestingly, however, private credit rationing has been generally prudent, and the greatest amount of debt has been accumulated by the "better credit" countries whose export proceeds are growing rapidly. Nevertheless, the issue warrants close monitoring as loan maturities have shortened and interest rates have risen in the last two years. *Michalopoulos* examines the rapidly changing world debt profile and proposes a number of alternative means for avoiding crises if particular classes of borrowers run into payments difficulties. The NIEO demand for a general debt moratorium has been dismissed by all but nearly-bankrupt borrowers. Yet, there are clear advantages in expanding current IMF facilities to permit smoother refinancing for some borrowers. Also, there must be public decisions on how to handle the debt accumulated by the world's poorest countries.

In sum, these chapters illustrate that the NIEO has raised some very worthwhile questions; and fortunately, on balance, there are pragmatic American responses that should yield adequate joint gains for successful North-South negotiations. What remains to be done now is to do further quantitative evaluations of the costs and benefits involved in these various proposals and integrate them with a broader U.S. geo-political strategy.

*　*　*　*

My acknowledgements in this effort are substantial. As in any group project, there were a large number of individuals concerned; and yet, what distinguished this activity was the remarkable level of cooperation which developed among those associated with the Economic Policy Council. It was, thus, a distinct pleasure to work with those involved in the EPC activities.

My greatest appreciation goes to Robert O. Anderson and Robert M. Ratner. Without their energy, enthusiasm, and continued assistance throughout the project, the management and coordination of the EPC's multifaceted activities would have been impossible. I am also especially grateful to Robert V. Roosa, Cyrus Vance, I.W. Abel, Jacob Clayman, and Colin Gonze, who were consistently available with thoughtful comments and advice during the summer of 1976, as the project took shape. I would also like to thank Peter Peterson, Stanley Ruttenberg, and James Grant who cooperated on the "Overview Statement" in the first EPC report. Their perspectives were very useful in helping the Council shape its approach to the competing claims about the preferable evolution of the international economic system.

Special regards also go to Sol Chaikin, Jack Parker, and

Gaylord Freeman, who chaired the EPC's three panels. They provided a continuing variety of questions, suggestions, and encouragement as we sought to analyze the disparate problems before us. Each of the panel coordinators, M.I. Nadiri, Vincent Ferraro, and Robert Hawkins, also played an essential role in organizing the panel meetings and discussion, and continuing intellectual stimulation.

Robert M. Seifman, my successor as Director of EPC, played an essential role, since he entered the project just as the final meetings were taking place on the EPC's policy recommendations; he not only ably completed the taxing job of editing our policy recommendations, but served as a superb critic as the manuscripts for this book evolved. Special thanks also go to Geraldine Caruana and Jane Pascale for their outstanding administrative and secretarial support throughout the project and preparation of the volume.

Arthur Day, Alan Tonelson, Edward Luck, and Joel Johnson showed a continuing interest in the project and provided a variety of interesting and useful comments as the work proceeded. Elmore Jackson provided some particularly worthwhile suggestions on how to make the optimal use of the resources of such a diverse group as the EPC.

In an edited volume, the quality ultimately depends upon the authors. I want to thank each of them for outstanding cooperation, and I believe additional appreciation will come in the reception that this volume receives. Finally, I would like to thank Despina Papazaglou for her continuing encouragement and assistance in the editing and production of the manuscript.

David B. H. Denoon
Vice President for
Policy Analysis
Export-Import Bank of the United States

March 1979

CONTENTS

Part I

THE SETTING

Chapter 1

FACING THE NEW INTERNATIONAL ECONOMIC ORDER

DAVID B. H. DENOON *

Assistant Professor of Politics & Economics
New York University

I. WHAT IS THE NEW INTERNATIONAL ECONOMIC ORDER ABOUT?

At the close of the Sixth Special Session of the United Nations General Assembly, the majority of delegates present enthusiastically supported the resolutions calling for the establishment of a New International Economic Order (NIEO).[1] It was an initiative, like many at the UN, which called for sweeping and wrenching changes of international political and economic relations. Not surprisingly, like many other expressions of intent at the UN, the NIEO declaration failed to provide either a blueprint for specific action or the mechanism for actually proceeding. Yet it would be a fundamental mistake to regard the call for

* Professor Denoon was on leave from New York University during 1978–79, serving in the federal government as Vice-President for Policy Analysis of the Export-Import Bank of the United States.

3

the NIEO as a trivial event. The date was May 1974, and the industrial world was still stunned by the effectiveness of the Organization of Petroleum Exporting Countries (OPEC) oil price increases. It looked to many observers as if the era of inexpensive raw materials was over and that the bulk of the low-income countries had found new, powerful allies in the oil producers. The tables in the grand game of world power seemed to have shifted irrevocably. Four years later, after thousands of man-hours of negotiation over policy proposals and countless assessments of North-South economic relations, the NIEO has clearly lost its luster but not its significance.

How can we evaluate the impact of the NIEO debates on the United States?

At the first level of analysis, the NIEO is a series of specific proposals for reorganizing the character of world economic relations. By stabilizing and raising raw materials prices, by providing increased tariff preferences to the less developed countries (LDCs), by expanding aid and waiving debt payments, by making more technology available at lower prices, and by allowing host countries to nationalize foreign assets on terms decided by their own judicial systems, the Group of 77[2] hoped to use the international system for their own internal development needs. Thus, it is essential to start with examining the predominantly economic aspects of the NIEO. In these terms, the NIEO is concerned with the world distribution of wealth and income. The Group of 77 and its theoreticians argued vehemently that the structure of international trade and monetary relations was biased against the low-income countries and that the purpose of changing the system was to get it to yield an adequate flow of benefits.

At the second level, the NIEO is concerned with the world distribution of power. For the political elites of the LDCs, the arguments of Neo-Classical economics are inherently frustrating because they ascribe the outcomes of much economic interaction to that ineluctable force, the market. Though a large part of twentieth-century economics deals with market imperfections and how to compensate for them, most LDC political leaders are unwilling on either a personal level or as a matter of policymaking to acknowledge the advantages of designing market-oriented systems for producing and distributing goods. Systems that are too open could limit the control over resources the elites possess, and it is increased control that these leaders seek. If the international economic system is producing inadequate results, then these leaders favor exerting political control.

Here it is important to realize that most of the LDC representatives to UN forums were raised in very traditional environments and find that the "uncertainty of the market" offends their sensibilities. The Marxists find the present international economic relationships predatory, while many of the non-Marxists are bothered by the lack of morality in a system where there is no "just price" for their commodities. We thus have the not unusual process of elites taking what appears to be a populist stance and using political pressure to achieve a different distribution of power than would have occurred if the market alone operated.

For those who look at the NIEO predominantly from this viewpoint, the essential readjustments that must come are in the political and psychological areas. To many who stress that the NIEO is a means for obtaining greater control over world decision-making, improved personal and national esteem may be just as critical as increased resource flows.

At the most fundamental level, however, the NIEO debate is about *restructuring* the international economic system. The rhetoric in the name NIEO would be more than verbiage if the basic proposals were implemented. If the international economic system became an explicitly agreed mechanism for international redistribution of income, it would be as fundamental a change in structure as occurred with the establishment of the Bretton Woods system or the shift from mercantilism to liberal trade in the nineteenth century.

From this "systems perspective," the focus of attention is on economic results; but the political and psychological elements of the present system that have contributed to the LDC resentment need to be dealt with simultaneously—so that an overall system can develop that is perceived as legitimate by an increasing number and range of actors. However, even if one accepts the premise that the NIEO is about systems restructuring, there is a critical difference beteen those who advocate: (1) a major one-time reorganization, or (2) a gradual evolution toward a new system through taking a planned series of marginal steps.

The basic theme in this chapter is that the NIEO is a call for a *World Social Contract*.[3] This means not only restructuring the system but creating new bonds of obligation.

In trying to conceptualize whether the creation of a World Social Contract is a worthwhile goal and, if it is, how it might be negotiated, there are a number of essential difficulties.

1. The *diversity of countries* involved and their myriad interests is staggering. Even if we divide the potential negotiators into four categories—low-income countries, middle-income countries, centrally planned economies, and developed industrial democracies—we see how heterogeneous the blocs would be and how difficult it would prove to satisfactorily aggregate their interests. On surveying this diversity, it is also striking to recognize how complicated any world economic planning would be, even if it were in the most rudimentary form. Thus, viewed in political terms, the market, decentralization, and national strategies that emphasize comparative advantage provide means for organizing the international economic system without requiring agreement on a central structure for decision-making.

2. As yet, there is no consensus on an appropriate *new model for world economic organization.* After World War II, at the time of the establishment of the Bretton Woods system, there was intense debate over the scope for the International Monetary Fund (IMF), the World Bank (IBRD), and the proposed International Trade Organization (ITO). Interestingly, it was precisely because the dominant views favored liberal trade with minimal government intervention that the IMF's purview was limited and the ITO's trade coordinating functions were never approved.

3.There is no agreed *forum for discussion* of the NIEO or even a neutral research body to do objective analysis on ways to construct a new international economic system.

4. A World Social Contract implies *bonds of mutual obligation.* To date, the LDCs have presented the NIEO as demands for

extracting more economic benefits and power from the wealthier countries. Although the developed industrial democracies might well be willing to provide more Official Development Assistance or negotiate on redesigning parts of the present North-South economic arrangements, it will almost certainly not be done unless there is a commonly agreed reciprocity and sense of mutual responsibilities. For example, in the individual commodity agreements now being formulated, the purchaser countries are supplying part of the capital for the buffer stocks, but this is done after clear understandings that access to supplies is assured.

Since the task of designing and beginning to negotiate a World Social Contract is so overwhelming in its scope and the outcome so dubious, the exercise has been mainly left to rhetoric or academics.[4]

It is important to see the concept of "international obligations" in its historical context. It has been extremely difficult for even the Western countries to achieve internal political support for the concept that the wealthy have obligations to the poor. Although the World Social Contract idea means more than just income redistribution, it is not surprising that an idea that has only recently taken hold at the national level would reach slow acceptance in the international arena.

In the absence of an agreed goal or method for a global economic reorganization, nations and agencies have been responding on a disaggregated basis to particular, narrow problems where agreement was feasible. The repeated droughts in the early 1970s have led to the initiation of the World Food Council and substantial improvements in emergency supply stocks; the massive fluctuations in commodity prices have provided an impetus for several individual commodity agreements and the current discussions on the Common Fund; and the great concern over growing LDC indebtedness was instrumental in providing support for the Witteveen and Extended Fund Facilities in the IMF and the current discussions on the capital expansion of the World Bank. Similarly, although the LDCs may not view these as entirely salutory results, the OPEC oil price increases and the Arab oil embargo clearly led to the initiation of the International Energy Agency. Likewise, the recession that followed the OPEC price increases created sufficient concern over macroeconomic demand management policies that the economic summit conferences (Rambouillet, 1975; Dorado Beach, 1976, London, 1977; and Bonn, 1978) were called. Both the International Energy Agency and the economic summits are groupings of wealthy countries, but they provide prototypes that could be expanded to encompass a North-South orientation as well.

A pragmatic approach that addresses individual sector problems is a congenial one for most economists and diplomats. It avoids a social visionary view. Nevertheless, if each of the key sectors of the world economy is dealt with individually, without an overall conception in mind, it is not likely to produce anything other than a series of ad hoc mechanisms.

The balance of the discussion in this chapter is designed to cover the events that led up to the NIEO, the initial responses, the current status of the NIEO, and some suggestions for U.S. policy.

II. WHAT SET THE STAGE FOR THE NIEO?

An intellectual challenge to Neo-Classical economics laid the groundwork for the ideas that surfaced as the NIEO on May 1, 1974. The Neo-Classical conception of a desirable international economic system is one where impediments to trade are minimized and where production decisions are based—to the maximum extent possible—on a country's comparative advantage. The entire Bretton Woods system was established to reify these principles. The economic nationalism of the 1930s (competitive currency devaluations and high tariffs) was viewed as anathema by the architects of the post–World War II economic arrangements.[5] Although many Western economic policymakers were willing to accept and plan major changes in the international trade and monetary system (witness the 1968 creation of IMF Special Drawing Rights (SDR) the U.S. move off the gold standard in 1971, and the 1973 steps to establish a fluctuating exchange-rate system), they continued to consider the system legitimate. As a fallback position, many claimed that at least the system worked and one "had to design a system for its main users."

The challengers to the Neo-Classical view and the Bretton Woods system fell into three main categories: (1) moderate, Western critics who resented the role of the dollar as an international reserve currency; (2) traditional Marxists who rejected the basic legitimacy of an open, capitalist trading environment; and (3) a growing number of analysts, predominantly from the developing countries, who saw few alternatives to open trade but wanted to shift the structure of the system to increase the LDC percentage of the benefits.

Interestingly, de Gaulle was one of the first to begin the challenge to the manner in which the Bretton Woods system had evolved. De Gaulle's claims that the dollar was overvalued, that U.S. payments deficits were merely being financed by domestic monetary expansion, and that the artificially maintained dollar was allowing Americans to buy up foreign assets at bargain rates were remarkably accurate. Although many of the other Europeans did not share de Gaulle's vitriol, they became sufficiently worried about the situation to press for an internationally controlled means of liquidity creation. Thus, the Special Drawing Rights (SDR) system emerged after extensive negotiation.

The Marxist critics stressed the inherently exploitative character of a capitalist-dominated system. Their advocacy of greater autarky, import substitution, and state-controlled trading had attracted a fair number of adherents in the 1950s, but was not meeting with overwhelming acclaim by the early 1970s. State trading had certain advantages when there were numerous other countries willing to participate in barter deals and when a country possessed an honest, efficient bureaucracy capable of managing the trade, but these criteria are only sporadically met.

The most fundamental challenge, however, came from intellectual ferment in the developing countries. As the leading economist at the Economic Commission for Latin America (ECLA) during the 1950s, Raoul Prebisch provided careful empirical research to demonstrate that after the Korean War period the terms of trade between LDC exported raw materials and imported manufactured goods had declined. This argument combined with earlier work by Ragnar Nurkse,[6] which stressed that the income elasticity of demand for raw materials was inevitably going to be less than for manufactured goods, helped lay the basis for the LDC attack on the legitimacy of the international economic system. By the mid-1960s, an entire school had developed that emphasized how international patterns of trade and investment created an ever growing dependent relationship between the LDCs and the industrialized countries.[7]

It was this "Dependency School" that provided the major theoretical underpinnings for the New International Economic Order proposals. By strongly asserting that the existing structure of international economic interaction was biased against their interests, the LDC intellectuals and governments were pressing for what they termed "a fair distribution of the benefits from trade." In essence, their argument was: "the system is too important to be left to 'the market.'" This theme was persistently pushed at the first three United Nations Conferences on Trade and Development,[8] and it had a modest effect on the wealthy countries through their agreement to establish the Generalized System of Preferences (GSP) for tariffs. Yet the LDCs had bigger stakes in mind. After more than a decade of experimentation with export duties, protection of domestic industries, and increasingly tight regulations over foreign investment, the LDC governments had few inhibitions about proposing more massive forms of market intervention.

The Dependency School argues that economic development has never proceeded entirely on the basis of comparative advantage. During the colonial era, investments were channeled into LDC agriculture and raw material extraction, and even the transportation and service facilities were geared to providing produce for the "metropolitan" country. Dependency theorists assert that the postcolonial period has essentially reinforced the earlier patterns of North-South economic linkages. They argue that strong links have grown between the wealthy countries and the urban areas in the LDCs; and, in the same manner that the wealthy countries dominated the LDCs, the LDC urban areas dominate their own rural hinterlands. To avoid perpetuating this reputedly insidious pattern, Dependency School advocates favor both a reduction of North-South economic links and a substantive change in the character of trade and investment to yield a greater share of the economic benefits for the LDCs.

Once again, we see that the LDC representatives object to dealing with economic matters on only a technical level because they do not accept the legitimacy of viewing the end results as just the outcome of "the market's efficiency." the LDC loyalty is not to abstract laws of Neo-Classical economics but to self-interest. This is in fundamental opposition to the common Western view and thus produces the developed country complaints that the LDCs are "asking for changes that constitute unwarranted tampering with the present system." Regardless of its merits as economic analysis, the political popularity in the LDCs and in certain international forums of the Dependency School policy prescriptions is obvious.

The Neo-Classical view of international economic policymaking thus came under increasingly intense intellectual attack during the late 1960s and early 1970s. Moreover, the LDCs began to see the growing mercantilistic practices of the industrial countries. Japan and France had developed to a high art various techniques for export promotion and protection of domestic industry, and LDC governments saw no reason why they should refrain from attempts at tilting the system in their favor. So not only was the diversity of countries involved in international economic negotiations growing, but the intellectual consensus that had shaped the early post–World War II period had disintegrated as well.

Several other trends *set the context* for the May 1974 call for a New International Economic Order.

Although there is a certain irony in this, the relative decline of the United States as a world power produced increased demands for American resources. Clearly, many of the LDC governments felt they could "extract" resources from a country they previously had to approach as supplicants. The Vietnam era had shown some basic failures in U.S. economic policymaking: Americans were reluctant to acknowledge the overvaluation of the dollar; President Johnson had been unwilling to propose a quick increase in personal income taxes to finance the war's escalation of 1965-66; and the U.S. government was left with a series of partial options (tight monetary policy and controls over capital exports) that bespoke disarray and contributed to the growing perception of U.S. weakness.

Linked with the declining dominance of the United States was a broader pattern of politicization of international economic policymaking. This politicizing of economic debates was a logical result of the growing disillusionment with Neo-Classical views that the market should determine resource allocation. If one were dissatisfied with what the market was providing and could assemble a coalition to achieve different results, then, under certain circumstances, political action would be preferable to accommodation with the price signals given by the market. The bloc voting at UNCTAD conferences, increased rancor in UN General Assembly debates on economic questions, and even LDC aggressiveness in IMF and World Bank meetings all were signs of dissatisfaction with the end results. The politicization of what formerly were technical discussions fit with other extant trends in the late 1960s. With the declining salience of Great Power rivalry issues for many middle-sized countries and the widening evidence of ethnic and subnational pressures, previously august international economic agreements appeared less sacrosanct.

Therefore, at the same time the intellectual underpinnings for the Bretton Woods system were being challenged, the process of international governance for economic matters was becoming less centralized and more politicized.

In combination with this broad background, several *specific events* raised LDC confidence to the point where it appeared possible to fundamentally reorganize the system into a New Order.

The *devaluation of the dollar* and Nixon's decision to move off the gold-exchange standard in August 1971 was a seminal event. U.S. difficulties were painfully obvious, and the government took a unilateral step that shocked the international economic system. Although economists could view the temporary import tariff surcharge and the subsequent move in February 1973 to a fluctuating exchange-rate system as merely pragmatic choices, the LDCs interpreted these steps as signs that the United States was weakened and that the system was no longer sacrosanct.

Another specific event, the *1973 Arab-Israeli War,* contributed to the momentum that led to the NIEO. Although it is common for the public to make no distinction between the war period and the oil price increases, it is important to recognize that the Arab oil exporters first showed the strength of the "oil weapon" through the embargo of those countries that continued to support Israel. Even though the embargo was only partly effective (because non-Arab OPEC members increased production and some pro-Arab receiving countries were willing to re-export their oil), the threat of economic disruption was adequate to bring about further pro-Arab moves by the French and also to bring about a complete reversal of Japanese policy toward a pro-Arab position. These signs of weakness by major industrial countries made the oil price increases plausible and added to the LDC conviction that the global balance of power had been noticeably shifted in their direction.

The Organization of Petroleum Exporting Countries (OPEC) price hikes during the four months after the October 1973 Mideast war were probably the single most important factor in convincing the LDC governments that there was a real chance of reorganizing the international economic system. Although this quadrupling of price for the world's most important traded commodity has been analyzed ad nauseam, its significance for the NIEO debates was not so much the resources being redirected to a small number of countries but more from the vulnerability shown by the major industrial democracies. In the same manner that the trauma of the Vietnam War illustrated weaknesses in the world position of the United States, the oil price rise dramatically raised the curtain on possible change. The drama was staged on a worldwide scale.[9]

The conclusions drawn about the significance of the oil price increases would have been less stark if the oil moves had not been preceded by an extraordinary *worldwide business expansion* in the first three years of the 1970s. Despite the fact that macroeconomic demand management techniques were known to economic policymakers throughout the 1950s and 1960s, there was never a period when the major economies (the United States, Europe, and Japan) were simultaneously at the peak of a business cycle. The odd occurrence of a synchronized business boom in the early 1970s thus tended to drive up prices of internationally traded goods (both manufactures and raw materials). Many of the LDC strategists hoped that the cause of the raw material price increases was a "fundamental scarcity" rather than a curious quirk of events. It thus appeared to some that raw materials prices were high and going to stay high and that the quadrupling of oil prices was merely the first step in a permanent shift in the ratio of raw materials and manufactured goods prices. It was only in the midst of the 1975-76 recession when raw materials prices had dropped precipitously that the certainty over "commodity power" began to wane.

For a variety of reasons, the excitement and enthusiasm that invigorated the LDCs during the winter of 1973 and spring of 1974 did not last.

III. WHY DID THE ROSE FADE: 1974-78?

When the cheering stopped in the fall of 1974, the LDCs had to decide what aspects of the broad-sweeping NIEO to pursue. In fact, it is probably reasonable to take the passage of the Economic Charter of the Rights and Duties of States in December 1974 as the pinnacle of LDC solidarity on NIEO questions. Although the original call for the NIEO had not been the result of a formal vote, the Economic Charter was passed over the vigorous opposition of the major Western trading nations by a vote of 86 to 10.

Not surprisingly, the cross-pressures of the different constituencies proved so complex that the developed countries were given time to regroup and make attempts at forming a common position. With Secretary of State Kissinger taking the lead, the United States tried to define the problem as essentially one of "energy supply"; he thus publicly proposed the formation of an oil reserve network to limit the effects of any future embargoes. The Europeans, who were even more dependent on imported

OPEC oil than the Americans, were unwilling to cast the problem in this light, as they saw themselves as too vulnerable to future economic threats. Thus, the Europeans took the lead in proposing talks on a "North-South basis" that would encompass a very wide agenda.

In January 1975, President Gerald Ford signed a new trade act that authorized new trade negotiations and permitted the United States to formally enter the Tokyo Round of the Multilateral Trade Negotiations (MTN). By April 1975, the Europeans had gotten their way; Kissinger's strategy of focusing on energy and confronting the LDC governments in other areas was thwarted, and the developed countries had agreed to the establishment of the Paris Conference on International Economic Cooperation (CIEC). Although it took the CIEC conferees ten months just to agree on an organization structure for the "North-South dialogue," the air of economic confrontation had subsided. Similarly, by the time the United Nations convened the Seventh Special Session in September 1975, there was an ample quota of rhetoric but much more emphasis on finding economic cooperation schemes that would be feasible.

Some of the more radical members of the Group of 77 were dissatisfied with the evolving character of the North-South dialogue and succeeded at engineering a new set of demands, known as the Manila Declaration, which they hoped would set the basis for the UNCTAD IV discussions in Nairobi during April 1976. Some pyrotechnics did develop at Nairobi, but they were mild, and it is startling to realize that the Paris CIEC discussions dragged on until May 13, 1977.

What combination of factors turned the New International Economic Order from an avalanche into a glacial advance?

First, the oil price increases proved to be a mixed blessing. Most of the LDCs were quick to discover that, despite the pride they took in seeing OPEC exert its economic muscle, they were not oil exporters and they were going to have to pay four times as much for their imported oil. Although some of the Arab OPEC members set up aid programs and concessionary oil-pricing schemes for fellow Moslem regimes, this proved to be only a minor palliative. Moreover, many LDC governments found that petroleum feedstocks had become central to their agricultural performance, since the new varieties of rice and wheat needed large amounts of urea fertilizer.

Second, the oil price jump had led to a massive redistribution of income from the oil-consuming to the oil-producing countries. This wrenching change had triggered almost panic levels of inflation in the developed countries, and their governments responded with tight monetary and fiscal policies. The world's major trading economies, therefore, moved in a period of two years from a widespread boom to a major recession. Since the LDCs still produce predominantly raw materials (and the demand for raw materials is a direct function of the demand for finished goods), the LDCs still depended on developed country markets for their products, and the global recession reduced the growth of their exports and national income as well.

Third, it became more and more widely recognized that the rapid increase in raw materials prices that had occurred in the 1971-73 period was the result, not of any fundamental scarcities, but rather of the highly unusual coincidence of business peaking in each of the major industrial markets. It thus became important to distinguish between oil prices that were maintained at high levels by the OPEC cartel and other raw materials prices that would (without organized market management) continue to fluctuate given more normal cycles of supply and demand. This forced those LDCs that relied primarily on raw materials exports to put their main effort into negotiating commodity price stablization schemes like the Common Fund.

Fourth, tension between the moderate Arab states and the West diminished considerably after 1973 as: (1) the United States began to put increasing pressure on Israel to negotiate, and (2) the Europeans and Japanese turned actively supportive of Arab positions. More importantly, the less militant Arabs recognized that extra income was far less critical to them than world political stability and a smoothly expanding world economy. In addition, with increasing Soviet influence in Africa, Southern Yemen, and Afghanistan combined with turbulence in Iran, the non-Marxist Arabs were anxious to encourage rather than threaten the Western powers. Although the New International Economic Order was a convenient tool for achieving solidarity among the developing countries when the Arabs wanted concessions from the West, it was largely irrelevant to their purposes by the late 1970s.

Fifth, the OPEC countries never provided the aid bonanza the non-oil LDCs anticipated. Although the "oil surplus" was approximately $40 billion in 1974, the OPEC members proved quite conservative in their investments; and by 1976 and 1977 they were spending at a rate that left them with only moderate surpluses. The non-oil LDCs also found that the Arabs were directing the bulk of their aid funds to countries that bordered Israel. Thus, the combination of a more moderate Arab political stance and the lack of any substantial new resources for joint LDC action produced a weaker Group of 77 bargaining position.

Sixth, the actual brokerage among the LDCs in the political arena proved exceptionally difficult. The belabored CIEC discussions in Paris were a good example of how intractable the negotiations became:

> The talks concluded with two tangible results: (1) an agreement in principle on the establishment of a Common Fund; and (2) a pledge on the part of the rich to provide an additional $1 billion in aid to the poorest countries. The industrialized countries were unable to get any concessions on energy issues; the developing countries, on the other hand, did not get the agreement on debt relief that they wanted.[10]

On the surface, these two results seem like some evidence of North-South compromise. Yet, eighteen months after the CIEC conference concluded, the size and method of operation for the Common Fund remain unresolved, and the $1 billion in aid was pledged with no specific countries or time limits agreed upon.

Moreover, the problem of brokerage among the LDCs goes beyond these negotiations to secure economic concessions from the wealthy countries. The diversity and heterogeneity of interests among the Group of 77 members is growing each year as

certain countries develop the capabilities to effectively participate in, and benefit from, the evolving patterns of world market
industrialization and specialization. Although the Group of 77 is
likely to be able to marshal solidarity for bloc voting on certain
symbolic questions, when it comes to vital issues the fissures will
become explicit. For example, at the CIEC conferences, the
LDCs were represented by seventeen of the largest, most technologically advanced, and most industrial of their members.
Most of these LDC governments were active users of the private
capital market and clearly had nothing to gain from aggressively
pushing for some of the debt rescheduling proposals of greatest
interest to the poorest countries. Similarly, for many of the
seventeen, the outcome of the Multilateral Trade Negotiations
were of greater significance than the intricacies of the Common
Fund.

Seventh, the adjustment in the industrial countries to the oil
price changes and the subsequent shifts in resource flows proved
far more difficult than most observers anticipated. In fact, the
worldwide boom in the early 1970s combined with the OPEC
price increases strained the basic elasticity of the system. Adjustment has taken a wide variety of forms[11] and caused major
dislocations through price, income, investment, and employment changes. This book, for instance, could be viewed as a
series of quantitative studies on alternative U.S. policies for
minimizing the disruptive effects of adjusting to post-1973 economic trends.

Adjustment to energy price changes in the United States was
particularly wrenching—given that most of the twentieth-century
industrial and housing investment had been widely dispersed on
the assumption that energy would be inexpensive. Similarly,
though it is theoretically possible to shift workers from one
sector to another if cheaper products are available through importing, many workers resist learning new trades and are especially reluctant to move their families as their ties are often
closer to their communities than to their work. This obsoles-
cence of human skills, equipment, and even infrastructure is
politically unpalatable under any circumstances, but it is definitely volatile when the causes are "Arab oil sheiks," "unfair,

low-wage competition," or "Japan, Inc." Thus, although political leaders in the industrial democracies may be able to count on a modest amount of humanitarian sentiment to support increased resource transfers to the LDCs, the political costs of even addressing the NIEO are too high unless the results help mute the dislocations caused by foreign economic events.

In sum, the LDC enthusiasm for the NIEO grew out of disillusionment with their share of the benefits from the international economic system and the hope that the oil price increase presaged a fundamental shift of world income in their direction. Though a basic shift in income did occur, it ended up hurting most of the members of the Group of 77 since they were not oil exporters. Moreover, the worldwide recession in 1975-76 destroyed any hope that raw materials prices were going to stay at their recent high levels. As certain visions faded and the complexity of the brokerage among the LDCs became more evidence, the developed countries recognized that the NIEO was not an overly forbidding menace that could be dealt with as a series of separable proposals—to be accepted, rejected, or modified on a case-by-case basis. The central question, then, for American policymakers becomes how to integrate the diffuse topics of the NIEO debates into a long-range strategy which optimally advances U.S. interests.

IV. WHAT IS APPROPRIATE U.S. STRATEGY NOW?

In the coming eighteen months, the U.S. government will need to: (1) define its basic position on the international development strategy for the UN's Third Development Decade; (2) decide how to proceed with the NIEO talks now scattered in various UN forums; and (3) enunciate a series of positions and negotiate them through the upcoming UNCTAD V conference in Manila, and special sessions of the UN General Assembly planned to review the progress on the NIEO. All of this must be done while dealing with the problem of excess dollar liquidity and inflation during the throes of a U.S. presidential election.

At these assorted sessions, there is likely to be only a minimal amount of rational discussion concerning the causes of the current international differences in income. Similarly, the goals of the Group of 77 are likely to be stated in such broad, sweeping terms that they could well inhibit serious consideration of even the worthwhile elements. To avoid such a deadlock, both the developed and developing countries should focus on specific schemes or proposals so that the participants can claim some tangible result from the exercise.

Unfortunately, the basic dichotomy that has pervaded similar past conferences could well persist. The Group of 77 could claim that the basic purpose of the NIEO is to transform the *international* aspects of economic relations between the developed and developing nations; while the wealthy countries could counter that they are willing to make compromises on certain international questions but only with explicit commitments from the LDCs that the enhanced resource flows will actually reach the most disadvantaged *inside* the poorer societies.

The typical LDC response to this impasse is to claim that if the international economic system is producing inequitable results, then there is no reason to delay changing it and there is good reason to avoid the demeaning circumstance of "making promises for something that should be remedied anyway." The typical developed country response is to claim that, though the system may need minor modifications, present results are not consistently inequitable, and that parliamentary governments cannot be expected to tax their own citizens unless they are convinced that the aid or concessions granted will help the less fortunate in the LDCs.

This type of LDC-DC repartee is not very edifying unless it provides the initial negotiating positions from which some mutually beneficial compromise can be achieved. Although the LDCs are demanding a new World Social Contract, the developed countries have so far appeared reticent to link their concessions to explicit guarantees from the LDCs. What is clearly needed is cooperative action to reinforce the stability of the international economic system. In trying to sculpt a U.S. position on these disparate issues, it is useful to organize a strategy by integrating objectives in three areas: microeconomic choices, means for adapting the international economic system to enhance its resiliency, and the relationship between economic and political/military questions.

MICROECONOMIC ISSUES

Interestingly, both the Ford and Carter Administrations have been relatively skillful in dealing with the individual proposals put forward in the New International Economic Order dialogues. Kissinger's intent was delay. He originally hoped to form a grouping of wealthy countries that would be a counter-response to OPEC. Yet, when that proved infeasible, he chose a dual strategy of simultaneously (1) suggesting a plethora of new institutions, and (2) allowing the grinding of the bureaucracies involved in slow action.

The September 1975 Kissinger speech to the UN General Assembly's Seventh Special Session (actually delivered by Ambassador Daniel P. Moynihan) emphasized individual commodity agreements rather than the Common Fund and proposed new means for agricultural development and capital investment (see appendix to this chapter). In the same vein, the major U.S. proposal at the May 1976 UNCTAD IV conference in Nairobi was for an investment and guarantee facility on International Resources Bank) to encourage greater private capital investment in LDC mineral and energy extraction. Kissinger's strategy was to assume "a good offense is the best defense," and his counterproposals to the NIEO clearly consumed considerable staff time at the working-party level. Moreover, even when his particular proposals were neglected, the intense scrutiny of repeated meetings helped deflect some of the least desirable NIEO proposals. This was important, as the more relaxed working sessions showed that there was not, in fact, unity in LDC interests and illustrated that there were few areas where even symbolic solidarity could be maintained.

The Carter administration took a more conciliatory attitude toward the NIEO. Though Kissinger had succeeded at stymying any progress in the CIEC or UNCTAD forums between May 1974 and January 1977, Secretary of State Cyrus Vance recognized that he would need to make some kind of concession or face renewed LDC intransigence. The decision to accept the

Common Fund "in principle" thus became the sacrificial offering at the last session of the CIEC meetings and part of the joint communiqué agreed to by all participants.

Despite their differences in orientation, both the Ford and Carter administration approaches have avoided dealing item for item with the NIEO demands and have allowed time for activities in other arenas. The delay has not only permitted some of the NIEO euphoria to subside, but it has also allowed the detailed, time-consuming discussions on the Code of Conduct for Transnational Corporations, the International Fair Labor Standards guidelines, and the International Wheat Agreement to achieve fruition during the period.

It is also important to remember that the executive branch must consider congressional mandates that bear on NIEO issues. The congressional strictures in the Foreign Assistance Act clearly require that U.S. developmental efforts provide essential services (i.e., basic human needs) for the poorest strata of society in the recipient countries. This means that the U.S. focus is likely to remain on such questions as health care, population, agriculture, employment and education as the key targets for improvement. Therefore, even though it may be desirable from a negotiating standpoint to make some concessions on proposals that deal exclusively with international resource transfer, the administration is never certain that it could ultimately get congressional endorsement.

Thus, on the microeconomic questions of responding to individual parts in the NIEO, the United States has done rather well. Delay followed by selected concessions has avoided tension over the most unacceptable NIEO proposals, while simultaneously facilitating the construction of an agreement that appeared to have some permanence and a chance of congressional support. If some blend of these tactics can be pursued through the coming eighteen months, the United States should emerge with minimal damage from the NIEO episode. The major failing during the past period, however, was that the consuming interest in tactics led to a neglect of broader economic policy questions. The most fundamental weakness was in failing to articulate the type of international economic system the United States sought.

The United States thus failed to show how the system should be adapted or to mobilize support for the changes.

ECONOMIC SYSTEM ADAPTATION

If the LDCs are to willingly participate in an open, competitive international economic system that they now consider biased against them, there must be some adaptations to win their allegiance and constructive behavior. The Ford Administration chose to ignore this problem by having Secretary of the Treasury William E. Simon repeatedly claim that free markets were the answer to virtually all economic problems. Simon saw no problem with the fluctuating exchange-rate system, was unconcerned with internal or external effects of the gyrating dollar, and was apparently willing to accept the unbuffered effects of sharp changes in international comparative advantage. Although the British saw a certain humor in a nineteenth-century liberal running the U.S. Treasury, none of the industrial countries was willing to follow Simon's regimen and the LDCs saw it as both unresponsive and ideologically unacceptable. Without adequate coordination on how to respond to the OPEC price increases, the industrial democracies basically chose economic slow-downs as their means for freeing resources to pay for their oil.

The Carter administration entered the scene with a flourish emphasizing U.S./European/Japanese coordination, but Secretary of the Treasury W. Michael Blumenthal initially sounded remarkably like Simon in his pronouncements on the dollar. Although by 1978 Blumenthal had changed his story and was trying to buttress the dollar, a period of almost two years was lost with only minimal attention paid to systemic questions.

In trying to conceptualize how the system may evolve in the next three to five years, it seems reasonable to make the following four assumptions:

(1) There is no other single commodity like oil that can be effectively cartelized and have a major effect on world price levels and the international distribution of income. Nevertheless, the developed countries will con-

tinue to rely extensively on raw materials from the LDCs, and it will be in the interests of the wealthy nations to provide adequate terms so as to keep the LDCs willing to guarantee supplies at predictable prices.

(2) Governments will become increasingly dissatisfied with the fluctuating exchange-rate system and will intervene more aggressively to moderate swings in the price of their currency.

(3) Although the deutsche mark will become an ever more important reserve asset and the development of the European monetary system may dampen the fluctuations in the price of the dollar, the dollar will, nevertheless, remain as the dominant international medium of exchange.

(4) The interests of the OPEC countries and the middle-income LDCs will steadily diverge from those of the poorest LDCs, as the rapidly growing countries will not only want greater access to the system but will eventually want to preserve it as well.

If these moderate assumptions come to pass, then radical adaptation will not be necessary. It may be more appropriate to view the changes as increasing flexibility and the system's elasticity.

On *trade* issues, assuming a satisfactory resolution to the Multilateral Trade Negotiations, there appear to be two major concerns: (1) obtaining agreement on an equitable monitoring procedure to insure that governments do not use nontariff barriers like export subsidies, procurement regulations, or tax schemes to unfairly promote exports; and (2) resolving the difficulties faced by exporters trying to compete in nonmarket economies or with barriers set up by customs unions of free trade associations. As governments are less willing to tolerate the disruptive effects of exposing their markets to a growing range of potential imports, the art of maintaining the benefits from trade will be in convincing the nations involved to accept comparative advantage but with "adequate safeguards to ease the transition into and out of specific industries."

In *investment and industrial policy,* there will need to be substantially greater international coordination. Although some countries will persist in building inefficient steel, petrochemical, computer, and aircraft industries for "strategic" reasons, it may well be possible to get cooperation in harmonizing industrial development plans—particularly when the economies of scale are obvious. Countries are already increasingly willing to enter into "coproduction" agreements where parts of one final product are manufactured in several nations; if this principle could be extended, there could be massive savings in research and development and capital expenditures.

On *monetary* questions, the central debate will be over how to avoid the uncertainties that have arisen from depending on the dollar as the prime international reserve asset. Measures like the enlarged Swap Agreement and foreign currency borrowings (announced by President Carter on November 1, 1978) are only termporary palliatives. It will be very much in the U.S. interest to get the oil surplus countries, Europeans, and Japanese to take responsibility for creating new, stable reserve assets. If the Special Drawing Rights (SDRs) is not sufficiently attractive and the European currency unit proves unworkable, then there will be no alternative to greater use of the deutsche mark and the yen. Also, to increase stability in the system, there will need to be far larger amounts of resources available to the International Monetary Fund for intervention in crisis situations.

Although this is only a brief sample of the types of system adaptations that are necessary and obtainable, it will be critical to present proposals like these as part of an integrated whole that warrants adherence and supportive action when NIEO questions of "system restructuring" arise.

POLITICAL/MILITARY CONSIDERATIONS

The NIEO is typically seen as an economic challenge with a high political content. Yet, to view it accurately, one must also consider the national security issues as well. From the standpoint of long-term U.S. needs, Canada, Mexico, Japan, Europe, the Caribbean, and the Middle East oil-exporting countries are the areas of greatest strategic significance. Except for Jamaica, and to some extent Mexico, in the Caribbean and some of the more radical Middle East oil exporters, none of these countries has taken a consistent, high-visibility role in the Group of 77. However, our trade with all LDCs is now more important to us than our trade with Europe and Japan combined. Thus, there is the possibility that there will be an increasing divergence between our trading interests and our perceived national security interests.

At this time, there are three new geopolitical developments that will be affecting our long-term calculations: (1) the increasing Soviet-Cuban role in Africa and the Red Sea: (2) the turbulence in Iran and the possibility that it may spread to other oil-exporting countries with which we cooperate; and (3) the growing prominence of the People's Republic of China as an international economic actor and the possibility that China will use its market as an inducement for countries to side with it in the growing Sino-Soviet competition. While it is too soon to tell, it would not be inconceivable for there to be a major political realignment, with the middle-income LDCs, moderate Arabs, and Chinese joining the West in an anti-Soviet amalgam.

There is still another major strategic question: How should the United States respond if the middle-income LDCs adapt satisfactorily but the poorest LDCs stagnate? On first glance, this appears not to be a military question but more one of humanitarian concern. However, with the increasing effectiveness of terrorism and the apparent upsurge in conventional conflicts (e.g., Ethiopia/Somalia, Algeria/Morrocco, and Vietnam/Cambodia) it could well be a military question if the evolving economic order appears to have only minimal benefits for the lowest-income LDCs. It will thus be critical to avoid a situation where the world economic system appears closed and the populous nations of Central Africa and Southern Asia sense the intense frustration of being left behind by even their former NIEO compatriots.

This brings our argument back full circle to the criteria for an acceptable World Social Contract. If adequate bonds of mutual obligation are not formed, the NIEO episode could repeat itself in the 1980s.

U.S. strategy should thus be to continue to look after our "critical allies" but to stress the delicate nature of the international economic system and try to form cooperative arrangements that could mute the "rich versus poor country" schism that made the early NIEO debates such an emotional confrontation.

In conclusion, a remarkable set of circumstances precipitated the New International Economic Order. Though the United States should be reasonably pleased with the results of its tactical response during the Ford and Carter administrations, steps need to be taken to avoid a recurrence. Several substantive agreements were negotiated and the most objectionable NIEO proposals were deflected. Yet some longer-term structural issues about the evolution of the international economic system have not been adequately handled. The system does need to be more resilient, and the LDCs need to see that there is a workable construct that will be able to cope with their particular concerns. Despite the reduced relative role of the United States on the world economic scene, there is no other single actor which can so clearly mold outcomes. Thus, the United States should actively pursue its own interests, seek possible new alignments for cooperative ventures, but present a New Economic Order that is a valid World Social Contract—both inducing and obliging constructive behavior.

NOTES

1. See the appendix to this chapter for a brief chronology of the main events relevant to the NIEO declaration.

2. The Group of 77 is the formal name for the caucus of developing countries when they meet in U.N. forums. Although the group now has 114 members, it was originally formed at the third United Nations Conference on Trade and Development session (UNCTAD III) where the LDC representatives concluded their only chance for increased power would come through various forms of collective action.

3. This argument is similar to that developed by J. and M. McHale in *The Planetary Bargain: Proposals for a NIEO to Meet Human Needs* (Aspen Institute Policy Paper, Palo Alto, 1977), but is different in that I am stressing the political accommodations that are necessary before substantive economic concessions are likely to be made.

4. Although neither author directly discusses the NIEO, the debate over income distribution principles in J. Rawls, *Justice*, (Boston: Beacon Press, 1972), and R. Nozick, *Anarchy, State and Utopia* (New York: Basic Books, 1975), nicely encapsulates the divergence of views on the obligations of the wealthy to the poor. Harland V. B. Cleveland and T. W. Wilson, Jr., in *Humangrowth*, Aspen Institute Policy Paper, Palo Alto, 1978, and J. and M. McHale, *The Planetary Bargain*, try to envisage the values and physical targets that new types of international cooperation may entail.

5. See, e.g., C. Kindleberger's defense of liberal trade in his *International Economics* 3rd ed., Homewood, Ill.: Irwin, 1963). In chapter 16, Kindleberger considers arguments against open trade, but his examples come predominantly from customs union theory—not from an LDC perspective.

6. R. Nurkse, *Problems of Capital Formation in Underdeveloped Countries* (New York: Oxford University Press, 1953).

7. The most lucid, single exposition of dependency theory is by A. G. Frank in "The Development of Underdevelopment," *Monthly Review* (1966).

8. The United Nations Conferences on Trade and Development (UNCTAD) were, respectively: UNCTAD I (Geneva, 1964); UNCTAD II (New Delhi, 1968); UNCTAD III (Santiago, 1972); and UNCTAD IV (Nairobi, 1976). UNCTAD V is planned for Manila in May 1979.

9. The debate in the Spring 1974 issue of *Foreign Policy* between C. Fred Bergsten's "The Threat Is Real" and S. Krasner's "Oil Is the Exception" is a good example of the uncertainty among analysts in the developed countries. The LDC governments naturally chose the interpretation that suited their objectives.

10. J. Singh, *A New International Economic Order*, rev. ed. (New York: Praeger, 1978); Postscript, p. 127.

11. See Chapter 2 in this volume for a more detailed exploration of the mechanisms for adjustment to trade changes.

Appendix

SUMMARY OF KEY EVENTS OF SIGNIFICANCE
TO THE NEW INTERNATIONAL ECONOMIC ORDER

1971 August   President Nixon announces a devaluation of the U.S. dollar and a decision to go off the gold-exchange standard as well as a temporary import surcharge.

December   The United States retracts the temporary import surcharge but only after devaluing for a second time and inaugurating a modified float for the dollar.

1973 February   The fluctuating exchange-rate system is agreed upon on a trial basis by the world's major trading nations.

October   The Arab-Israeli War leads to the Arab oil exporters' boycott of countries supporting Israel.

November-   Rapid increases in the Organization of Petroleum
December   Exporting Country (OPEC) oil price.

1974 March   Lima Conference of UNIDO, which the LDC governments dominate and use to endorse positions on nationalization of foreign assets, commodity prices, and commodity-producer cartels.

April-May   Sixth Special Session of the UN endorses a Declaration and Program of Action on the Establishment of the New International Economic Order. The program includes sections calling for: increased prices for commodity exporters, greater food aid and food reserves, use of the Special Drawing Right-Link proposal, greater technology transfers from the wealthy to the LDCs, tighter controls on the activities of transnational corporations, targets for LDC industrialization, targets for Official Development assistance, and special programs for LDCs most seriously affected by economic circumstances in the 1970s.

December   The Charter of Economic Rights and Duties of States is passed by the UN's Twenty-ninth General Assembly. The provisions that proved most controversial were the ones that declared states had the right to nationalize, expropriate, and transfer ownership of foreign property, with the compensation to be determined by the laws and regulations of the host government.

1975 February The first serious intergovernmental discussions of the UNCTAD Integrated Commodity program take place.

April French President Giscard d'Estaing hosts a conference on North-South questions. The industrialized countries want the topic to be energy supplies and pricing, but the LDCs will not participate unless the energy discussions are linked to issues of raw materials pricing and other development questions. From this meeting, the Conference on International Economic Cooperation (CIEC) is established and meets periodically until May 1977. It becomes the key forum for the North-South economic dialogue.

1975 September The UN's Seventh Special Session is held and takes on a very different cast from the confrontation positions expressed in the Sixth Special Session. The LDCs take a less antagonistic position, and the United States proposes a broad range of new alternatives: a special development facility of the IMF to stabilize foreign-exchange earnings, establishing consumer-producer forums for each major traded commodity, increased capitalization for the International Finance Corporation, a willingness on the part of the United States to hold and finance the bulk of the world's international grain reserves, the establishment of an International Energy Institute, and greater technological exchange between the developed and developing countries.

1976 January The formal acceptance (at a special meeting of the IMF in Kingston, Jamaica) of the fluctuating exchange-rate system as the agreed international currency regime. There is also agreement to return some of the IMF member states' gold and to sell some gold to generate income to be used for LDCs facing particularly difficult balance-of-payments problems.

May The UNCTAD IV Conference is held in Nairobi. Although Kissinger's idea for an International Resources Bank is not accepted, there is agreement to hold discussions on the Integrated Commodity Program and the Common Fund.

1977   May   The CIEC meetings in Paris adjourn with agreement in principle to establish the Common Fund and for the industrialized countries to contribute $1 billion in special aid funds to LDCs facing particular difficulties. No resolution is reached, however, on energy supply or pricing questions.

Part II

TRADE

Chapter 2

CRUCIAL ISSUES FOR CURRENT
INTERNATIONAL TRADE POLICY *

ROBERT E. BALDWIN

F. W. Taussig Research Professor of Economics
University of Wisconsin—Madison

JOHN H. MUTTI

Associate Professor of Economics
University of Wyoming

J. DAVID RICHARDSON

Associate Professor of Economics
University of Wisconsin—Madison

* The authors would like to thank David B. H. Denoon for careful commentary and the Ford Foundation for supporting part of the empirical work that underlies the paper in a grant to the Universities of Wisconsin and Wyoming to encourage research in International Economic Order.

I. INTRODUCTION

In our judgment, two issues are of paramount importance for trade policy today. The first is how trade policy should be shaped or augmented in light of its heightened impact on dislocation and income distribution within countries. The second is whether and how trade policy should be applied to narrowing the increased inequality of income distribution among countries.

Both issues have a long history. But both have become more crucial in the profound global economic flux of the 1970s. Virtually worldwide stagnation has raised unemployment rates toward pre-World War II highs. More important for trade policy, stagnation has lengthened the duration of both the average job seeker's unemployment, and the operation of capital at suboptimal rates of capacity utilization. As a result, any men and machines that are displaced by trade liberalization are involuntarily unproductive for longer periods of time than during the 1950s and 1960s. Both their personal burdens and the overall social cost of their unproductivity are offsets to the gains from freer trade—offsets that loom larger now than at any time since the Great Depression.

Worldwide inflation, on the other hand, has significantly altered the internal income distribution in most countries. Owners of natural resources and land have fared well; semiskilled and unskilled workers have fared poorly. Unlike inflationary boomlets during the 1950s and 1960s, the much more dramatic outburst of the 1970s has probably been regressive in its internal distributional impact. Pressures to "catch up" and to maintain former standards of living have heightened the vigilance with which policies are examined for adverse incidence. Trade policies are increasingly suspect, given the nearly worldwide growth in the openness of economies (measured by share of tradables in overall production).

As a result of the recent import pressures in an economic environment of high and enduring unemployment and inflation rates, protectionism is currently stronger than at any time since the early 1930s. Moreover, evidence that protectionists are achieving some of their goals is very apparent. In the spring of 1977 the U.S. government entered into Orderly Marketing Agreements (OMAs) with South Korea and Taiwan for shoes and with Japan for color television sets. Under such arrangements, foreign countries agree to quantitative limits in their exports of particular products. The trigger (reference) pricing systems for steel recently adopted by the United States and the European Community represent another significant protectionist step. A study by the Federal Trade Commission estimates that this cartel-like, price-raising arrangement will cost U.S. consumers more than $1 billion a year. In Europe, a tightening of existing curbs on textile imports as well as the application of market-sharing pressures on Japan in shipbuilding are additional instances of the "new protectionism."

Worldwide stagnation and worldwide inflation have both been influenced importantly by macroeconomic policies that were reluctantly adopted in the face of predatory pricing by OPEC (Organization of Petroleum Exporting Countries). Oil prices sextupled between 1970 and 1974, and the terms of trade deteriorated dramatically for oil-importing nations. By making them suddenly poorer, OPEC heightened still further the jealousy/equity impulses that rivet attention on income inequality. Because neither the increased oil prices nor their stagflationary influence imposed comparable burdens from nation to nation, interest in the distribution of income among nations has been revitalized. OPEC's success at pursuing transfers of wealth from other countries, rather than wealth creation, has prompted developing countries to do likewise. Their commitment to succeed, along with OPEC's explicit and implicit support, has led to the formulation of plans for a New International Economic Order.

Our feeling is that other issues confronting trade policy today pale by comparison with dislocational and distributional issues. Some of these other issues are controversial primarily because of their impacts on dislocation and distribution. Among them are how multinationals and technology transfer affect commodity trade, jobs, and incomes; [1] and how increasing import dependence on resource-rich developing countries alters international income inequality. [2] Still other issues are controversial and important in their own right, such as the merits and disadvantages of increased recourse to bilateral, discriminatory, nontariff barriers to trade; increased East-West trade; increased South-South trade (regional economic cooperation among developing countries); or increased agricultural trade.

We suppress our discussion of these other issues below in order to focus on the two we find most critical. We begin in section II with a summary of the various ways in which international trade strengthens (and occasionally weakens) a national economy. Observations made there set the stage for section III's exploration of the short-term adjustment costs from trade liberalization, and for section IV's evaluation of the proposals for a new international economic order. Conclusions are presented in section V.

II. INTERNATIONAL TRADE AND NATIONAL ECONOMIC STRENGTH

Much of what follows is, on reflection, straight-forward. Yet neglecting it seems to be responsible for the irrelevance of much classroom international economics, for the propagandistic artifice of much congressional testimony, for the inflammatory rhetoric that engulfs discussions of international income inequality, and for the obtuseness of much journalistic reporting on all.

THE GENERAL CASE FOR FOREIGN TRADE

International trade strengthens the U.S. economy for many reasons. Having some is better than having none, although more and more is not necessarily better and better. The pattern of U.S. trade, and not merely its existence, may also be strengthening. The United States has comparative advantage in goods that are believed to have special economic and strategic production value: goods that feature stable export earnings and a monopolistic position in the world market; high-technology, growth-promoting manufactures; [3] armaments. The United States also has a comparatively well diversified set of stable suppliers and customers, few of which can match the market power of the U.S.

economy. This enhances U.S. bargaining power, and mitigates uncertainty. In sum, both the industrial and geographical pattern of U.S. trade is favorable.

But international trade is, of course, not the only source of U.S. economic strength, nor even the most important. Other sources include still abundant natural resources, energy, and productive equipment; rich and growing technology; and a highly motivated, energetic, and skilled labor force.

For any country, international trade sometimes provides indirect strength through these other sources, as well as independent strength of its own. Imports can be the channel for tapping abundant foreign capital and technology. Exports of technology, by itself or embodied in goods, can stimulate further domestic innovation by raising its rewards. On the other hand, international trade can also increase a nation's economic and political vulnerability. And it can create pressures on selected labor groups and capital owners alike that are productively debilitating.

Overall, however, one of the most robust of all economic theorems is that some international trade is better than none at all. Thoroughgoing national self-sufficiency may be a virtue in some ways, but any country that attempts it pays a huge economic price.

Robust as this theorem is, it is often superficially proved, then cavalierly applied in problems to which it has no real relevance.

The superficial proof goes like this:

"Obviously, certain countries produce some things more cheaply than we do, such as textiles, and we produce some things more cheaply than they, such as aircraft. Therefore both exports and imports are beneficial. Exports provide jobs and income to U.S. labor and resource owners; imports reduce the U.S. cost of living because they are priced lower than their U.S. equivalents." While these observations are true, they do *not* "prove" that trade is beneficial to the United States—any more than fears that exports raise U.S. prices and imports displace U.S. workers "prove" the case false. In fact, all the descriptive observations are usually simultaneously true. Somewhat crudely, exports can generate employment and upward pressure on prices; imports can "take away" employment but hold down prices. It is necessary to go beyond these superficial statements to prove that some international trade is preferable to none and to demonstrate how trade's existence strengthens an economy.

Impossible as it sounds, trade enables every country to get more and give up less. It can increase every country's consumption of real goods and services without any increase in its use of resources, or it can free up resources for voluntary leisure, while still allowing a country as a whole to consume the same goods and services it did without trade.

International trade performs this "magic" because it is completely analogous to superior technology. It allows inputs to be transformed into outputs more productively than would be possible without trade [4]—only exports are the inputs into creating physically different outputs called imports. Just as superior technology allows a country to get more for less, or something for nothing, so does trade. Nations thus choose to trade internationally out of self-interest, not altruism. The added economic strength obtained thereby is not due to the weakening of other countries either. All can gain simultaneously, just as they can from superior technology.

These insights alone, however, shed little light on the practical concerns of trade policy. They deal with comparisons of some trade to none. Two questions thus go unanswered: Is free trade better than restricted trade? and Is freer trade better than the status quo? Neither question can be answered glibly, although both free traders and protectionists sometimes try to do so in the heat of controversy. Trade policy is like situation ethics, unfortunately for the purists at either extreme. Appropriate answers to these questions under one set of circumstances are not necessarily appropriate under another. There is no universal, timeless answer to either practical trade-policy question.

The list of circumstances under which restricted trade can conceivably make an economy stronger (and freer trade can make it weaker) is quite long. It includes exploiting national monopolistic power in export sales, or monopsonistic power in import purchases. It includes using trade policy to combat foreign monopoly, felt perhaps through predatory dumping, when superior antimonopoly policy is unavailable or administratively more costly. It includes protecting economic sectors that possess positive production externalities (e.g., national defense, or high-technology industries with significant spillovers into the rest of the economy), when more direct, first-best production subsidies are infeasible or sufficiently costly to implement. And most important in current world conditions, it includes defending the status quo when trade liberalization would lead to a sufficiently large and enduring rise in national unemployment and excess capacity—one that could not be alleviated quickly (or at all) by conventional government policies.[5]

INTERNAL DISLOCATION AND DISTRIBUTION OF INCOME

The last entry in the list is a direct consequence of downward inflexibility of prices. Economists often refer to such inflexibility as a "distortion." But it seems more appropriate to treat it as a fact of life—and not even necessarily a regrettable one, since one person's inflexibility may be another person's predictability. Most prices, including wages, rents, and interest, are contrac-tually determined between buyers and sellers, and cannot legally be altered in the short run. The familiar result of such rigidity is short-run unemployment and excess capacity when any demand declines. Layoffs take place, assembly lines are idled, and whole plants are shut down. Both people and capital are made invol-untarily unproductive. National product declines by the value of the goods that could have been produced but were not. And national welfare declines further to the extent that the very real subjective and psychic costs of unemployment reduce future productivity of those displaced. Problems of unemployment and excess capacity are further exacerbated by other inflexibilities—unwillingness of labor to move from job to job or place to place; unwillingness of management to move from industry to indus-try; difficulties and costliness of retraining, retooling, and refurbishing.

In the longer run, of course, these inflexibilities moderate, and almost all prices cease to be rigid as contracts expire and are renegotiated. Yet as we will see below, even *temporary* displacement caused by trade liberalization can in some circumstances undermine its desirability, despite the indefinite recurrence of its familiar benefits. And there is some tendency in the current world setting for even long-run flexibility of prices to be less than it once was, thus lengthening the duration of any temporary displacement.

The list of ways in which freer trade might potentially be unfavorable is sometimes dismissed by U.S. economists, who doubt that it could ever convincingly overrule their presumption that, in practice, freer trade is almost always desirable. But the grounds for their doubts and presumptions are rarely more than gut feelings. Only recently, in some of the research we summarize below, have firmer foundations been provided for the usual practice.

Whether firmly founded or not, economists' skepticism about the practical application of the list often reinforces the arguments of those who favor freer trade out of self-interest (e.g., U.S. wheat farmers, aerospace companies, and retailers). And the list is frequently abused by those who favor restricted trade and who want to wrap their self-interest in the flag of national welfare.

The abuses of the list suggest one more important entry to it. Except in ideal worlds, there are always gainers and losers from trade liberalization. To design and carry out practical mechanisms whereby *every* loser was duly compensated (and more) would require a frightening diversion of resources from wealth-producing to wealth-transferring activity. Yet in the absence of such mechanisms, there may be instances in which trade liberalization should be rejected because it undermines a society's sense of equity. In other words, the absence of compensation makes any reference to national economic welfare tenuous and a matter of opinion. Suppose that trade liberalization increased consumption possibilities for 99 out of every 100 individuals by 2 percent. For the 100th, however, it led to temporary dislocation that reduced consumption possibilities to zero (or to the basket that unemployment compensation will buy). In the aggregate, as a lump, the society's average standard of living would rise even in the very short run.[6] But a small minority of society would be made desperately worse off, and a large majority somewhat better off. The possibility must be accepted that the moderately increased satisfaction of the many could be insignificant compared with the dramatic unhappiness visited upon the few. Significant enough distributional consequences of trade liberalization could in turn weaken an economy through social malaise and unrest, and then through their indirect impacts on incentives, confidence, and certainty.

This discussion also makes clear why it is insensitive to dismiss the self-interest of either free traders or protectionists as "self-serving" or "selfish." It is simply impossible often to define any alternative "public interest" to which to recommend adherence. Besides, one person's selfishness is another person's concern for home and family. The problems of trade policy are not conflicts between pure motives and cupidity, nor between intelligence and stupidity. They are problems of resolving legitimate, well-taken differences. My opposition is justified from my point of view; your support is justified from yours. Understanding this is only the beginning of a resolution.

National politicians (and sometimes even economists), of course, resolve such differences to their own satisfaction in practice. But there can be no objective guidelines for doing so. One source becomes immediately apparent for the notorious disagreement among equally intelligent people on whether international trade liberalization is socially desirable or disastrous. Some weight severe losses for the few more heavily in national welfare than others. They feel that poor New England textile workers are already victims of an ungenerous society, and they will recommend forgoing large gains to avoid victimizing them further. Others feel that poor New England textile workers have largely victimized themselves by not being willing to move and adjust when all the signals prompted them to. (Trade liberalization is rarely a surprise.) There is no such thing as a "correct" position on these matters of opinion, interpretation, and subjective judgment.[7]

INTERNATIONAL DISTRIBUTION OF INCOME

Distributional conflicts and contradictory perspectives aggravate relations among nations as well as within them.

None of the insights provided in the general case for international trade sheds any light on the way in which the gains from trade (or, for that matter, from advanced technology) are distributed among nations. It is comfort indeed, but cold comfort, for developing nations to suspect that although trade strengthens their economy, it strengthens the economies of developed nations far more. They are confronted constantly with the exasperating anomaly that international trade may well make the rich richer relative to the poor, and thus increase international income inequality.

Exasperation is compounded by the belief that the gains from international trade are distributed among nations roughly in proportion to their market power. To the strong go most, to the weak go only what their residual veto ("we will not trade") can extract. Distribution based on market power is worse than arbitrary from the perspective of developing countries; it is inimical. It condemns them to a vicious circle of relative poverty, from which they can emerge only by chance. Their relative poverty requires national spending on the necessities of the day, on penalty of collapse. Little is left over for the accumulation of capital and technology at a faster rate than developed countries, which would enable them to close the international gap in living standards and end their relative poverty.

In this context, OPEC's successful oil cartel is a two-edged sword. It confirms the belief of developing countries that the gains from trade are distributed arbitrarily and inimically according to market power (no oil importer ceased to trade with OPEC, so their gains from OPEC trade must not have dried up completely). Yet while validating their view of the world, OPEC impoverishes them still further, heightening their demands that international income inequality be alleviated.

Pleas and proposals for a New International Economic Order fall on comparatively deaf ears in developed countries. In their view, international trade *does* alleviate the absolute poverty of the world's developing countries. To alleviate their *relative* poverty more than a certain amount would be to concede too much to jealousy, however well disguised as equity. Most important, it would require them to sacrifice, unlike engaging in trade, where all nations can gain. They have poor enough at home; they view their prosperity primarily as a bequest of capital and technology from diligent and prudent past generations, not from arbitrary manipulation of the international terms of trade; and they see international income inequality as a red herring, diverting attention from the fundamental proposition that trade strengthens all.

We will elaborate these conflicting points of view regarding international income inequality in section IV. We now turn in section III to the other crucial issue facing current trade policy, whether dislocational and distributional impacts of trade liberalization can practically undermine its benefits.

III. INTERNAL DISLOCATION AND ADAPTATION TO INTERNATIONAL TRADE

THE GENERAL PROBLEM OF INTERNAL INFLEXIBILITY

Developing policies that facilitate shifts in productive resources among various industries in response to economic change must become one of the major aims of the more advanced industrial nations. For domestic reasons alone such a goal is imperative. A large part of the labor force in industrial countries is no longer willing to accept politically the severe economic and social burdens that have often been imposed upon them by economic change. We see evidence of this unwillingness to pay the entire costs of adjustment in many ways: social legislation dealing with unemployment compensation, retraining efforts, and migration allowances; special tax and lending policies designed to foster new industries in depressed areas; union attempts in contract negotiations to protect the jobs of their members against laborsaving technological changes; and various trade and immigration laws restricting the inflow of goods and people.

In such efforts it is sometimes forgotten that the success of one group in maintaining its jobs or capital position is often at the economic expense of some other group. One manifestation of this is the difficulty industrial countries are encountering in reducing unemployment, even during prosperous periods, below what once were minimum acceptable levels. Continued economic change coupled with growing economic rigidities introduced by groups seeking to protect themselves against such change has resulted in pervasive structural inflexibilities that prevent the attainment of so-called full employment. Moreover, the unemployment burden falls heavily upon the young, the uneducated, women, the elderly, and various minority groups— all of whom lack the economic and political organization necessary to match the job-protecting achievements of most other economic and social groups.

There is also a close relationship between economic growth and the flexibility of a country's resources. When countries are in the early stages of industrialization, the problem is minimal. New economic opportunities can usually be exploited quickly by attracting young, opportunistic workers from the low-productivity agricultural sector and capital from abroad or other domestic industries. Yet once a nation is predominantly industrial and even its smaller agricultural sector is mechanized, the problem can become a very difficult one. Change now often requires shifts of older, less mobile, more narrowly skilled workers from one industrial sector to another, with the prospect of only comparable or even lower wages for many workers. No longer is there an "industrial reserve army" in agriculture on which to draw. The collective, often organized resistance of workers and industrialists in those sectors adversely affected by economic change to move their resources into new areas and adjust to the new earnings situation slows the potential rate of economic growth. This in turn makes it even more difficult to achieve full employment and improve the distribution of income.

In attempting to formulate sensible adjustment policies, a first step is to try to understand the nature of the adjustment process and then actually to measure the magnitude of adjustment costs and benefits in response to particular economic changes; for example, the lowering of import duties. The next subsection will discuss in general terms the impact on productive agents and consumers of economic change in the international economy, while the subsection following that will summarize some results from our attempts to measure adjustment costs and benefits from trade liberalization. The last subsection will discuss particular policy proposals.

THE PROCESS OF ADJUSTMENT TO TRADE LIBERALIZATION

Traditionally, economists have tended to dismiss the costs of domestic adjustment associated with a lowering of tariffs with the remark that they disappear in the long run, while the benefits from lower import prices continue indefinitely. Yet the following familiar quotation from Lord Keynes' *A Tract on Monetary Reform* reminds us that this view often cloaks a cavalier social attitude: "In the long run we are all dead. Economists set themselves too easy, too useless a task, if in tempestuous seasons they can only tell us that when the storm is long past the ocean is flat again." Besides, the typical dismissal of short-run adjustment costs is just bad economics. Every day people indicate the manner in which they compare present benefits or costs with future benefits or costs through the discount mechanism in money markets. One can legitimately argue that when estimating costs and benefits for society as a whole a discount rate different from the market rate should be employed, but there can be little quarrel with the discounting principle. The short-run costs of adjustment must be compared to the long-run benefits. Since discounting gives greater weight to near-future costs or benefits than long-run costs or benefits, it is possible that a particular tariff cut, for example, does not raise collective social welfare even though the absolute sum of the costs is less than the absolute sum of the benefits.[8]

Let us trace through in a general way the effects of a reduction in the cost of foreign products due to a duty reduction or perhaps to some relative technological advance abroad. The first effect, of course, is a reduction in the price of imports. This is likely to be less than the duty or cost reduction and may not occur at all for a while if competition among importers is slight.

But eventually import prices are likely to decline, or at least not rise as fast as they otherwise would have. As this takes place, purchasers of domestic substitute goods tend to shift their purchase toward the import goods and away from similar domestic items. Here too, however, purchasers are cautious, especially if items are used as intermediate inputs in further production. Firms do not want to jeopardize the goodwill of traditional suppliers unless they are convinced that the relative price decline is likely to be permanent.

Unless domestic firms respond by lowering their prices, too, domestic sales and employment fall. Of course, if other countries are also reducing their tariff and an industry is a net exporter, sales and employment will rise. But let us focus on net importing industries that tend to be hurt by greater importation. The nature of the price response of domestic firms to increased imports varies widely among industries. It seems reasonable, however, to assume that wage rates, rents, and many borrowing costs are relatively inflexible downward in much of the industrial sector for the year-or-so, short-run period upon which we are concentrating. However, if the duty reduction is general, the costs of imported goods used as intermediate inputs fall and lower domestic production costs. Firms that follow a markup pricing system, therefore, tend to reduce their domestic price because of lower costs. Moreover, if considerable excess capacity develops despite this price decline, the price is likely to be reduced still more. Since wages are rigid, the income burden of this cut falls most significantly on the owners of the plant and capital equipment that is industry-specific.

It is possible that the relative prices of domestic import substitutes fall enough to prevent any immediate decline in the volume of sales and employment. However, even if this were the case, capital owners would not replace all their plant and equipment as it depreciated because of the low rate of return, and output and employment would eventually begin to decline. But this would be a gradual process and could be offset by the normal growth in the industry's market.[9] Thus, the adjustment process *could* be carried out without any increase in unemployment and with capital owners bearing all the adjustment costs.

However, the losses to the owners of domestic facilities are matched by gains to consumers in the form of lower prices for domestic goods. In addition, consumers benefit from lower import prices.

Nevertheless, sales in some industries are likely to decline in the short run. Even this may not lead to an immediate decline in employment, however. Because of the costs of hiring and training new employees, employers tend to retain their labor force until they are convinced that the sales decline is more or less permanent.[10]

When employees are released, however, they and society begin to suffer real losses. The cost to society of this unemployment is the output the workers could have produced plus any additional output used by the unemployed or others in helping them find other jobs. While much more information is needed, we now have some data on how long it takes displaced workers to find new jobs. A study by the U.S. Department of Labor in 1972 of workers displaced as a result of increased imports indicated the average period to be thirty-six weeks.[11] As might be expected, women, older employees, and minority groups had a considerably more difficult time in finding new jobs than young white males. A 1975 sample survey indicated the average duration of unemployment to be forty-nine weeks (thirty-nine for males and sixty-one for females).[12] Still another study by James E. McCarthy of the shoe industry in Massachusetts indicated an average length of unemployment of eighteen weeks.[13] Besides the relationships mentioned above, the studies found that the higher the general unemployment rate, the longer it took to find alternative employment. A surprisingly large proportion of workers in McCarthy's sample (26 percent) never worked again. Most of these workers, whose mean age was sixty-one, retired.

The new jobs obtained by displaced workers open up in part because some industries are expanding in response to growing markets and in part because the workers in effect do accept wage cuts. Though established rates may not change, they agree to work for lower wages at less skill-intensive jobs. Employers hire such workers over new entrants into the labor force with less skills. This sets up a chain reaction that finally lowers the going wage rates for the least skill-intensive jobs. If the import effects are significant enough to cause an exchange-rate change, the currency depreciation will lead to an expansion of export industries and some reduction in the adverse effects in the import-competing sectors. Both of these reactions also provide new jobs for the displaced workers. Of course, if foreigners are also reducing duties, the export expansion will occur without any exchange-rate change.[14]

Offsetting these social costs of import displacement are the conventional benefits from lower prices of imports. As alluded to earlier, these benefits appear in two ways. First, individuals gain directly from cheaper consumer-good imports. But they also gain indirectly. Most domestically produced goods use some imports as intermediate goods. Since the costs of these fall, the prices of domestically produced consumer goods also tend to decline. The benefits from these lower prices as well as those for consumer goods directly imported continue indefinitely, while the costs associated with unemployment last a comparatively short period.

Another matter that must be considered in any framework of adjustment costs associated with increased imports is the possible effects on a country's terms of trade, that is, the ratio of its average export prices to its average import prices. Some countries are large enough in world markets to possess some market power. Consequently, when they impose import duties, this has the effect of improving their trading terms and thereby raising their real income in the same way an individual monopolist can do by raising his price.[15] Consequently, when these countries lower their duties, they incur a loss that must be balanced against the gains just mentioned. Some studies indicate, for example, that the United States would lose on balance by a unilateral tariff reduction because of this effect—quite aside from the temporary losses from unemployment. However, if one is considering a multilateral tariff negotiation, where all the major countries reduce import duties, the reduction in the use of monopoly power on the part of any one country is likely to be roughly offset by the reduction in the use of monopoly power by all other countries.[16]

MEASURING ADJUSTMENT COSTS

On the basis of the framework outlined above, it is possible actually to estimate on a detailed industry basis the changes in trade, employment, and net social welfare associated with such economic changes as the general reduction in tariffs among the industrial countries that currently is being negotiated in Geneva. The three of us have done so under various hypothetical tariff-cutting formulas, and it would be useful to summarize some of our results here.[17]

It is wise to say a few words about the usefulness of such estimates. Obviously we would not have attempted the study unless we thought it was worthwhile. But our tools are still crude and our lack of adequate data considerable. The best way to make sensible social decisions is, in our view, to continue to refine such types of studies. However, for the present, policy makers should take the results of such studies as only one among several data inputs into their decisions. The views of commodity experts, businessmen, labor leaders, and the like, should still receive considerable weight in deliberations about what will happen when import duties are reduced. But they should also be scrutinized with the same care as should such studies as ours.

Let us indicate the type of impact effects we obtain when it is assumed that all major developed countries reduce their import duties by 50 percent. We do, however, exclude from the tariff-cutting exercise manufactured goods subject to quantitative controls, mainly textiles, as well as agricultural products whose import levels are independent of duty levels, mainly those covered by the variable-levy system of the European Economic Community and certain U.S. agricultural imports subject to quantitative restrictions.[18]

A major conclusion of our studies is that the overall aggregate effects of a significant multilateral duty reduction, namely, a 50 percent cut, on the U.S. trade balance and employment picture are negligible. As Table 2.1 indicates, the particular 50 percent cut examined improved the U.S. trade balance by $4 million and reduced employment by 15,000 jobs. For manufacturing

Table 2.1

TRADE AND EMPLOYMENT EFFECTS ON THE
UNITED STATES OF A 50 PERCENT,
MULTILATERAL TARIFF REDUCTION

| | Exchange Rate | |
	Fixed	Flexible
Trade Changes (millions of U.S. $)		
Exports	+ 1.750	+ 1.747
Imports	− 1.746	− 1.747
Net trade effect	+ 4	0
Employment Changes (man-years)		
Export-related	+ 136.000	+ 135.800
Import-related	− 151.200	− 151.200
Net employment effect	− 15.200	− 15.400
Exchange-rate Change (percent)	−	+ .003

alone, the figures were: −$126 million and −32,000 jobs. Both
sets of figures are very small when compared with total U.S.
exports and imports, which now each amount to over $100
billion and to total employment that is around 90 million. Thus,
the exchange-rate change needed to maintain the initial balance
of trade is also negligible. However, even in countries where the
balance of trade might tend to improve or worsen significantly,
the exchange-rate mechanism will operate to offset such pressures. Given the political difficulties countries face in using fiscal
and monetary policies to change employment, it is reassuring to
know that in the U.S. case no such policies would be needed
and, even if they were, we must recognize that this policy measure is also becoming increasingly politicized, thus reducing the
ability of policymakers to respond quickly to international economic shocks that affect trade and employment.

The fact that the aggregate effects were minimal does not
mean that changes in all industries were insignificant. One way
of summarizing the distributional impact of trade liberalization
is to compare its employment consequences from industry to
industry. In 189 or 61 percent of the 310 traded-goods industries
there was some loss of employment. Most of these declines were

small, however. There were only 54 industries in which the loss of employment was more than one half of 1 percent of the industry's labor force. It would seem that an industry should be able to absorb the loss of 1 job in 200 without too much difficulty. Normal retirements and voluntary quits should easily handle this.

In only 31 of the 310 industries was the loss in employment more than 1 percent of the industry's labor force. These industries appear in Table 2.2.[19]

On the other hand, there are seven industries in which employment *grows* by 1 percent or more. These industries appear in Table 2.3. The shorter length of this list and the generally smaller impact perhaps help explain the absence of strong, freer-trade pressures from very many individual industries.

We next considered whether the market growth rate of each industry in recent years could absorb the employment losses in some of the 54 severely affected (employment loss greater than one half of 1 percent) industries if the tariff cuts were phased over ten equal annual cuts, as the new U.S. tariff law permits. For thirty-three of the fifty-four industries past growth rates would have been sufficient, so that no absolute decline in employment was needed. The remaining twenty-one included non-rubber footwear, various leather products, ceramic tile, pottery, lead and zinc, and certain textiles not covered by the long-term agreement.

Other breakdowns of the short-run gainers and losers from trade liberalization relate to labor skills and geography. In the United States, the portion of the labor force that gains on balance in employment opportunities consists of professional, technical, and managerial employees. Skilled craftsmen and unskilled laborers lose somewhat, while semiskilled workers lose the most. The percentages are all very small, however. The loss for the semiskilled group, for example, is only 0.15 percent of their size. The geographical pattern of incidence for the tariff cuts indicates what one would expect: the New England states suffer the most.

Thus far, we have described the adjustment problems only in terms of numbers of jobs lost or gained. However, it is possible

Table 2.2

INDUSTRIES ESTIMATED TO FACE
REDUCED LABOR REQUIREMENTS GREATER THAN
1 PERCENT FROM MULTILATERAL TARIFF REDUCTION

Industry	Percentage Employment Loss
Food utensils and pottery	20.6
Rubber footwear	13.1
Cutlery	12.4
Motorcycles, bicycles, and parts	12.0
Artificial flowers	11.3
Pottery products	9.7
Scour and combing plants	4.6
Other leather products	4.0
Games and toys	3.1
Industrial leather tanning	3.1
Ceramic wall and floor tile	2.7
Jewelry	2.7
Nonrubber footwear	2.7
Sewing machines	2.6
Radios and TV sets	2.5
Sport and athletic goods	2.5
Watches, clocks, and parts	2.4
Buttons, needles, pins, and fasteners	2.2
Lace goods	2.1
Musical instruments	1.9
Optical instruments and lenses	1.9
Textile machinery	1.9
Veneer and plywood	1.7
Primary zinc	1.6
Miscellaneous manufactures	1.6
Electrical equipment	1.4
Electronic tubes	1.4
Primary lead	1.3
Sugar	1.2
Vegetable oil mills	1.1
Other nonferrous mining	1.0

to value the stream of lost income due to unemployment and compare this with the stream of consumer benefits from lower import and domestic prices. By relating the various economic

Table 2.3

INDUSTRIES ESTIMATED TO FACE
INCREASED LABOR REQUIREMENTS GREATER THAN
1 PERCENT FROM MULTILATERAL TARIFF REDUCTION

Industry	Percentage Employment Gain
Semiconductors	6.3
Computing machines	3.2
Tobacco	3.0
Office machines	2.3
Mechanical measuring devices	1.5
Electronic components	1.4
X-ray tubes and apparatus	1.1

characteristics of the labor force in any industry—such as age, skill, sex, and racial composition of the workers—to the study previously mentioned dealing with the length of the job search depending on these characteristics, one can determine the number of days of lost employment in each industry. By valuing this unemployment at the income levels workers could have earned if employed, and discounting the stream of lost income at plausible rates, one finally obtains the social cost of the net labor made idle by the duty reductions. The stream of net benefits can be determined in a similarly straightforward manner. Of course, the same discount rate should be used for both the cost and the benefit streams.

It is striking that for the United States as a whole our estimates indicate that benefits in just one year considerably outweigh the present value of the stream of adjustment costs at any reasonable discount rate. At a 10 percent discount rate for both benefits and costs, the value of the benefits from a 50 percent cut amounted to $1,056 million, while the value of the costs came to only $37 million. There are twenty-six industries in which the net welfare effect exceeds $10 million. Moreover, these industries account for $600 million of the $1,019 million net welfare gains to the economy. These industries are: tobacco; canned fruits and vegetables; sugar; alcoholic beverages; veneer and plywood; rubber footwear; miscellaneous plastic products; non-rubber footwear; other leather products; glass, excluding containers; food utensils and pottery; cutlery; computing machines; radio and TV sets; semiconductors; electronic components; motor vehicles; aircraft; aircraft equipment; aircraft equipment, not elsewhere classified; motorcycles and bicycles; mechanical measuring devices; jewelry; games and toys; sport and athletic goods; and miscellaneous manufactures.

Although the largest welfare changes by industry are all positive, there are negative net welfare effects in thirty-two industries. These are: cotton; iron and ferroalloy mining; copper ore mining; coal mining; stone and clay mining; felt goods; pads and upholstery filling; logging; sawmills and planing mills; hardwood flooring; special-product sawmills; wooden containers; paper containers and boxes; newspapers; periodicals; synthetic rubber; industrial leather and tanning; footwear cut stock; glass containers; structural clay, etc.; concrete blocks and bricks; ready-mixed concrete; lime; minerals; ground; primary nonferrous metals; nonferrous castings, not elsewhere classified; metal cans, fabricated steel products; architectural metal; coating and engraving service; and steel springs.

There are also twenty-four nontraded-goods industries in which the net welfare change is negative. Furthermore, even though the number of industries in which the total welfare change is negative is comparatively small, there are ninety-five traded-goods industries and twenty-four nontraded-goods industries in which the welfare impact for the first year is negative. Nevertheless, as pointed out earlier, there is a net gain in welfare for all industries combined for the first year.

Thus, although a number of arbitrary assumptions were made and imperfect data were sometimes used, it appears that taking account of the short-run adjustment costs involved in trade liberalization does not significantly alter the traditional conclusion concerning the merits of multilateral trade negotiations. The benefits calculated are so much larger than the costs that it seems unlikely that reasonable variations on the assumptions and procedures will alter this conclusion. Nevertheless, the unemployment caused in some industries is significant, and the net welfare effect in certain industries also is negative. The implication of these results is not that duties should never be cut in such industries but that tariff reductions should be introduced gradually in order to take greater advantage of normal market growth and retirements to ease the costs of adjustment.

Before we would claim conclusively that the United States is better off from a 50 percent multilateral cut, it is necessary to address the distributional issue. Are there mechanisms that assure that the $37 million of losses are not so severe in human terms that the rest of society would be "collectively willing" to forgo its $1,056 million of gains? It is here that policies like unemployment compensation, trade adjustment assistance, and wage subsidies [20] have a role to play.

SELECTING OPTIMAL INDUSTRIAL ADAPTATION POLICIES

The manner in which the estimates described above can be used to achieve needed adjustments at minimal social costs is fairly obvious. For example, to assist negotiators in the current round of trade negotiations, we are testing in detail the trade, employment, and welfare effects of the various tariff-cutting rules that are being proposed. Obviously the U.S. aim is to choose a rule that gives a significant average cut in a manner that minimizes adjustment costs. Any government that is not making similar estimates is not doing its homework properly.

There are many ways of reducing the costs of adjustment and still obtaining the benefits of adaptation. Clearly, staging duty reductions over time periods that enable normal market growth to provide increases in labor demand that match the decreases due to duty cuts is an important method.[21] Industries in which adaptation is rapid can be cut more quickly in order to increase net benefits. Duties in some industries where employment is already declining and adjustment problems are already significant should perhaps not be reduced at all. They are already bearing enough adjustment pressures. Indeed, we would not hesitate to recommend temporary safeguard measures for such industries if it is clear that they will not impede long-run adjustment. From a broad viewpoint, if countries wanted to move ultimately toward free to near-free trade, studies like ours can be used to help policymakers decide how fast to proceed. If we are given certain constraints, such as that the relative cost of employment should not exceed such-and-such an amount in any one year, we can solve for the maximum speed at which the country could cut duties in any industry in any year without exceeding this constraint. While similar studies for other countries are needed before strong generalizations can be made, the U.S. evidence suggests that the significant industrial adaptations likely to be required by the developed countries in the future can be made within the framework of socially and politically acceptable domestic adjustment costs, even at presently exceptional high levels of unemployment.

Our problem now seems *not* to be that the costs are too high overall, but that too many groups identify personal costs with social costs and apply political pressures leading to nonadjustment policies. Export and import quotas, both mandatory and voluntary, run the danger of turning into such nonadjustment policies, if past experience is any guide to generalization. If quotas are to be imposed or even tariffs raised, these measures should perhaps be supplemented with means other than market pressures in order to achieve the needed adaptations that the market pressures are signaling. For example, industries requesting such aid might be required to produce meaningful rationalization programs that reduce employment gradually. Older workers might be given lump-sum payments or retirement incomes in order to achieve their early exit from weak industry. Young workers might be discouraged from entering such industries through various tax or subsidy systems. With early retirements and the minimal use of young workers, many firms should be able to continue to provide jobs to middle-aged workers until their retirement. There are a number of other specific adaptation measures that might be tried, but a discussion of these would require another paper.

The point we would like to make strongly is that our reactions in the trade area to the need for industrial adaptation have thus far been essentially ones of nonadjustment. We must combine acceptable international market pressures with positive domestic programs to foster active industrial adaptation.

IV. INCOME INEQUALITY AND THE NEW
INTERNATIONAL ECONOMIC ORDER

PERSPECTIVES ON THE PROBLEMS OF DEVELOPING COUNTRIES

While the difficulties that the advanced industrial countries have faced from resource inflexibility have been considerable in recent years, these are, we believe, only a moderate indication of what is to come. Much more severe adjustment pressures will emanate in the future from the developing nations of the world. Just as poorer groups in modern industrial societies have vigorously demanded a large share of the economic pie, so too are the developing countries. The whole system of proposals covered under the New International Economic Order is a manifestation of this pressure. Their growing political, economic, and military strength is posing questions that the industrial nations can no longer turn aside or treat in a piecemeal fashion. Are the developing nations going to be permtted to raise their income levels by the developed nations opening their domestic markets to these countries? Or will the developed nations attempt essentially to maintain the status quo? Considerable political and economic turmoil is likely to be ahead no matter what policy is followed, but experience and common sense would suggest that some form of the first policy simply must be followed in our own long-run interests. The second policy holds out only the prospect of chronic structural unemployment, economic stagnation, and increased international political instability. This does not mean that we should immediately dismantle all our trade barriers and accept what imports result from this action. This would impose economically cruel and politically intolerable burdens on significant parts of the labor force. Instead we must devise compromise policies that balance not only our own short-run and long-run interests but help to meet the legitimate goals of the developing nations.

The last ten years have been ones of deep frustration for most of the developing countries in the world. Their high hopes of the 1950s and early 1960s to reduce the income gap between the rich and poor nations have not been fulfilled. The gap has in fact continued to widen. While rapid growth in the industrial sector was generally achieved during initial development efforts directed at substituting domestic production of manufactures for imports of such goods, continued high growth rates in the industrial sector have become increasingly difficult to maintain. Moreover, these efforts have been plagued by periodic balance-of-payments crises involving extensive foreign-exchange and import controls and often eventual sharp exchange-rate depreciations that heighten internal political tensions.

Attempts to grow by exporting manufactured goods to the advanced industrial nations have been successful for a few, generally small countries, but the overall results have been disappointing. Specifically, the "gang of four"—Taiwan, Korea, Hong Kong, and Singapore—have done well, whereas such large economies as India, Indonesia, and Pakistan have performed poorly in export markets. Brazil, however, is a recent example of a large country that has shifted successfully from a predominantly import-substitution policy to one of export promotion. It took ten years after the first United Nations Conference on Trade and Development (UNCTAD) in 1964 to attain zero-duty treatment in the developed countries for the manufacturing exports of the developing nations. And the schemes that are in effect are encumbered by quantitative restrictions and outright prohibitions or special treatment for a number of the goods most easily produced in the poorer countries; for example, textiles and apparel. Moreover, recent protectionist actions by the European Community and the United States toward textiles, color television, steel and shoe imports give little encouragement for any significant further liberalization of import restraints for labor-intensive goods on the part of the industrial countries.

The exhaustion of import-substitution possibilities and the uncertain outlook for export promotion to developed countries suggest one visionary alternative: regional economic cooperation among developing countries exclusively (the "South-South" model of trade). Experience to date with developing country integration has been too thin to provide encouragement or discouragement, but the phenomenon may loom larger in the years to come, both in practice and in proposal.

One recent encouraging development from a developing country perspective was the increase in the price of primary products, including commodities other than oil, relative to prices of manufactured goods in the first few years of the 1970s. But part of this gain was lost during the 1975-76 worldwide recession. This experience served to reemphasize the problem of the high instability of export prices and export earnings of commodity producers. The compensatory financing scheme established in the IMF as a result of the first UNCTAD conference has not come close to meeting the goals of the developing nations in the commodity field. The great bulk of the population of these countries is still engaged in agricultural activities that are subject to wide fluctuatons in profitability.

Clearly the one most important event that has forced upon the developed countries a new awareness of the developing nations has been the very sharp increase in oil prices engineered by the OPEC nations through coordinated monopolistic action. This price increase introduced a major shock into the world economy that caused both significant inflation and unemployment in the industrial (and developing) countries. The unemployment situation was exacerbated by a general cyclical downturn in economic activity. While the short-run effect was to turn attention away from the basic problems of the great majority of developing countries who did not produce oil, the gradual realization that price-raising cartels might be formed in other commodities exported by the developing countries seems to have caused the developed countries to be more forthcoming and receptive in their responses to the economic demands of the former nations. Indeed, it was the developed countries who proposed the recently concluded eighteen-month Conference on International Economic Cooperation (CIEC), which became the main forum in which the key elements of the New International Economic Order were negotiated. Yet there has been a sense of bitterness and frustration on the part of the developed nations in these negotiations, based on what they regard as the "unfair" sudden oil shock deliberately imposed upon their economies. Of course, for years leaders of the developing countries have regarded the activities of the rich countries toward them in this way, and perhaps such attitudes may be necessary to achieve significant reforms in international economic relations.

A final view shared by many individuals in the developed world is that the income gains sought by the poorer countries must stem mainly from domestic rather than international economic forces. Further, it appears to these individuals that a number of developing countries have pursued policies that actually have thwarted the establishment of strong domestic economies capable of generating significant economic growth. The domestic economic structures fashioned in these countries produce high-cost economic goods incapable of competing in world markets or of generating significant further domestic backward and forward production linkages. In addition, the misuse of foreign aid for the selfish gain of special interests, coupled with the disregard for human rights in some developing countries, has engendered a cynicism toward the views of these countries. The demands for special international treatment strike many in the developed world as attempts to turn attention away from the real domestic roots of their problems. Moreover, even on the international level, many who sympathize with the long-run goals of the developing nations question the wisdom of the particular policies being pressed upon the developed countries. Whether these various views have merit is not the issue at this point. What is important in seeking progress in the North-South dialogue is that both sides appreciate the underlying conflicting attitudes toward each other and work toward allaying some of the misconceptions on which they are based.

THE PROPOSAL CONSTITUTING THE NEW INTERNATIONAL ECONOMIC ORDER

Spurred on by the growing per capita income gap between poor and rich nations, worldwide inflation, major changes in the international monetary system, and a growing awareness of their political and economic strength, the developing countries succeeded in obtaining adoption in the UN General Assembly in May 1974 of two major resolutions: a Declaration on the Establishment of a New International Economic Order and a Program of Action on the Establishment of a New International Economic Order.

The essence of all the various policies recommended is that they give preferential treatment to the developing nations (compared with the treatment of developed countries to each other). In the first UNCTAD meeting in 1964, the key issues were preferential tariff treatment for the poorer nations and some form of compensatory financing to meet their balance-of-payments problems. While these programs were justified by the developing countries on equity grounds, Raul Prebisch, the first secretary general and leading intellectual in suggesting policies, also argued (convincingly to many people) that world resource allocation would be improved by adopting the recommended measures. For example, he employed the infant-industry argument to justify preferences for manufactured and semimanufactured goods. In the current discussion there seems to be less emphasis on promoting economic efficiency and greater stress on economic "rights" and privileges of developing countries because they are poor. It is important to recognize that this greater stress on equity considerations continues a trend evident in international affairs at least since the 1950s. Moreover, this trend is an extension of the much greater emphasis in the twentieth compared with the nineteenth century on social measures providing special help to the poor and disadvantaged within countries.

The most controversial trade policies recommended as part of the New International Economic Order are stabilizing commodity prices and increasing exports of manufactured goods to the developed nations. We turn to each now in more detail.

STABILIZING COMMODITY PRICES

Primary-product producers everywhere in the world understandably complain about the greater price fluctuations they encounter than producers of manufactured goods. It seems "unfair" that prices of manufactures are relatively more stable over the business cycle. (It should also be remembered that workers in the industrial sector object with equal vigor to the "unfairness" of suffering periodic unemployment as prices and wages in this sector remain rigid in the face of an economic downturn.) When much of a country's economic activity is devoted to producing primary products subject to wide price fluctuations, the prospects of undertaking sound development policies involving extended time periods for successful completion appear bleak. Consequently, it is not surprising that the goal of commodity price stabilization has recently been in the forefront of the goals of developing countries.

The key commodity proposals of the developing countries at the Conference on International Economic Cooperation, which was concluded at the end of May, were the establishment of commodity agreements for each of from ten to eighteen commodities of export interest to the developing countries, and the creation of a Common Fund of $3 billion to finance the commodity buffer stocks that would be a part of these commodity agreements.[22] The rationale behind setting up a Common Fund to finance buffer stocks is that besides achieving certain management economies, Fund members can take advantage of "complementarities" in commodity price movements. While some schemes will be borrowing in order to buy commodities and hold prices up, others will be selling stocks to keep prices from rising too much and thus will be paying back previous borrowings. The total resources needed to operate buffer-stock programs will supposedly be less than if each scheme were independent of the others. In addition to the creation of commodity-stabilization schemes for a wide range of products and of the common financing fund, the developing countries also pressed for tying or indexing the prices of commodities to the prices of manufactured goods in order to maintain the purchasing power of their commodity exports.

Despite early opposition on the part of some of the key developed countries represented at the Conference on International Cooperation—for example, the United States, West Germany, and Japan—the developing countries finally succeeded in gaining agreement on the part of the developed nations to set up a Common Fund to finance buffer stocks for a range of commodity agreements. Details of the Fund are to be negotiated at UNCTAD, but the industrial countries did pledge "to ensure a successful conclusion" of these negotiations. However, the indexation proposal was essentially set aside, at least for the time being.

In evaluating commodity agreements generally, it seems fair to say that they sound good in theory but do not work out in practice, at least as far as past experience is concerned. In theory it sounds plausible that we should be able to reduce the degree of price instability of commodity prices over cycles in economic activity. But there are several practical difficulties with carrying out this goal successfully. A key one is the problem of judging the length of cyclical fluctuations and disentangling short-run fluctuations from long-term trends.[23] This is not to say that it is impossible to moderate prices with buffer stocks, but that the stocks required and the cost of carrying these stocks are much larger than many have thought were adequate. When the managers of buffer stocks run out of funds to buy commodities or supplies of the goods to help hold prices down, precipitous price changes tend to occur that increase rather than decrease the degree of price instability.

A related cause of the breakdown of past commodity agreements has been the breakthrough of the ceiling due to the depletion of buffer stocks. As a result of this, consuming nations feel that they should not be held to their part of the bargain, namely, agreeing to buy in the future at no less than the established minimum prices. This was the fate of the International Grains Agreement that collapsed in 1969. Another common breakdown cause has been cheating among suppliers during surplus times. Suppliers with small market shares, who often feel that their quota allocation is too small in terms of current production-cost realities, see the opportunity to increase their market supplies enough to reap significant gains but not enough to depress the price so much that the larger producers engage in a price war. Of course, quite often the independent actions of the various small producers do bring about such a price decline, and the agreement collapses completely. This was the fate of most commodity agreements in the 1930s.

While compensatory financing schemes such as the present

IMF program are considerably more efficient in stabilizing export *earnings* of primary-product producers than are commodity price-stabilization schemes (and it is earnings that the developing countries are frequently concerned with), it is now evident that commodity agreements will be a major means of establishing a New International Economic Order. To the developing nations, short-run loans and even grants appear merely to emphasize their dependency upon the developed countries, whereas commodity schemes that stabilize (and raise, if possible) prices are not only "just" but permit a more dignified arm's-length economic relationship with the industrial world. The modest sums involved in past compensatory financing schemes also suggest that in actual practice the commodity agreement route will bring about a greater transfer of income to the developing countries. But it seems reasonable to predict that the new commodity schemes will be beset by the same problems as the old ones and that one cannot be too optimistic about their success.

INCREASING EXPORTS OF MANUFACTURES BY DEVELOPING COUNTRIES

Despite what might be said about the inefficient manufacturing structure built by many developing nations, there is no doubt why these countries were encouraged to develop in this manner. The developed countries have erected tariff structures that highly protect manufactures and semimanufactures. Moreover, by means of quantitative restrictions on such items as textile and apparel products, shoes, certain electronic goods, and a number of agricultural products, they have greatly curtailed export markets for developing countries in lines in which the latter have a comparative advantage.

Since the first UNCTAD conference, the developing countries have stressed the attainment of a Generalized System of Preferences (GSP) as the major means of increasing exports of manufactures to the developed countries. Under this system, manufactured goods from developing nations are admitted duty-free in the developed countries. Currently, the European Community, Japan, the United States, Australia, Austria, Canada, Finland, New Zealand, Norway, Sweden, and Switzerland have implemented preferential arrangements. The more developed socialist countries of Eastern Europe have also introduced such schemes. However, all of the present schemes have a number of restrictions in terms of country and commodity coverage, as well as in terms of permissible import volumes.[24] Therefore, in the current world trade negotiations, the developing countries are directing most of their energies toward improving and extending the existing arrangements. But it is an open question whether it would be more in their interest to devote attention to seeking general tariff cuts, that is, cuts that apply to all exporters.

In the so-called Tokyo Round of trade negotiations currently under way under the auspices of the General Agreement on Tariffs and Trade (GATT), the developing countries have adopted a rather passive attitude toward the particular tariff-cutting formula to be chosen. They have instead concentrated on trying to insure that no matter what formula is chosen their margin of preference is maintained, either under the tariff system or by means of some other form of compensation. In particular, they have not exerted any significant negotiating pressure toward influencing the extent of the average duty cut made by the industrial nations.

Should all duties be cut, say, by 50 percent, there would of course be a trade loss to the developing countries due to the erosion of their preference margin. For example, if the particular duty in a developed country is now 30 percent for all other developed countries but zero for developing countries, a decrease of the duty to 15 percent would tend to reduce exports of the developing countries to the developed country. However, there are also forces operating to increase the exports of the poorer countries. Some commodities not covered by preferences will be included in the general most-favored-nation (MFN) cuts, and the developing countries will share in the increased trade related to the duty reductions. These countries will also obtain trade gains in those lines on which proportional value limitations for duty-free preference trade exist. They will be able to share in the increased trade at the lower MFN duty rate. Those developing countries presently excluded from preferences will also benefit, since MFN cuts apply to all countries. Finally, the MFN reductions will last indefinitely, while the various preference schemes have a limited duration.

Estimates by one of the authors and Tracy Murray yield a trade loss due to the erosion of preference margins from a 50 percent cut of $32 million annually to the countries covered by preferential schemes.[25] However, increases in exports of countries enjoying preferences would be $150 million annually due to the MFN cuts; $106 million of this $150 million stems from increased exports of preferentially treated goods; the remaining $44 million stems from increased exports of goods not covered by preference schemes. Thus, the export increase just to the participants in existing preferential arrangements would be more than 4.5 times their trade loss due to the erosion of preferential tariff margins. In addition, trade increases will accrue for the 50 percent cut to developing countries not covered by preferences. In annual terms these amount to $268 million under our estimation procedures. Thus, net benefits to all developing nations from a 50 percent cut in addition to the trade increases from preferences are estimated to be $386 million annually.

It would appear from these estimates that the developing countries have much to gain from a significant MFN cut by the developed countries. It is probably tactically wise to seek to maintain the existing preference margin and to improve the existing preference schemes, but it is also important for the developing nations that the average MFN cut be significant. Still another route, but one that raises special rancor in the United States because its exports suffer, is to negotiate new or more comprehensive reverse preferences with the European Community. A difficulty with this, however, besides its obvious violation of GATT principles, is that it may be even more discriminatory than the widespread GSP.

V. SOME CONCLUSIONS

While, as noted at the outset, it is easy to become discouraged with respect to the development progress of the poorer countries of the world, we should keep in mind that there have been solid accomplishments. The average growth rate of around 5.5 percent annually for gross domestic product between 1960 and 1975 is actually quite remarkable in terms of past performance. Population in these countries has also grown rapidly, but per capita income has still managed to expand at nearly 3 percent annually.

Fortunately, under the rubric of the New International Economic Order the problems of the developing countries are receiving more attention from the advanced nations than at any time since the 1950s, and there is thus a possible opportunity for improving upon this growth performance. Whether in fact this goal is achieved, of course, remains to be seen. But there are some reasons for not being too optimistic. The tremendous energies and resources that will go into establishment of a number of additional commodity agreements and a Common Fund to finance buffer stocks will obviously result in a significant transfer of resources to the developing countries. But whether these efforts are the best feasible way to further the long-run goal of closing the income gap between rich and poor countries is debatable. Past experience with commodity agreements suggests that they do not work effectively and often result in increasing the bitterness of producers and consumers toward each other when they break down. Moreover, there is no evidence that price stability increases growth rates. A better means of achieving both greater stability in export earnings and more rapid growth may be to work toward greater product diversification in the commodity field. The greater willingness by the developed countries to finance such efforts offers an important opportunity that should be seriously considered.

Regardless of what occurs in the commodity field, a major point to keep in mind is that greater industrialization offers the best opportunity for high incomes, greater employment, and a better income distribution for most of the Third World. While industrialization history amply demonstrates from the case of England to that of Japan that success rests fundamentally on the development of internal markets, there is no doubt that industrialization can be promoted to a significant extent by international trade. In this area the leaders of the developing countries have chosen to exert most of their negotiating pressure on achieving improvements in the preference arrangements granted by the industrial nations.

But political leaders in developed countries cannot provide trade concessions such as zero-duty preferences without also establishing controls guaranteeing that these concessions will really not hurt competing domestic industries. Political pressures from these domestic industries make this result inevitable. The growing restrictions on trade not covered by preferences, shoes, for example, also illustrate this political reality. Developing countries have also not granted reciprocal concessions for MFN cuts made by the developed countries. Thus, the latter countries feel perfectly justified in taking steps to insure that their unilateral concessions do not cause market disruption in their countries.

It appears to us that the interests of the developing countries call for a significant reversal of their traditional attitudes on trade matters. The more rapid growth of industrial exports from these nations than from the developed countries is a manifestation of their growing ability to compete in a highly successful manner in a growing list of manufactures. To continue to take advantage of competitive ability, it is essential that world trade be permitted to expand rapidly. Tariff and nontariff trade distortions impede the expansion of trade. Of course, it is easy to argue for liberalization by the developed countries alone, but as pointed out above this tends to lead eventually to the blocking of trade expansion by the developing nations. The developing countries would seem to gain more in the long run by beginning to negotiate for trade liberalization on a reciprocal basis with the developed countries. In this way they have an opportunity to make meaningful penetrations of developed country markets in products where they have a strong comparative advantage and at the same time strengthen their own economies.

Exports of capital goods and skill-intensive consumer goods to developing nations already constitute an important market for the developed countries and, if growth rates in the former countries continue to exceed those in the latter, this market will become even more vital for the industrial economies. It is clear that negotiators from the industrial nations are prepared to make concessions in the labor-intensive manufacturing lines in return for increased access to developing country markets for skill-intensive and technology intensive manufactures. But, as Richard Cooper, U.S. Undersecretary of State, has often said, these negotiators cannot politically make such concessions unilaterally. As far as the developing countries are concerned, not only can they profit from an expansion of their export trade, but they can facilitate the rationalization of their domestic industrial structure. It has become abundantly evident that import-substitution policies have been pushed too far in some countries and have resulted in the creation of a number of capital-intensive industries requiring relatively large amounts of imported inputs for their operations. These industries do little to solve the employment and income-distribution problems in developing countries, and they drain away scarce foreign exchange. Yet, as in the developed countries, it is not easy politically to retrench in inefficient product lines. However, if political leaders can demonstrate that substantial gains in other product lines can be achieved if domestic activity in these industries is gradually reduced, then these costs can be made acceptable to domestic pressure groups.

Finally, to return to the first important theme of this paper, a key part of the export strategy of developing countries should be an understanding of the adjustment problems in industrial nations. To expect the developed nations to open their local markets in a manner that causes large-scale unemployment of labor and capital is completely unrealistic. At the same time, without hard bargaining that promises substantial alternative gains, the developed nations will adopt policies resulting in little or no real adjustment. Domestic political pressures will press for the maintenance of existing market shares, and these pressures are likely to succeed when there are no attractive alternatives. Besides opening up markets for capital goods in developing countries, the developing nations can bargain with respect to access to their supplies of primary products. Agreeing to bind export charges on primary products or permitting sufficient foreign investment to insure a continued flow of raw materials to the industrial countries are examples of policies for which these latter countries are prepared to make significant concessions in terms of opening up their markets for manufactured goods.

Above all, the developing nations should urge that the expected changes in Article XIX of the GATT, dealing with safeguard procedures, include provisions insuring regular, multilateral review within the GATT framework of measures taken to restrict imports. General periodic justifications are not sufficient to protect the smaller nations; panels should be established to monitor the restrictionist actions taken, as well as the steps adopted to bring about the necessary resource adjustments. The developed countries will, we think, agree to such provisions, but unless the developing countries press for them, they are not likely to be given much attention in the redrafting discussions.

NOTES

1. On the multinational dislocational and distributional issues, see the contribution to this United Nations Association Trade and Planning panel by Kaj Areskoug, "Foreign Direct Investment and Industrial Activity in the United States: A Reappraisal," August 1977. On the technology-transfer issues, see Rachel McCulloch, "Technology, Trade, and the Interests of Labor: A Short-Run Analysis of the Development and International Dissemination of New Technology," n.d., and a great many brief discussions in position papers and congressional testimony from spokespersons for the AFL-CIO.

2. One of the earliest and most readable accounts is C. Fred Bergsten, "The New Era in World Commodity Markets," *Challenge* (September-October 1974): 34-42.

3. Despite well-publicized import penetration by now standardized, once high-technology goods (e.g., consumer and business electronic equipment), there is no convincing empirical evidence that the United States is losing its comparative advantage in the *most* technologically advanced goods. United States exports of technology-intensive manufactures grew at an average annual rate of 23.3 percent over the years 1973-75, faster than either Germany's or Japan's. Furthermore, the United States comparative advantage has been relatively unaltered even though the U.S. absolute technology advantage has clearly deteriorated. That is, even though the United States is losing much of its across-the-board technological leadership of the 1950s and 1960s, compared with other nations it is still much more competitive in innovative,

high-technology goods than in established, standardized goods. In fact, it is probable that the United States will retain comparative advantage and exports in high-technology goods even if sometime in the future it slips to a position of absolute technological inferiority, compared with Germany and Japan. On these points, see the *International Economic Report of the President* (Washington, D.C.: U.S. Government Printing Office, March 1976), pp. 117-120.

4. These points are persuasively and engagingly illustrated in James C. Ingram's "Fable of Trade and Technology," *International Economic Problems* (New York: Wiley, 1970), pp. 43-45.

5. Given the "structural" character of much unemployment and excess capacity today, for example, it is not clear even that the familiar tools of fiscal and monetary policy are sufficiently effective to rule out all opposition to trade liberalization.

6. If the average standard of living were 100 to start with, the new standard of living under liberalized trade would start at $100.98 \, [= (0.99 \times 102) + (0.01 \times 0)]$ in the very short run.

7. For historical examples of the internal political dynamics of policy formation on international trade, see (for just two examples): Robert E. Baldwin, *"The Political Economy of Postwar U.S. Trade Policy,"* New York University, Graduate School of Business Administration, Center for the Study of Financial Institutions, *The Bulletin,* 1974-6, and Raymond A. Bauer, Ithiel de Sola Pool, and Lewis Anthony Dexter, *American Business and Public Policy: The Politics of Foreign Trade* (Chicago: Aldine-Atherton, 1972).

8. A further modification of this discount factor may be called for if there is considerable uncertainty with respect to the duration of the benefit stream over time. The issue might arise in dealing with goods that become obsolete very quickly, or more important, if foreign countries explicitly or implicitly withdraw concessions through escape clauses, offsetting nontariff barriers, or exchange-rate policy. Possible ways of dealing with this uncertainty are to shorten the relevant time horizon or to increase the discount rate. This observation seems particularly relevant if any offsetting costs arise that may be quite immediate and certain, in contrast to the more long-run and uncertain nature of benefits.

9. The salutary effect of growth may be rather limited if there is considerable geographic dispersion of output in the industry, yielding the result that attrition of workers in plants that are expanding output will not reduce the necessary adjustment in plants that are contracting. Analyses that suggest that much of the necessary adjustment is possible through attrition rest on a national labor-market interpretation that sometimes misses the true nature of the adjustment problem.

10. The phenomenon is known sometimes as "labor hoarding" and has been documented in M. Ishaq Nadiri and Sherwin Rosen, *A Disequilibrium Model of Demand for Factors of Production* (New York:

National Bureau of Economic Research, 1974). On the other hand, a decline in output may result in a greater than proportional decline in employment. For example, if capital is fixed and receives only a residual rent, then there is an immediate incentive to substitute this cheaper factor for rigid-wage labor. Another theoretical rationale for labor adjustments to be proportionately greater is based on the concept of vintage capital. If the oldest vintages that tend to be most labor-intensive are displaced first, the labor adjustment is understated by the average labor/output ratio, as suggested by James M. Jondrow in "Effects of Trade Restrictions on Imports of Steel," in William G. Dewald, ed., *The Impact of International Trade on Investment and Employment,* mimeographed (Washington, D.C.: U.S. Department of Labor, 1977).

11. This study is analyzed in Malcolm D. Bale, *Adjustment to Freer Trade: An Analysis of the Adjustment Assistance Provisions of the Trade Expansion Act of 1962,* National Technical Information Service, Springfield, Virginia, Report No. DLMA 91-55-73-05, 1973.

12. George R. Neumann, "The Direct Labor Market Effects of the Trade Adjustment Assistance Program: Evidence from the TAA Survey," in Dewald, ed., *The Impact of International Trade.*

13. James E. McCarthy, "Trade Adjustment Assistance: A Case Study of the Shoe Industry of Massachusetts," Ph.D. dissertation, Fletcher School of Law and Diplomacy, 1974, p. 58.

14. It is important to note, however, that the export expansion due to foreign duty reductions probably falls short of that due to an equivalent depreciation of the dollar. Given a depreciation of the dollar relative to all foreign currencies, the price of U.S. goods facing Spanish buyers, for example, will fall relative to goods produced in Spain and also relative to other imports, such as those from Japan. Under multilateral tariff reductions, a cut in the Spanish tariff results in both U.S. and Japanese goods being cheaper relative to domestically produced Spanish goods. The competitive gain to the United States is not as great in the latter situation. If a major share of U.S. exports is sold in markets where the greatest competition is from other exporting countries, this distinction is important, and the export gains from the multilateral aspect of trade liberalization may be very small indeed.

15. Even though a country may face infinitely elastic import supply curves, it can still affect its terms of trade if the elasticity of demand for its exports is finite. The reason this factor is relevant is that removing trade barriers results in a trade deficit that requires a currency depreciation. The size of this depreciation will depend upon the relevant demand elasticities in markets for exports and other imports. The smaller the demand elasticities in these markets, the larger the depreciation necessary. Giorgio Basevi has demonstrated the welfare significance of this factor for the United States in "The Restrictive Effect of the U.S. Tariff and Its Welfare Value," *American Economic Review,* 58 (Septem-

ber 1968): 840-852. Recent analyses by Lance Taylor and Stephen L. Black for Chile ("Practical General Equilibrium Estimation of Resource Pulls Under Trade Liberalization," *Journal of International Economics*, 4 [(February 1974]: 37-58) and by Alan V. Deardorff, Robert M. Stern, and Christopher F. Baum for a variety of countries ("A Multi-Country Simulation of the Employment and Exchange-Rate Effects of Post-Kennedy Round Tariff Reductions," paper presented at the Eighth Pacific Trade and Development Conference, Pattaya, Thailand, July 1976), both rest on relatively small supply elasticities. Not surprisingly, the exchange-rate changes they calculate are considerably larger than in the case of infinite supply elasticities (as assumed, e.g., by Robert E. Baldwin and Wayne Lewis, in "U.S. Tariff Effects on Trade and Employment in Detailed S.I.C. Industries," in Dewald, ed., *The Impact of International Trade.)*

16. Although the United States suffered a terms-of-trade loss even from the multilateral Kennedy Round, according to a study by one of the authors. See John H. Mutti, "A Retrospective View of Multilateral Tariff Reductions," March 1977.

17. Our data sources and methodology are described in a number of places, most recently in Robert E. Baldwin, John H. Mutti, and J. David Richardson, "Welfare Effects on the United States of a Significant Multilateral Tariff Reduction," paper presented to a Ford Foundation Conference on Trade and Employment at the University of Wisconsin—Madison, November 11 and 12, 1977. Another notable attempt to measure dislocation, as well as price and exchange-rate changes, from trade liberalization is the contribution to this UNA Trade and Planning Panel by Alan V. Deardorff, Robert M. Stern, and Mark N. Greene, "The Implications of Alternative Trade Strategies for the United States," August 1, 1977. Both their data sources and methodology differ at points from ours.

18. Our grounds for excluding these are that they are subject to special treatment in the negotiations, and calculating the welfare benefits and adjustment costs from liberalizing them is a unique project in itself. The magnitude of the measured benefits and costs from such a project is *not* likely to be small, however, to judge from calculations made by Stephen P. Magee in "The Welfare Effects of Restrictions on U.S. Trade," in *Brooking Papers on Economic Activity*, no. 3 (1972): 645-701.

19. It is important to note that the figures we report are job gains less job losses within an industry. In many economic comparisons, these net figures are appropriate because each job gained removes someone from the pool of the unemployed even if that person was not directly displaced by trade liberalization. However, the net figures will understate the true cost of adjustment when the unemployment experience of trade-impacted workers is less favorable than would have been the case for the individuals hired due to greater export production (which seems

to be true). In other economic and interpersonal comparisons, the gross number of individuals displaced by trade liberalization may be important. These numbers are always larger than those we report in any given industry. Gross displacement is furthermore the relevant datum in calculations of the budgetary cost of trade adjustment assistance, such as those carried out by George R. Neumann in another contribution to this UNA Trade and Planning Panel, "Adjustment Assistance for Trade-Displaced Workers," n.d.

20. See George Neumann's paper cited in note 12.

21. In fact, a policy of phased, partial reduction may yield greater net benefits than one-shot reduction of the same cumulative size. The gains from further reduction become progressively smaller as a larger percentage of the initial barrier is eliminated, but the adjustment costs are proportionally related to the cut (see John H. Mutti, "Adjustment Costs and the Non-Optimality of Unilaterally Removing Tariffs," *Review of Economics and Statistics*, 60 [February 1978]).

22. The ten most important candidates for commodity schemes are sugar, copper, cotton, coffee (already in existence), rubber, cocoa (already in existence), tin (already in existence), tea, jute, and sisal.

23. Studies of the tin and copper markets indicate that stabilization would require the managers of a buffer stock sometimes to remain on either the buying or selling side of the market for five or six years. It is estimated that buffer stocks valued at nearly three times the $3 billion Common Fund proposed by the developing countries would have been necessary to stabilize these commodity prices alone over the past twenty years. Or consider the cocoa case. Who could have forecast in 1973, when the cocoa pact was put into effect and a ceiling price of 32 cents per pound set, that the price would soon exceed this ceiling and be around $1.50 recently? Is this four-year period in which the price has exceeded the initial ceiling merely a temporary phenomenon? It is hard to find a cocoa producer who is now willing to consider 23 cents a reasonable floor, nor a consumer who will accept $1.50 as a reasonable ceiling. The coffee situation is rather similar and accounts for the absence of a meaningful agreement.

24. The U.S. arrangement excludes Hong Kong, OPEC countries, Turkey, Greece, Spain, Portugal, and Cuba. The EC does not grant preferences to Taiwan or the Mediterranean countries, while Japan excludes from preferential treatment imports of many products from Hong Kong. Nor do all manufactured goods qualify for duty-free treatment. Textile trade is excluded outright by the U.S. and Japan, and the EC grants preferential treatment only when a developing country exporter abides by the "voluntary restraints" under the Long-Term Textiles arrangement. Shoes, petroleum products, and industrial raw materials are not covered, and the United States also excludes watches, certain steel products, and products subject to escape-clause action.

Perhaps even more significant is that the United States, the EC, and Japan place limits on the value of imports that can be treated preferentially.

25. Robert E. Baldwin and Tracy Murray, "MFN Tariff Reductions and Developing Country Trade Benefits Under the GSP," *Economic Journal,* 87 (March 1977): 30-46.

Chapter 3

THE IMPLICATIONS OF ALTERNATIVE
TRADE STRATEGIES FOR THE
UNITED STATES

ALAN V. DEARDORFF, ROBERT M. STERN,
AND MARK N. GREENE

University of Michigan

I. INTRODUCTION

As the Multilateral Trade Negotiations (MTN) approach a critical juncture, decisions have to be made by the United States and other negotiating countries with regard to the depth and industry coverage of reductions in tariffs and nontariff barriers (NTBs). The purpose of our paper is to analyze the implications, especially for the United States, of alternative negotiating strategies. We examine in particular the output and employment, price, and exchange-rate effects of several different tariff-cutting rules. We also consider, although much more tentatively, possible reductions in NTBs. Our analysis is based upon a disaggregated, general equilibrium model of world production and trade for twenty-nine sectors in each of the eighteen major industrialized countries.

Governments have committed themselves to mutual reductions in trade barriers in the belief that the resulting welfare benefits from more efficient resource use in production and lower prices to consumers will outweigh the adjustment costs that may be experienced due to worker displacement in industries that are vulnerable to import competition. In selecting a negotiating strategy, each country must then weigh the benefits and costs. Difficulties arise, however, because countries may differ in their assessments of benefits and costs and thus in the strategy they believe is most appropriate for their national interest.

The situation is further complicated by macroeconomic considerations, since countries may be reluctant to liberalize import barriers at a time when they are experiencing general underemployment. In what follows, we abstract from these macroeconomic issues even though they will have a direct bearing on the nature and outcome of the negotiations. This should not be a serious omission because, as our results indicate, the overall employment impacts are not particularly large for any of the negotiating strategies that have been put forth to date. With this in mind, we can focus on the more purely microeconomic effects of the alternative strategies.

The plan of the paper is as follows. In section II, we provide a brief description of our model and how it was used. In sections III-V, we report and comment on a variety of results based upon several alternative tariff-cutting rules that have been proposed in the course of negotiations. In section VI, we consider some possible reductions in quantitative restrictions on trade, with particular reference to textiles and wearing apparel. Finally, in section VII, we comment on how the exclusion of the developing countries from our model may have affected the results. Section VIII provides some summary remarks.

II. DESCRIPTION OF THE MODEL AND ITS USE

A more complete description of our model is given in Deardorff et al.[1] For present purposes, a brief overview should therefore suffice.

The model includes world markets for each of twenty-two tradable industries, with separate functions for the supply of exports into these markets and for the demand for imports out of these markets in each of eighteen countries. Separate "home" markets for each country and industry are specified in these twenty-two industries as well as in an additional seven nontradable industries. This division of the tradable industries into home and world markets reflects an assumption that home-produced and imported products are regarded by both producers and consumers as imperfect substitutes. All supply and demand functions are constructed to incorporate some substitution between home and imported goods, as well as a complete network of interindustry interactions taken from the U.S. input-output table.

The equations for equilibrium in all of these world and domestic markets can be solved simultaneously for equilibrium world and domestic prices. By adding equations for the exchange markets of each country, we can solve for the equilibrium exchange rates as well.

Tariffs enter the model in two ways. First, they cause the domestic price of imports to exceed the world price by the percent of the tariff. And second, all tariff revenue is assumed to be redistributed to consumers. This second assumption is used to neutralize the effect that tariff changes would otherwise have on the amount of aggregate expenditure that reaches producers.

Labor markets are not assumed to clear in the model. Wages instead are taken as constant, and changes in demands for labor are assumed to change levels of sectoral employment. Thus, the model is able to generate the initial impact of tariff changes on labor-market disequilibrium.

As mentioned above, we abstract from macroeconomic considerations. That is, we have chosen to maintain aggregate expenditure at levels that will keep world economic activity approximately constant. Thus, our results reflect exclusively microeconomic behavior.

In contrast to our earlier modeling efforts referred to above, the version of the model used in the present paper includes quantitative trade restrictions and changes in those restrictions.

As noted in Deardorff and Stern,[2] we introduce quantitative restrictions in a manner that permits domestic prices to adjust automatically to prevent imports from changing. For those industries in which quantitative restrictons affect only a fraction of trade, that fraction is used to construct an average of the two hypothetical prices that would prevail with no quantitative restrictions at all and with restrictions on the entire industry. The result is to make trade in restricted industries less responsive to changes in tariffs and other variables than it would have been had restrictions not been considered.

As already mentioned, our model provides estimates of changes in production and employment in each of the eighteen major industrialized countries, with reference to twenty-two tradable and seven nontradable industries. We can also obtain estimates of changes in consumer price indices and exchange rates for each country. The model therefore furnishes some insight into the potential costs of trade liberalization as reflected in the employment displacement from imports and the potential benefits arising from the employment expansion due to exports and the reduction in consumer prices. The exchange-rate changes indicate the adjustments in imports and exports that will take place to restore trade balance after trade has been liberalized.

It would be desirable if we could translate our results on output, employment, prices, and exchange rates into comparable measures of costs and benefits. To do so, however, would require more information about the welfare implications of these economic variables than our model is presently able to provide. The difficulties are most obvious with respect to employment, for the costs of unemployment must include not only the forgone output but also the financial and psychological hardship of the unemployed workers. Other problems are encountered if we try to measure the welfare implications of output, price, and exchange-rate changes. Thus, we are unable to produce dollar estimates of the welfare effects of tariff reductions. Any conclusions regarding the overall desirability of alternative trade strategies must therefore be interpreted with caution—a caution that would be appropriate in any case in view especially of our findings, to be noted below, that costs and benefits of trade liberalization may well be distributed unevenly across sectors of the economy, particularly as between tradable and nontradable industries.

It should also be noted that for some problems our approach would not be optimal. Since our model is static, it does not provide information about the dynamic response to trade liberalization. Also, for this and other reasons, the model cannot be tested against actual experience with tariff reductions so as to assess its accuracy. These are admitted drawbacks, but it must be realized how complex the problem at hand actually is. Even for a single tariff reduction, there are many complicated interactions that must be taken into account. Add to these the need to consider many tariff changes simultaneously and our desire for information about many separate industries, and the problem becomes far too large to be handled in a testable, dynamic, econometric model.

On the other hand, it should be emphasized that our model incorporates a great deal of empirical information, giving us some confidence in its accuracy. Supply and demand functions are both based on published econometric studies of behavior, and other parameters of the model are derived from carefully gathered data on production, trade, and employment. All of this, together with our very detailed modeling of intercountry and interindustry interactions, convinces us that our results may well be more reliable, and are certainly more useful, than could have been obtained from a simpler and more highly aggregated model.

The model covers the following eighteen major industrialized countries, which are listed together with the abbreviations that will be used to refer to them in subsequent sections. The choice of countries was dictated by the availability from GATT [3] of detailed trade and tariff information at the line-item level. We treat the eighteen industrialized countries as if they were a closed system. The developing countries could not be included because of the lack of data. We shall comment in section VII on the implications of this omission.

ALA—Australia
ATA—Austria
BLX—Belgium-Luxembourg
CND—Canada
DEN—Denmark
FIN—Finland
FR—France
GFR—West Germany
IRE—Ireland

IT—Italy
JPN—Japan
NL—Netherlands
NZ—New Zealand
NOR—Norway
SWD—Sweden
SWZ—Switzerland
UK—United Kingdom
US—United States

World industry was categorized into twenty-nine classifications, of which twenty-two are tradable. They are identified by numbers adapted from the International Standard Industrial Classification (ISIC) and are described in the accompanying table.

NONTRADABLES

ISIC Group	Description
2	Mining and quarrying
4	Electricity, gas, and water
5	Construction
6	Wholesale and retail trade, restaurants and hotels
7	Transport, storage, and communication
8	Finance, insurance, real estate, etc.
9	Community, social, and personal services

TRADABLES

ISIC Group	Description
1	Agriculture, hunting, forestry, and fishing
310	Food, beverages, and tobacco
321	Textiles
322	Wearing apparel (except footwear)
323	Leather; leather and fur products

324	Footwear
331	Wood products (except furniture)
332	Furniture and fixtures (except metal)
341	Paper and paper products
342	Printing and publishing
35A	Industrial chemicals (351): Other chemical products (352)
35B	Petroleum refineries (353): miscellaneous petroleum and coal products (369)
355	Rubber products
36A	Pottery, china, and earthenware (361): other nonmetallic mineral products (369)
362	Glass and glass products
371	Iron and steel basic industries
372	Nonferrous metal basic industries
381	Metal products (except machinery, etc.)
382	Machinery (except electrical)
383	Electrical machinery, apparatus, etc.
384	Transport equipment
38A	Plastic products, not elsewhere classed (356): professional, photographic goods, etc. (385): other manufacturing industries (390)

To give some idea of how the eighteen countries interact with one another in the twenty-two tradable industries, we present a summary of the basic trade and trade-policy data in Table 3.1. For each tradable industry, the first column gives U.S. net exports (exports minus imports) for 1970 with the total U.S. trade balance at the bottom.[4] Then we report average nominal post-Kennedy Round (1972) tariff levels by industry for the United States and for the world as a whole (the eighteen countries, including the United States). Average tariffs have been obtained by using 1970 levels of imports as weights. In this case, the bottom entries in the table are the import-weighted averages of the columns above, rather than their sums. Finally, in the last two columns we report an index that we have constructed to indicate the importance of quantitative restrictions on trade. This index is intended to represent the percentage of trade within each industry and country that is subject to quantitative restrictions. Further details on its construction are available upon request. Again, as with tariffs in the preceding columns, import-weighted averages were used to get the figures for the world and for all industries together.

Since our focus in this paper will be on the United States, it is worth noting from Table 3.1 how the United States compares in its level of protection with the other industrialized countries. It appears that U.S. tariffs are, on average, lower than those in the rest of the world. In fact, while it is not apparent from Table 3.1, there are only two of the eighteen countries whose average tariffs are lower than those of the United States (Norway and Switzerland). And among twenty-two separate industries, there are only six in which the U.S. tariff exceeds the average for the world. As for quantitative restrictions, the United States is again slightly below average.

Among industries, the most heavily protected are clearly food, beverages, and tobacco (ISIC 310), textiles (ISIC 321), and wearing apparel, excluding footwear (ISIC 322). Textiles and wearing apparel (321, 322) are especially notable in being subject to quantitative restrictions.[5] This means that the tariffs that are also present in these industries do not affect prices. That is, the tariffs serve merely to provide revenue to the government out of the tax on profits of those who control the limited allocation of imports arising from the quantitative restrictions.

III. THE EFFECTS OF EQUIVALENT MULTILATERAL TARIFF CHANGES

We turn now to the analysis of results generated by our model. We begin by considering several formulas for tariff change in which all countries are treated identically. That is, a single formula for determining a tariff change is constructed based upon the level of the existing tariff. The formula is then applied to all countries at the same time. Thus, there is no attempt to discriminate among countries, except to the extent that their existing tariffs may make them unusually vulnerable to a particular tariff formula.

TABLE 3.1

THE PATTERN OF U.S. TRADE AND PROTECTION COMPARED WITH AN AVERAGE OF THE WORLD'S INDUSTRIALIZED COUNTRIES

ISIC Industry	U.S. Net Exports, 1970 (millions of U.S. $)	Average Post–Kennedy Round Tariff		Index of Post–Kennedy Round Quantitative Restrictions	
		U.S. (%)	World (%)	U.S. (%)	World (%)
1	1924.7	3.14	10.66	1.4	21.38
310	− 791.2	7.40	16.78	45.4	28.08
321	− 191.1	20.44	12.41	100.0	100.0
322	− 423.4	26.32	18.74	100.0	100.0
323	− 12.3	6.72	4.02	0	1.04
324	− 444.9	10.08	11.62	0	16.12
331	159.7	1.95	2.94	0	0
332	− 68.1	7.14	9.36	0	0
341	− 852.9	0.43	5.81	0	0.53
342	203.5	0.76	5.46	60.6	9.07
35A	1661.7	6.34	10.12	0	4.52
35B	311.3	2.89	3.14	56.2	41.39
355	28.4	4.31	7.70	0	3.72
36A	− 74.6	11.26	6.29	0	7.25
362	− 5.0	12.95	10.77	0	0
371	− 844.4	6.32	5.72	0	0.23
372	− 278.0	2.29	2.56	0	4.75
381	− 70.6	8.79	9.02	0	2.74
382	2943.1	4.97	7.13	0	2.68
383	179.6	7.23	9.63	0	5.03
384	1300.4	3.51	7.81	1.8	12.20
38A	− 232.6	8.47	8.86	0.5	3.40
All	4423.6	6.26	8.23	12.36	15.45

NOTE: The trade and tariff data were compiled from GATT, *The Basic Documentation for the Tariff Study* (Geneva, 1974). The tariffs are post–Kennedy Round (1972), ad valorem equivalents and are import-weighed, using 1970 trade. Details on construction of the index of quantitative restrictions are available upon request.

The simplest formulas (1-3) of this sort consist of changing all existing tariffs by the same percentage, independently of their initial size. More complicated formulas (4-6) make the percentage tariff cut dependent on the initial tariff. The individual formulas are as follows:

Formula 1: a 10 percent increase in all tariff rates;

Formula 2: a 50 percent reduction in all tariff rates;

Formula 3: a 100 percent reduction in all tariff rates;

Formula 4: a "harmonization" formula consisting of three applications of a tariff cut equal to the initial tariff rate.[7]

Formula 5: a "nonlinear" formula in which all tariffs below 5 percent are removed entirely, tariffs above 40 percent are cut to 20 percent, and all other tariffs are cut in half; and

Formula 6: a "linear with intercept" formula in which all tariffs are set equal to 3 percent plus 40 percent of their initial value (but with no tariff allowed to rise).

With the exception of formulas 1 and 3, which are included in order to determine the effect of changing the overall level of tariff reduction, all of these formulas are very similar in terms of their overall effects. In addition, they all approximately represent actual tariff formulas that have been proposed by different participants in the current round of trade negotiations. They differ primarily in terms of their differential treatment of high, medium, and low initial tariffs.

Formulas 4 and 6 both cut high tariffs the most and low tariffs the least, with the difference being most pronounced for formula 4. Formula 5, on the other hand, requires large cuts of both very high and very low tariffs and has its smallest effect on tariffs in the middle range (5 to 40 percent). In addition, the tariff reductions implied by formula 5 are all at least as large as for formula 2, so that the average tariff reduction under formula 5 is likely to be somewhat greater than under the others.

In principle, each of these tariff formulas is intended to apply to all industries as well as to all countries. In fact, there are certain industries that are likely to be excluded from tariff cuts in the current negotiations. We therefore assume in all of our calculations in this paper that—regardless of the formula applied—tariffs in these industries are unchanged. These industries are: agriculture, etc. (ISIC 1); food, beverages, and tobacco (ISIC 310); textiles (ISIC 321); wearing apparel (ISIC 322); and petroleum products (ISIC 35B). In section V, we will take a further look at two of these industries, textiles and wearing apparel, to determine the effect of their being excluded.

The results of these six tariff formulas are summarized in Tables 3.2, 3.3, and 3.4. Table 3.2 reports effects on employment, first in man-years, then in percentages. Since space does not permit reporting the detailed employment results for all industries, we have included the maximum and minimum countries and the U.S. industries affected in order to show the range of results. In Table 3.3, we report price effects for both the United States and the world (all eighteen countries); and in Table 3.4 we report exchange-rate changes. Readers who wish to see more detailed results of the effects on employment and other variables should request them from the authors. For example more complete results of the effects of formula 2—the 50 percent tariff cut—are available. Likewise tables for the results based upon the remaining formulas are obtainable from the authors.

The first thing to notice in all of the employment results in Table 3.2, is that they are not very large. With only a few exceptions, none of the employment changes is more than a fraction of a percent, and even the exceptions never much exceed 3 percent. Similarly, the effects on consumer prices (Table 3.3) and exchange rates (Table 3.4) are all comparatively small in percentage terms. For example, the reduction in U.S. consumer prices is an estimated 0.044 percent, based upon formula 2—the 50 percent tariff cut. With consumer expenditures of, say, $1 trillion, this would be equivalent to $440 million. Thus, whatever the costs and benefits may be from tariff reductions, neither are likely to be very large.

We had intended, before looking at the employment results, to report also the amount of time that would be required for the economy to reabsorb workers who had been laid off due to the tariff changes. However, as we look at the bottom part of Table 3.2, it is clear that even a mere 1 percent annual rate of growth

SUMMARY OF EMPLOYMENT EFFECTS OF ALTERNATIVE TARIFF-CHANGE FORMULAS

	1 10% Up	2 50% Down	3 100% Down	4 Harmonization	5 Non-linear	6 Linear with Intercept
Absolute Change in Man-Years						
All U.S.	2.509	−12.550	−25.099	−3.226	−21.158	−1.044
Maximum country	JPN 8.438	UK 28.339	UK 56.677	UK 8.373	UK 42.709	BLX 5.166
Minimum country	UK −5.668	JPN −42.190	JPN −84.380	ALA −26.680	US −21.158	JPN −27.781
Maximum U.S. Industry	ISIC 9 2.603	ISIC 5 7.239	ISIC 5 14.478	ISIC 5 3.948	ISIC 382 3.328	ISIC 5 5.179
Minimum U.S. Industry	ISIC 5 −1.448	ISIC 9 −13.017	ISIC 9 −26.033	ISIC 9 −4.390	ISIC 9 −12.283	ISIC 9 −3.307
Percentage Changes						
All U.S.	0.003	−.016	−.033	−.004	−.028	−.001
Maximum Country	IRE 0.106	BLX 0.465	BLX 0.930	BLX 0.151	BLX 0.390	BLX 0.138
Minimum country	BLX −0.093	IRE −0.531	IRE −1.062	NZ −0.582	CND −.212	ALA −0.481
Maximum U.S. Industry	ISIC 358 0.317	ISIC 382 0.348	ISIC 382 0.696	ISIC 384 0.212	ISIC 323 0.405	ISIC 35A 0.256
Minimum U.S. Industry	ISIC 382 −0.070	ISIC 35B −1.587	ISIC 35B −3.173	ISIC 35B −0.977	ISIC 355 −0.384	ISIC 35B −1.035

TABLE 3.3

SUMMARY OF PERCENTAGE PRICE EFFECTS OF ALTERNATIVE TARIFF-CHANGE FORMULAS

		Formula					
		1 10% Up	2 50% Down	3 100% Down	4 Harmoni- zation	5 Non- linear	6 Linear w Interce
Export Prices	U.S.	.052	−.259	−.519	−.107	−.068	−.110
	World	.008	−.044	−.088	−.015	−.030	−.013
Import Prices	U.S.	.278	−1.388	−2.777	−.737	−.262	−.86(
	World	.256	−1.281	−2.562	−.573	−.494	−.578
Consumer Prices	U.S.	.009	−.044	−.088	−.015	−.030	−.01?
	World	.034	−.168	−.337	−.082	−.049	−.084

TABLE 3.4

PERCENTAGE EXCHANGE-RATE EFFECTS OF ALTERNATIVE TARIFF-CHANGE FORMULAS

		Formula				
Country	1 10% Up	2 50% Down	3 100% Down	4 Harmoniza- tion	5 Non- linear	6 Linear Interc
ALA	.317	−1.585	−3.171	−1.710	−.186	−1.5'
ATA	.101	−.503	−1.005	−.451	.018	−.5
BLX	−.091	.457	.915	.185	.143	.1
CND	.035	−.173	−.345	−.157	.142	−.1
DEN	.047	−.235	−.471	−.082	−.061	−.0
FIN	.028	−.014	−.028	−.020	.019	−.0
FR	.067	−.334	−.667	−.134	−.013	−.1
GFR	−.024	.118	.237	.046	.092	.0
IRE	.010	−.048	−.096	−.043	−.006	−.0
IT	.006	−.032	−.064	.019	−.019	.0
JPN	−.058	.288	.576	.209	.164	.1
NL	−.026	.131	.262	.051	.020	.0
NZ	.127	−.636	−1.272	−.567	−.018	−.5
NOR	−.009	.047	.094	.012	.041	.C
SWD	−.039	.193	.387	.113	.095	.1
SWZ	−.069	.347	.694	.242	−.171	.?
UK	.003	−.015	−.031	.064	.006	.C
US	−.010	.048	.096	.130	−.207	.1

of each industry would be sufficient to reabsorb most of the unemployed workers back into their original industries within a year. And, with a 3 percent rate of growth, this would be true in even the most seriously affected industries.

Variation among the six formulas is also comparatively minor, except of course that all results are reversed in sign when tariffs go up, as in formula 1, instead of down. Otherwise, the results tend to be of the same general order of magnitude, regardless of the formula used.

The minor variations that do appear among the formulas seem to follow a pattern. From the point of view of the United States, formulas 4 and 6 generate the smallest employment reductions. Similarly, the U.S. dollar appreciates the most with formulas 4 and 6. On the other hand, the benefit in the form of reduced consumer prices is smallest for the United States with these same formulas.

The reason for these results is of course that formulas 4 and 6 cut low tariffs the least, and as we have already noted, U.S. tariffs are already comparatively low. In contrast, New Zealand and Australia, both of whose tariffs are quite high, become the greatest losers of employment only when formulas 4 and 6 are applied.

IV. U.S. PARTICIPATION IN TRADE LIBERALIZATION

In the previous section, we noted that with the multilateral application of tariff formulas 4 and 6, which impinge most severely on high-tariff countries, the average tariff reduction in the United States would then be smaller than in other countries. This seems to lend support to the idea that any country will benefit most if it can exclude itself from a general round of tariff reductions by other countries. To examine this proposition in more detail, we used our model to calculate the effects of three more tariff formulas in which the extent of U.S. participation in trade liberalization was varied. As we shall see, whether or not the United States can be said to gain or lose from unilaterally excluding itself from a round of tariff reductions elsewhere depends upon the weights one gives to the costs and benefits mentioned in our introductory remarks.

The additional formulas which we consider here are the following:

Formula 7: 10 percent increase in all U.S. tariffs; 50 percent reduction in all tariffs of all other countries;

Formula 8: no change in U.S. tariffs; 50 percent reduction in all tariffs of all other countries; and

Formula 9: 100 percent reduction in all U.S. tariffs; 50 percent reduction in all tariffs of all other countries.

As before, we exclude industries 1, 310, 321, 322, and 35B from tariff changes in all countries.

The results for each of these formulas are summarized in Table 3.5, together with results for formula 2, with which they are readily compared. As we move to the right in the table, we have U.S. tariffs being made lower and lower, until they are completely eliminated in the far-right column.

As might be expected, overall employment in the United States falls more the more the U.S. tariffs are reduced and actually rises if U.S. tariffs are increased. However, even with complete removal of U.S. tariffs, the fall in total employment is a tiny three hundredths of 1 percent.

If we look at the industry detail of employment effects, however, we find a surprise. The most adversely affected industry (ISIC 35B) actually suffers a *smaller* loss of employment when U.S. tariffs are reduced than when they are not. Similarly, the industries that expand the most do so by a greater percentage when U.S. tariffs are reduced than when they are raised. Now, obviously it is not possible for all industries to expand with greater U.S. tariff reductions and still have the aggregate effect to be negative. To see what was happening, we looked at the detailed industry results that space prevents us from reporting here. We found that the pattern reported in Table 3.5 for industry 35B is also observed in 16 of the 22 *tradable* industries. On the other hand, all but one of the *nontradable* industries were hurt by larger U.S. tariff reductions. The apparent explanation

TABLE 3.5

THE SENSITIVITY OF U.S. VARIABLES TO
UNILATERAL VARIATIONS IN U.S. TARIFFS

% Change	U.S. Across-the-board Tariff Change			
	+10% (formula 7)	0 (formula 3)	−50% (formula 2)	−100% (formula 9)
U.S. Total Employment Change	.002	−.001	−.016	−.031
Maximum U.S. Industry Employment Change	ISIC 35A .328	ISIC 35A .329	ISIC 382 0.348	ISIC 382 .698
Minimum U.S. Industry Employment Change	ISIC 35B −2.373	ISIC 35B −2.242	ISIC 35B −1.5887	ISIC 35B −.931
U.S. Consumer Price Change	.010	.000	−.044	−.089
Maximum U.S. Industry Home-price Change	ISIC 384 .032	ISIC 384 .019	ISIC 6 −.023	ISIC 6 −.046
Minimum U.S. Industry Home-price Change	ISIC 372 .044	ISIC 323 −.005	ISIC 324 −.085	ISIC 324 −.166
U.S. Exchange-rate Change	.655	.554	.048	−.458

for these results, in terms of our model, is that U.S. tariff reductions cause U.S. consumers to substitute away from nontradables toward tradables as the latter become less expensive.

Turning now to the benefits from tariff reductions, we find that consumer prices fall more, the greater the U.S. tariff reductions are. This is not surprising, since tariff reductions cause import prices to fall. Note, however, in the next two lines of the table that the prices of home-produced goods also fall more as tariffs are reduced. Thus, the benefits to consumers from reduced prices are not confined to the goods they happen to import.

Together, these results again suggest the problem noted earlier of weighing the costs and benefits of tariff reduction. Broadly speaking, those who derive their livelihoods from tradable industries tend to gain income, while those dependent on nontradable industries tend to lose income. At the same time, both groups share the benefit of reduced consumer prices. Now, it can be argued that the latter effect is enough to tilt the scale in favor of a net benefit for society as a whole, and that the U.S. should therefore take the lead in reducing its own tariffs as far as possible. But the question remains whether the losers in this process should be adequately compensated. If so, the process of compensation is likely to be difficult, since our analysis suggests that the bulk of the losers will not be located in the import-competing industries, but in those vast industries that deal in nontradables.

V. ANALYSIS OF SELECTED INDUSTRIES

So far, we have reported results for specific industries only when they were indentified by the solution of the model as experiencing extreme responses to the tariff changes being considered. In this section, we report the results for several industries in more detail.

Table 3.6 contains the percentage output changes that we calculated for each of the nine tariff formulas considered so far, for the selected industries. Since the main differences within the table are between the first two columns and the last four, we will comment on these two groups of industries in turn.

TEXTILES AND APPAREL

Textiles (ISIC 321) and wearing apparel (ISIC 322) were selected because they were excluded from the tariff reductions in our calculations. Nonetheless, we see from Table 3.6 that the tariff reductions elsewhere caused these industries to contract. This result would probably come as a surprise to workers and manufacturers in those industries, who surely feel the "protection" afforded them by tariffs to be desirable.

In fact, what is happening is that by exempting an industry from multilateral tariff reductions, that industry is denied the benefits of the consumer substitution toward tradable goods that we mentioned earlier. Instead this substitution acts against it,

TABLE 3.6

PERCENTAGE OUTPUT CHANGES IN SELECTED U.S. INDUSTRIES FOR ALTERNATIVE TARIFF-CHANGE FORMULAS

Multilateral Changes	Industry					
	321 Textiles	*322* Apparel	*324* Footwear	*371* Iron & Steel	*383* Electrical	*384* Transport
10% Up	.013	.023	−.044	.003	.027	−.052
50% Down	−.065	−.113	.219	−.015	.136	.262
100% Down	−.129	−.226	.439	−.030	.271	.523
Harmonization	−.065	−.039	.021	−.037	.072	.161
Nonlinear	−.017	−.131	.022	.111	.068	−.021
Linear Intercept	−.077	−.029	−.093	−.059	.075	.176
Unilateral Changes by U.S.						
10% Up	−.178	−.035	.069	−.124	.081	.166
No Change	−.159	−.048	.094	−.106	.090	.182
100% Down	.030	−.178	.345	.077	.181	.341

just as if it were a nontraded good. While not included in Table 3.6, the other excluded industries display the same pattern.

In the case of the textile industries, this effect is even stronger due to the presence of quantitative restrictions on trade. While these do not exclude imports entirely, they do make trade so unresponsive to price changes that the industries behave more like nontradables than tradables.

There is a difference between the results for industries 321 and 322 in Table 3.6 that should be noted, even though we cannot fully account for it. When unilateral variations in U.S. tariffs are considered in formulas 7, 8, and 9, we see that wearing apparel is hurt, but textiles are helped the greater is the U.S. tariff reduction. Since both industries are excluded from these reductions, we would have expected both to be hurt, as though they were nontradable. Our only explanation for this result is that textiles are primarily an intermediate product and that they may be benefiting from expansion of the industries in which they are used. However, since the principal textile-using industry is wearing apparel, this explanation is not very satisfactory. More detailed examination of the characteristics of these two industries would thus be in order.

FOOTWEAR, IRON AND STEEL, ELECTRICAL, AND TRANSPORT

Footwear (ISIC 324) was selected for study because of the recent pressure on the U.S. government to increase its level of protection. Electrical machinery, apparatus, and so on (ISIC 383), which of course includes television sets, and iron and steel basic industries (ISIC 371), were selected for the same reason. Transport equipment (ISIC 384) was selected because of its importance as a durable consumer good.

Given the different characteristics of these four industries and the fact that they are noticeably wary of competition from abroad, all but one respond similarly to most of the tariff-reduction formulas by increasing their outputs. The exception is iron and steel (ISIC 371) which contracts under all but one of the tariff-reduction formulas. The explanation for these results is easily found in the data of Table 3.1. There we see that iron and steel is the only one of these four industries in which the initial U.S. tariff is greater than that of the world average. Thus, it appears that a primary determinant of an industry's vulnerability to multilateral tariff reductions is whether its own tariff is greater or smaller than that of the world average.

VARIATION OF INDUSTRY TARIFFS

We have noted that tariff reductions tend to cause consumer substitution toward the affected industries and away from both nontraded industries and those traded industries which were exempted from the tariff reduction. As a check on this result, we have experimented with variations in the tariffs on the second group of selected industries considered above. For each of these four industries, we first tried setting their tariff changes equal to zero in all countries, then tried complete removal of their tariffs in all countries, and finally tried exempting only the U.S. industry from tariff reduction. In each case all other tariffs were reduced by 50 percent as in formula 2.

The results are reported in Table 3.7, including percentage

TABLE 3.7

PERCENTAGE OUTPUT CHANGES IN SELECTED
U.S. INDUSTRIES WITH ALTERNATIVE CHANGES
IN TARIFF OF SELECTED INDUSTRY
(T = TOTAL INDUSTRY, H = HOME SECTOR, X = EXPORT SECTOR)

Tariff Change in Selected Industry	324 Footwear		371 Iron & Steel		383 Electrical		384 Transport	
0 in All Countries	T	.888	T	−.056	T	.016	T	.039
	H	.896	H	−.006	H	.034	H	.045
	X	−2.28	X	−1.50	X	−.482	X	−.201
−50% in All Countries	T	.219	T	−.015	T	.136	T	.262
	H	.204	H	−.084	H	−.025	H	.023
	X	7.06	X	2.00	X	4.55	X	3.90
−100% in All Countries	T	−.450	T	.026	T	.256	T	.493
	H	−.487	H	−.162	H	−.083	H	.000
	X	16.41	X	5.51	X	9.58	X	8.00
0 in U.S., 50% Other	T	.964	T	−.014	T	.187	T	.328
	H	.960	H	−.084	H	.065	H	.141
	X	2.87	X	2.00	X	3.57	X	3.18

output changes both for the selected industries as a whole and for their home and export sectors. In three of the four industries (all except footwear) the pattern inferred earlier is reaffirmed: each expands more, the more tariffs are reduced multilaterally in the industry. The sectoral results indicate, however, that it is the export sector that expands while the home sector, in most cases, contracts. This distinction is important, of course, since the costs of shifting from home to export production are not likely to be borne equally by all firms within an industry.

An exception to the pattern was found for the footwear industry (ISIC 324), which loses (in the United States) from multilateral tariff reductions on footwear imports. The reason for this result seems to be the unusually small size of the export sector in the U.S. footwear industry. This prevents it from participating in the worldwide expansion of demand for footwear that tariff reductions imply.

Finally, the last lines of the table report the effects of unilaterally excluding the United States from tariff reductions in the selected industries. Here, as one could expect, most of the industries benefit from having tariffs on their products reduced elsewhere but not at home.

VI. THE ROLE OF NONTARIFF BARRIERS

It should be evident that we have confined our attention thus far only to the effects of tariff reductions. There are numerous nontariff barriers (NTBs) that impede trade in various industries that must also be taken into consideration. These include quantitative restrictions on imports, voluntary export restraints ("orderly marketing" arrangements), government procurement practices, customs regulations, health and safety requirements, and numerous other barriers that are too detailed to be documented here.

While these various NTBs are obviously important, they are, unfortunately, very difficult to analyze. The problem is one of translating them into their tariff equivalents, or otherwise estimating the extent to which they may restrict imports. For want of anything better, we have used the data on NTBs compiled by Murray and Walter,[8] based upon the coverage of trade that was subjected to NTBs in individual countries in 1973. These data by no means measure the restrictiveness of NTBs, but they nevertheless provide some indication of the degree to which imports in particular industry categories and countries are affected by NTBs. The detailed results are available upon request.

With respect to the United States, Murray and Walter [9] note that:

> Apart from the textiles sector ... U.S. quantitative restrictions at present cover imported meat, specialty steel, petroleum products, printed books and periodicals, aircraft, ships and boats, dairy products, oil seeds and fruits, margarine and other edible fats, sugar, chocolate and other food products containing cocoa, certain preparations of flour and starch containing cocoa, sweetened forages and

certain other food preparations. Imports of wild bird feath-
ers are controlled, as are narcotics and firearms.

We would have to add to the foregoing list the recently imposed
voluntary restraints on imports into the United States of shoes
and television sets and the restrictions on imports of steel. These
restraints are not reflected, however, in our data.[10]
It may be of interest to compare the coverage data for the
United States with those of other major industrialized countries.
Thus, as Murray and Walter[11] have noted, it appears that
France, Italy, Japan, Norway, the Benelux countries, and
Switzerland maintain fairly extensive NTBs on industrial products, in particular footwear, ceramic tableware, cutlery, and
tools. For agricultural products, besides the European Community's rather restrictive variable-levy scheme, Austria, Canada,
France, Japan, Norway, and Switzerland impose NTBs on many
items.
We have already seen how the presence of nontariff barriers
can affect the outcome of tariff reductions. That is, by limiting
the response of imports to price changes, they cause the protected industry to behave more as though it were nontraded
than traded. It remains to consider what effects changes in the
nontariff barriers themselves may have.
To determine this, we ran two more experiments with our
model, increasing the quotas on the textile and wearing apparel
industries (ISIC 321 and 322). The increases were assumed first
for the United States alone, then for all countries. The results
are summarized in Table 3.8.
The effects on the textile industry are similar to what we have
found before for tariff reductions. The U.S. textile industry
contracts if the quota increase is done unilaterally by the United
States, but expands when all countries raise quotas. The expansion in the latter case, however, is confined to the export sector.
The results for the apparel industry, however, are surprising.
Here there is expansion in both cases and in both the home and
export sectors. The reason turns out to be the heavy dependence
of that industry on textiles as an input and the extreme reduc-

TABLE 3.8

THE EFFECTS OF A 10 PERCENT INCREASE IN TEXTILE AND
APPAREL QUOTAS IN U.S. ONLY AND IN ALL COUNTRIES

| | | Quota Increase In | |
		U.S. Only	All Countrie
% Change U.S. Total Employment		.0007	.011
% Change U.S. Textile Employment		−.021	.304
Absolute Change in U.S.	Home	−.867	−.830
Textile Employment (Man-Years)	Export	635	4,214
% Change U.S. Apparel Employment		1.40	1.44
Absolute Change in U.S.	Home	16,055	16,080
Apparel Employment (Man-Years)	Export	261	758
% Change U.S. Consumer Prices		−.011	−.012
% Change U.S. Prices of Textiles	Home	−.012	−.012
	Import	−8.785	−8.785
% Change U.S. Prices of Apparel	Home	−.020	−.020
	Import	−2.569	−2.569
% Change U.S. Exchange-rate		−.080	−.095

tion in import prices that the quota increase there permits.
While this result is surely not representative of what would
happen to most industries if their nontariff barriers were relaxed, it does point up the importance of allowing for interindustry interactions as we do in our model.

We have seen that the effects of *changing* quotas can be very
similar to the effects of changing tariffs. However, this does not
mean that the effects of *maintaining* constant levels of tariffs and
quotas are the same when other things are changing. There is an
important difference. When quantities demanded or supplied
change, a tariff permits some adjustment to that change through
imports. A quota does not. When a quota is present, such adjustment must be accomplished entirely through prices. Tariffs are
therefore a much more flexible instrument than quotas.

Time and resources have unfortunately precluded a more
detailed examination of alternative strategies for liberalizing

NTBs. In principle, we could conduct experiments in which the United States and the remaining countries might reduce their existing quota coverage by some given percentages, and we could interact these changes with various tariff reductions. This would of course add to the plethora of results that the reader may already be finding difficult to assimilate.

Negotiated reductions in NTBs may nevertheless be important in selected industries, particularly in agricultural products and foodstuffs (ISIC 1 and 310) and textiles and wearing apparel (ISIC 321 and 322). Using the data on trade coverage, the United States could identify the instances in which its exports and imports were being restricted by foreign and domestic NTBs. Calculations of costs and benefits from liberalization of the NTBs could then be made along lines similar to ours for the purpose of developing an appropriate negotiating strategy for the United States.

VII. THE ROLE OF LESS DEVELOPED COUNTRIES IN U.S. TRADE

Data limitations have prevented us from incorporating the less developed countries (LDCs) into our model. In this section, we will attempt to assess the importance of this omission.

Two factors should be considered in evaluating the importance of omitting countries from our model. The first is simply the amount of trade accounted for by the omitted countries, and the second is the price responsiveness of that trade. For it is only the *changes* in rest-of-world trade that occur when tariffs and NTBs are reduced that matter for our results. These changes would necessarily be small if the volume of trade itself were minimal, but they could also be small for a large volume of omitted trade if that trade were relatively unresponsive to price variations. We shall consider each of these points in turn.

To give some idea of the volume of omitted trade and its possible importance for the United States, we report U.S. exports and imports by region, for 1975, in Table 3.9. The source of these data was not the same as was used elsewhere in the paper, and the industry and country classifications are accord-

TABLE 3.9

PERCENTAGE OF U.S. TRADE WITH
SELECTED REGIONS OF THE WORLD (1975)

Industry		Industrial Areas [a]	Eastern Trading Area	Developing Areas
Primary Products	Imports	30.6	1.0	68.4
	Exports	62.9	6.1	31.0
Nonferrous Metals	Imports	67.8	4.7	27.1
	Exports	75.6	3.8	21.4
Iron and Steel	Imports	93.0	0.6	6.4
	Exports	37.4	1.2	61.4
Chemicals	Imports	86.8	1.1	11.9
	Exports	56.0	1.0	42.9
Engineering Products	Imports	80.6	0.4	19.0
	Exports	57.0	2.4	40.6
Road Motor Vehicles	Imports	98.9	0.1	0.9
	Exports	70.7	0.4	28.9
Textiles and Clothing	Imports	32.0	1.9	66.4
	Exports	65.5	0.5	33.5
Other Manufactures	Imports	73.7	1.0	25.4
	Exports	72.3	0.9	26.7
Total	Imports	58.6	0.9	40.5
	Exports	61.3	3.0	35.7

SOURCE: General Agreement on Tariffs and Trade, *International Trade 1975/76* (Geneva, 1976).

[a] Includes the eighteen countries used in this study plus South Africa.

ingly not exactly comparable. Still, the column labeled "Industrial Areas" closely approximates U.S. trade with the industrialized countries included in our model. It is clear from this column that we have accounted in our model for well over half of U.S. trade in all industries except for imports of primary products, textiles, and clothing, and exports of iron and steel. Nonetheless, the quantity of trade with LDCs is fairly sizable in all but a few industries.

Even in quantitative terms, however, this result can be misleading, since it reflects only U.S. trade. Since the United States competes on world markets with all other countries, a better measure of the omitted trade would have been that of all eighteen countries together. This was not available on a disaggregated basis, but we can report the results for total trade. Of the total exports of the industrial areas, 70 percent was to the eighteen countries included in our model. The analogous figure for imports was 69 percent. Comparing with the last row of Table 3.9, it is clear that U.S. trade with LDCs is disproportionately large. Thus, the data in Table 3.9 for the United States alone tend to overstate the importance of the trade that was omitted from our model.

We turn now to the issue of the price sensitivity of the omitted trade. In our model, prices are determined so as to leave the balance between world supply and demand unchanged in each industry. Were we to add to the model additional trade with countries that are currently excluded, the estimates of equilibrium price changes would be altered only to the extent the additional net trade is responsive to changes in world prices.

Now, consider the nature of the omitted trade as indicated by Table 3.9. First, a portion, admittedly small, of that trade is with the centrally planned economics of the eastern trading area. Since this trade is negotiated by state traders in whose own economies market prices play only a minor role, it seems unlikely that such trade is very price elastic. Indeed the same argument might possibly be applied to the much larger volume of trade with the LDCs. These countries are notorious for their government intervention in export and import markets, either directly via export and import licenses or indirectly through exchange controls and other means. Thus, there may be limited scope for competitive supply and demand responses within these economies to be felt on world markets, particularly in the short-run period encompassed by our model. This conclusion might be altered, however, in the longer run, particularly if trade liberalization created new and permanent opportunities for LDC imports in the markets of the industrialized countries.

Finally, if we look at the particular industries for which the quantitative importance of LDC trade is greatest in Table 3.9, we see that there are reasons for these industries to be even less price responsive than normal, at least in the short run. In primary products, for example, short-run supply depends more on current weather conditions and on the pattern of historical resource exploitation than on current prices. In textiles and wearing apparel, on the other hand, supply is presumably much more price elastic. But here, as we have seen, the demand for imports on the part of the developed countries is severely constrained by quantitative restrictions. Thus, unless these restrictions can be relaxed significantly, the LDC exporters of textiles and wearing apparel will continue to find limited opportunities for these goods in industrialized country markets.

Our inability to include the LDCs in our model is a possibly important drawback for the United States especially. However, this omission may be less serious than it appears in view of the short-run orientation of our model and the difficulties that LDCs might have in adapting their industrial structure to export markets. Also, the maintenance of NTBs that restrict imports from LDCs, particularly of textiles and wearing apparel, enhances the plausibility of our results. We should mention, finally, that a full account of trade liberalization vis-à-vis the LDCs would have to take into account the mutual expansion of trade that would occur as LDCs increased their own imports from the industrialized countries. Clearly there is more work to be done to take all these factors into account.

VIII. CONCLUSION

In the earlier sections of the paper, we analyzed the effects of several different tariff-cutting formulas. Of these, only four (numbers 2, 4, 5, and 6 of section III) represent plausible outcomes of the current round of trade negotiations. All other formulas were included in order to highlight the effect of varying the extent of trade liberalization in particular countries, particular industries, and for the world as a whole. Two experiments were also performed in section VI with changes in quotas. While we found no notable difference in the analysis of quota changes and tariff changes, time and resource limitations prevented us from examining various alternative strategies for changes in quotas. Finally, while all of our results are somewhat inaccurate due to the omission of LDCs, the short-run orientation of the model and the difficulties that LDCs might experience in expanding their exports suggest that our results are reasonably plausible, at least for most industries.

Several conclusions of a general nature emerge from our analysis. First, we have seen that multilateral tariff reductions reduce prices in all countries. The greatest reductions are in the prices of imports themselves, but the effect extends as well to the prices of exports and to consumer prices generally (see Table 3.3). In addition, the price declines in any particular country tend to be greater, the larger the tariff reductions in that country are. This was noted in Table 3.3 in comparing the effects on U.S. consumer prices of formulas 4 and 6 *versus* the others and is also evident in Table 3.5.

Second, we have seen that the employment and output effects of tariff reductions are distributed quite unequally across sectors of the economies involved. There is some tendency for particular industries to be harmed by tariff reductions if their own tariffs are initially high compared both with other countries and with other industries. However, in general the particular tariff on a specific industry in a given country is less important than whether the tariffs are reduced elsewhere for that industry. Thus, we have seen that multilateral tariff reductions tend to cause expansion in most industries that share in the reduction. This expansion is at the expense of nontradable industries as well as of any tradable industries that are exempted from the reductions.

Third, the expansion of (nonexempted) tradable industries is accomplished by means of a considerable alternation of production within these industries. With some exceptions, the export sectors of these industries expand substantially while the sectors producing for the home market contract. This shifting of production within the industry may impose additional costs of adjustment, particularly if labor cannot easily move between the home and export sectors.

Finally, we have computed the effects on exchange rates that arise under the alternative strategies. As one would expect, a country's currency rises less or falls more in value, the greater its own tariff reductions are compared with the rest of the world. The welfare implications of exchange-rate changes are unclear, however, since a depreciation on the one hand stimulates most sectors of the economy but on the other hand raises prices, and it is sometimes viewed politically as a sign of failure.

Together, these conclusions indicate that any trade strategy that might be chosen will result in benefits to some parts of the population and costs to others. No trade strategy is possible that will, by itself, make everyone better off. Instead, one must try to balance the interests of producers (including labor) in tradable industries against those of producers in nontradable industries and in industries that are to be excluded from worldwide trade liberalization. The first group is likely to gain from tariff reductions both by receiving higher incomes and by paying lower prices. The second group is likely to lose by suffering loss of income in excess of the price reduction.

For the United States, this trade-off is apparent in the comparison of the more realistic of the tariff-reduction formulas we have studied (formulas 2, 4, 5, and 6 of section III). Because U.S. tariffs are low compared with those of the rest of the world, formulas 4 and 6, which reduce high tariffs the most and low tariffs the least, lead to comparatively small tariff reductions in the United States. This in turn means that the benefits to consumers are minimized (i.e., the fall in consumer prices is small) but that producers in nontradable and exempted industries lose less than they would with the other formulas. Furthermore, the effect on producers in tradable industries is unclear. The small U.S. tariff reductions under formulas 4 and 6 limit the extent of substitution by U.S. consumers toward these industries, but, on the other hand, the larger tariff reductions abroad stimulate these industries. All in all, then, it would seem that tariff-reduction formulas such as formulas 4 and 6 might be the most desirable from the U.S. point of view.

It should be noted, however, that whatever formula is applied none of the effects is likely to be very large. Even 100 percent tariff removal was seen to have very small percentage effects on output, employment, and prices in most countries and industries. Thus, it may not be of crucial importance for the United States and other countries that we succeed in calculating exactly all of the costs and benefits of alternative trade strategies, for the difference between the optimal strategy and other nonoptimal strategies is probably not very large. The importance of our analysis here, then, is not that it enables us to pick out the optimal trade strategy. Rather, it is useful in directing our attention to particular sectors of the economy that will be hurt the most by whatever strategy is chosen.

In this regard, we have shown that labor displacement in the United States would be small both absolutely and relatively. This suggests that policies of trade adjustment assistance might not be unduly costly. It also suggests, particularly in view of the larger macroeconomic issues in the economy as a whole, that general employment conditions may be of controlling importance in terms of the ease or difficulty that workers may experience in adjusting to changes in international trade policy.

NOTES

1. A. V. Deardorff, R. M. Stern, and C. F. Baum, "A Simulation Model of World Trade and Production," 1976 (mimeograph available from authors); "A Multi-Country Simulation of the Employment and Exchange-Rate Effects of Post-Kennedy Round Tariff Reductions," in N. Akrasanee et al. (eds.), *Trade and Employment in Asia and the Pacific* (Honolulu: The University Press of Hawaii, 1977); and A. V. Deardorff, R. M. Stern, and M. N. Greene, "The Sensitivity of Industrial Output and Employment to Exchange-Rate Changes in the Major Industrialized Countries," in J. P. Martin and M.A.M. Smith (eds.) *Trade and Payments Adjustments Under Flexible Exchange Rates* (London: Macmillan Press, 1979).

2. A. V. Deardorff, and R. M. Stern, "A Note on Calculating the Tariff Equivalent of Quantitative Restrictions," 1977 (mimeograph available from authors).

3. GATT, *The Basic Documentation for the Tariff Study* (Geneva, 1974).

4. Detailed information on imports at the line-item level was available for 1970 and 1971 and GATT, *The Basic Documentation.* We used the 1970 data to correspond with our data on employment by industry for this year, which was the latest available at the time we assembled all

the data for computational purposes. The basic data underlying our model are available upon request.

5. We set the coverage of quantitative restrictions for these industries at 100 percent in the absence of more detailed information.

6. Our choice of formulas has been influenced in part by the work of W. R. Cline et al., "Prospective Trade Effects of Tariff Reduction in the Multilateral Trade Negotiations," November 1975; and "Choice Among Alternative Tariff-Cutting Formulas in the Multilateral Trade Negotiations," January 1976.

7. An illustration of formula 4 would be that if there were an initial tariff rate of 50 percent, the successive reductions would be: $50 \times .50 = 25$; $25 \times .50 = 12.5$, and $12.5 \times .50 = 6.25$ percent. Thus, the negotiated reduction would be from 50 percent down to 6.25 percent, with the result that high tariffs get cut the most.

8. T. Murray and I. Walter, "Special and Differential Liberalization of Quantitative Restrictions on Imports from Developing Countries," paper presented to the Agency for International Development and Foreign Service Institute, February 22, 1977.

9. Ibid., p. 18.

10. Ibid., pp. 11-13. Murray and Walter have summarized the evidence on the costs of NTBs to the United States. On an aggregate level, it has been estimated, based on 1971 data, that the annual efficiency loss to the United States from NTBs was about $3.6 billion, or about 0.44 percent of national income. In terms of trade coverage, for 1972, about $100 billion of domestic consumption was estimated to be subject to NTBs on imports (including petroleum, which may have inflated the estimate). Estimates of costs of NTBs have also been made for specific industries and sectors. For example, these ran about 20 to 25 percent of total U.S. domestic expenditures on raw sugar in 1970, and about 10 percent of total expenditure on cotton and noncotton textiles in 1972. Estimates for more recent years are also cited for textiles, meat, and steel. While all of the available estimates are no doubt subject to criticism on various methodological grounds, there is nevertheless good reason to believe that many NTBs have been and will continue to be fairly costly to U.S. consumers.

11. Ibid., p. 19.

Chapter 4

ADJUSTMENT ASSISTANCE FOR TRADE-DISPLACED WORKERS

GEORGE R. NEUMANN

Graduate School of Business
University of Chicago

A primary obstacle hindering the expansion of trade among nations has been the large dislocation costs borne by individuals. Despite a more than twenty-year period of official concern with this problem in the United States, relatively little has been done to minimize the burden that falls on trade-displaced workers. Thus, even with the development of specific programs such as the Trade Adjustment Assistance (TAA) program in 1962, and the substantially expanded 1974 version, the political pressure against expanded trade continues to exist. In this paper we review the evidence on adjustment-assistance efforts, both domestic and foreign, and suggest an alternative approach to the issue. The plan of the paper is as follows.

In section I the development of adjustment-assistance programs in the United States is reviewed, and their major problems are discussed in section II. The third section of the paper examines the adjustment-assistance programs of other countries and suggests modification in the existing U.S. adjustment-assistance program. In the fourth section the costs of trade adjustment assistance commensurate with the employment changes estimated by Deardorff, Stern, and Greene are presented. The final section summarizes the major results. This paper is concerned with adjustment assistance for displaced workers. Related programs exist to provide aid to firms, but as few firms have made use of these programs, we have focused on programs designed for displaced workers.

I. ADJUSTMENT ASSISTANCE IN THE UNITED STATES

Prior to the Trade Expansion Act of 1962 the only means available for workers affected by increased trade was escape-clause relief. Although present in some earlier trade agreements, the idea of escape-clause relief was formalized in the Trade Agreements Act of 1951. Such actions, effective in principle, are costly, both in economic and political terms. Raising tariffs or establishing quotas reduces, or eliminates entirely, the benefits of trade; consequently, the directness of this approach has prevented its use in most circumstances. Between 1947 and 1962, the president invoked escape clause relief in only fifteen of forty-one cases.[1] Infrequent resort to escape-clause relief is due to two major factors: adverse foreign reaction and the bluntness of the instrument. In areas where only a few marginal firms were affected, relief would have to apply to the entire industry; consequently only major disruptions in trading patterns could be treated in this manner. While a temporary use of escape-clause relief may have been helpful, the tendency for "temporary" quotas and tariffs to become permanent has created obstacles for even limited usage. In the period 1947-62, the costs of labor market adjustments were borne mainly by individuals.

THE RANDALL COMMISSION

The inadequacy of escape-clause relief for reallocating the costs of increased trade were recognized by several observers, and various proposals were offered. The most important of these, from the viewpoint of subsequent adoption, was that offered by David McDonald, president of the United Steelworkers of America, in the Randall Commission Report of 1954.[2] The essence of the proposal was that trade-impacted workers should be compensated in some way to reduce their losses. Three programs were suggested by McDonald. The first provided unemployment benefits for up to one year, and for special training, job counseling, and moving allowances. The second program was an early retirement program—workers were to be given a certain number of weeks' pay for each year of service with the company, and for workers over fifty-five or sixty, benefits equivalent to the social security benefits that a sixty-five-year-old could draw were to be paid. The third program was a revised unemployment insurance, with benefits paid at a higher rate for a longer time.

Although influential in some regards, the Randall Commission had little success in generating a specific program for trade-displaced workers.

TRADE ADJUSTMENT-ASSISTANCE PROGRAMS IN THE U.S.

Formal efforts in providing adjustment assistance to workers can be separated into three periods: 1962-74, under the Trade Expansion Act of 1962 (TEA); 1966-68, under the Automotive Products Trade Act of 1965 (APTA); and 1975 to date under the Trade Act of 1974 (TA). Despite the appearance of overlap in the dating of the first two programs, they actually are distinct, since adjustment assistance was not available under TEA until November 1969. The essential features of the adjustment-assistance programs, which are outlined in Table 4.1, are quite similar. Differences that arise among the programs are due mainly to the differences in eligibility requirements.

Examination of the characteristics of these adjustment-assistance programs indicates congressional intent clearly. All three programs have the feature that the adjustment to changed trade conditions would be made primarily by individuals finding new jobs. No attempt was made to create new employment opportunities, and even upgrading of workers' skills was not stressed, as no additional training opportunities were created. To facilitate this adjustment, the cash payments made to individuals were significantly larger and were available for a longer period

TABLE 4.1

CHARACTERISTICS OF ADJUSTMENT ASSISTANCE UNDER TEA, APTA, AND TA

	TEA (1)	APTA (2)	TA (3)
I. *Benefits:*			
Cash Payments	65% of previous weekly earnings up to a maximum of 70% of average manu-facturing weekly earnings	65% of previous weekly earnings up to a maximum of 70% of average manu-facturing weekly earnings	70% of previous weekly earnings up to a maximum of 100% of average manu-facturing weekly earnings
Job Training and Counseling	Special services not avail-able, but individuals were eligible for services pro-vided under any federal law	Special services not avail-able, but individuals were eligible for services pro-vided under any federal law	Special services not avail-able, but individuals were eligible for services pro-vided under any federal law
Job Search Allowances	None	None	$500 maximum
Relocation Payments	Reasonable and necessary expenses plus 2.5 times average weekly earnings in manufacturing	Reasonable and necessary expenses plus 2.5 times average weekly earnings in manufacturing	80% of reasonable and necessary expenses plus 3.0 times the workers average weekly wage.
Maximum Benefit Period	52 weeks; 65 weeks if over 60	52 weeks; 65 weeks if over 60	52 weeks; 78 weeks if over 60
II. *Eligibility Requirements:*			
A. Individual:	Employment in 78 weeks of the previous 156 at wages of $15 per week, and 26 of the 52 weeks with the impacted firm	Employment in 78 weeks of the previous 156 at wages of $15 per week, and 26 of the 52 weeks with the impacted firm	Employment in 26 of the previous 52 weeks with the impacted firm
B. Group Determina-tion Made By	Tariff Commission	Automotive Agreements Adjustment Board	Secretary of Labor

of time, thus eliminating most of the short-term income loss that workers would incur.

The liberality of the benefits available was offset partially by the strictness of the eligibility requirements. Under TEA a recipient had to have been employed at least half-time for the previous three years at some firm, and also to have worked twenty-six weeks of the previous fifty-two at the trade-impacted firm. The effect of this restriction was to focus benefits at workers with "full-time" labor force commitment. Although these individual requirements restricted eligibility somewhat, the greatest restriction was occasioned by the group eligibility determination. Because the Tariff Commission linked adjustment assistance to escape-clause relief, groups were eligible for benefits only if their unemployment was "in major part [due to] . . . concession[s] granted under trade agreements."[3] Since the Kennedy Round tariff cuts did not begin until 1968, the availability of adjustment-assistance benefits under TEA was delayed until 1969.

Group eligibility requirements were loosened under the APTA by replacing the Tariff Commission with the Automotive Agreement Adjustment Assistance Board composed of the secretaries of commerce, labor, and the treasury, and by changing the legal wording of "in major part" to "a primary factor."[4] This severed the link between escape-clause relief and adjustment assistance for this act but had no bearing on other adjustment-assistance programs. In essence, this was a legal finesse, because escape-clause relief was never considered as an option by any of the parties.[5]

The greatest change in the group eligibility decision process was made by the TA of 1974. The Tariff Commission, renamed the International Trade Commission, was replaced entirely by the secretary of labor in determining eligibility, and determination of eligibility was made dependent on imports having *contributed importantly* to workers' separation. Essentially, this meant that changes in impacts for any reason—even if imports fell but domestic production declined at a greater rate—would make groups eligible for adjustment assistance.

Because of differences in eligibility requirements, these adjustment-assistance programs differed greatly in size. Evidence on the size differences among the programs is given in Table 4.2. Limiting eligibility to the automobile industry accounts for the small size of the APTA program, but the pronounced size differences between the TEA and TA programs must be attributed to the more liberal definition of trade impact.

TABLE 4.2

CHARACTERISTICS OF U.S. ADJUSTMENT–ASSISTANCE PROGRAMS

	TEA	APTA	TA (4/75 9/76)
	(1)	(2)	
Certifications	106	14	435
Denials	171	7	640
Number of Certified Workers	53,970	2,493	105,000
Benefits Paid	$86 million	$4.1 million	NA

SOURCE: Bureau of International Labor Affairs unpublished documents and P. Henle, "Trade Adjustment Assistance: Should It Be Modified?" *Monthly Labor Review,* 100, no. 3, pp. 40–45.

The size difference between the programs may be overstated somewhat due to the sharp recession of 1974-75, but this is unlikely to account for all of the sevenfold increase.

The development of trade adjustment programs in the U.S. has proceeded from an exclusive use of escape-clause relief to adjustment-assistance programs applicable to a single firm or to groups of workers. These latter effects, which rely mainly upon short-term income maintenance to smooth the transition to re-employment, have varied degrees of success. Adjustment assistance under the TEA was delayed until November 1969 because of a strict interpretation of eligibility. Further delays in benefit delivery also occurred during the program's operational period because of the eligibility requirements. In contrast, the adjustment-assistance program operated under the APTA is generally regarded as more successful, in part because of the absence of such delays. Although the adjustment-assistance programs were otherwise similar, the restriction of eligibility in this case to workers from one industry facilitated eligibility determination and benefit delivery. It is not clear how much of this success was due to the program being restricted to one industry and how much was due to the industry being the automobile industry—an industry that has relatively few firms, most of which are organized by one union.

The adjustment-assistance program contained in the TA of 1974 is only slightly different from its predecessors in terms of the kinds of benefits provided but is significantly more available to workers because of the more liberal eligibility requirements. Because of this expanded eligibility, the current adjustment-assistance program far exceeds previous efforts in attempting to aid trade-displaced workers.

In essence, then, the sixteen-year history of adjustment-assistance effects in the United States can be summarized as a continual expansion of the beneficiary population with little change in the basic structure of the programs. Emphasis has been, and is, on the provision of short-term income maintenance with almost no attention to longer-run problems of reemployability and earnings loss.

II. ADJUSTMENT ASSISTANCE: PROBLEMS OF IMPLEMENTATION

Experience with adjustment-assistance programs, despite the numerous changes that have occurred, has generally been less than favorable in the United States. To be fair, the APTA is often considered to have been successful,[6] but this was a very small program, limited to one industry. It is more comparable to private adjustment programs, such as negotiated by the railway workers on Amtrak, or the arrangements negotiated in the West Coast longshoring industry. Larger programs such as the TAA program in the 1962 act and its successor in the 1974 act have found few strong supporters. Organized labor regards these programs as at best "burial insurance," and the opinion of the business community is no higher.[7] Independent observers offer no great support for the program either and even question the conceptual basis for such programs. That the program survives at all in the face of such opposition is surprising and can be explained more by political expediency than by any economic benefit-cost calculation.

Since the experience of the past is often a guide to the future, a critical examination of the deficiencies of past and present adjustment-assistance programs is in order. Before evaluating the problems that have occurred, a knowledge of the population the programs were designed to serve is essential.

WHO ARE THE TRADE-IMPACTED WORKERS?

Several studies of trade-impacted workers have appeared in recent years, all of which focus on workers who received benefits under the TAA program of the 1962 Trade Expansion Act.[8]

One consistent picture emerges from these studies: TAA recipients tend to be older, less educated, and less skilled than the average unemployed individual. This lack of general skills is usually counterbalanced by a significant amount of time spent with one employer. Consequently, the prelayoff earnings of these individuals were not noticeably atypical of the industry. However, the attribution of such a substantial part of earnings to firm-specific factors implies that a job separation will have much larger effects on this group. Since women appear to be over-represented among trade-impacted workers, this problem is emphasized.

An important caveat should be added to this description of the trade-impacted worker. The characteristics reported refer to those workers who actually received benefits under the TAA program. Not all workers who are affected by increased trade receive these benefits, and for several reasons one would expect that workers who do receive benefits would differ significantly from other trade-impacted workers. For example, the impact of increased trade does not usually occur immediately—firms generally experience a reduction in demand, or poor growth, several periods in advance. Therefore, mobile workers, reacting to the adverse situation, may quit to find employment in firms or industries that offer more attractive long-run opportunities.[9] Also, since adversely affected firms tend to react by not replacing normal attrition, the net result is that the workers employed when the full trade impact occurs are likely to be those who have the greatest difficulties in making the transition to alternative employment.

This review of the characteristics of TAA recipients who were permanently displaced from previous employment indicates that trade-displaced workers face unusually severe problems when laid off. In general, they are older, less educated, less likely to be skilled workers, and have a significant portion of their work experience with one firm. Prior studies of the relationship of earnings to personal characteristics would lead one to expect poor prospects for reemployment and, if reemployed, a significant decline in earnings, which are also observed. While evidence from the current adjustment-assistance program is limited, there are several reasons to expect that permanent job losers would be as disadvantaged now as previous individuals were. The normal workings of the labor market would result in those workers with the greatest opportunities either leaving a trade-impacted firm earlier, and thus not being eligible for benefits, or finding employment quickly after impact and thus not applying for benefits. This "screening" effect can be expected to be present whenever there is advance notice or expectations of a plant closing. A further reason to expect these characteristics to apply to future job losers is based on the industries that are most affected by impacts. With a few notable exceptions, such as steel, impacts have had their greatest effect in low-wage, labor-intensive industries such as footwear, textiles, and some parts of the electronics industry. Workers in these industries tend to be less skilled than the average U.S. worker, and thus the effect of increased trade tends to concentrate unemployment in these sectors. This effect is likely to diminish as production in the United States becomes more specialized in capital—both human and physical—intensive sectors, but it will still have effects in the near future.

BENEFITS PROVIDED BY TAA: SOME GENERAL CRITICISMS

Although access to adjustment-assistance benefits has been increasing since 1962, and thereby meeting some of the objections to increased trade, the TAA programs continue to be criticized about the structure of the programs. The major areas of complaint are: (1) benefits are received with a sometimes substantial lag; (2) the amount and type of benefits are inadequate; and (3) inequities exist in that individuals facing the same problems are treated differently according to the reason for unemployment. In discussing these criticisms, we will be concerned primarily with their applicability to the current program. However, since experience with the current TAA program is limited, we will have to infer some information from the earlier program.

Benefit Delay. Benefit delivery under the 1962 program was characterized by extremely long lags—on average, benefits were received seven months after layoff. The reason for this long lag was the cumbersome eligibility determination process. Investigations had to be made by the Tariff Commission and, following an affirmative finding, the Department of Labor. The information required for these investigations was often not available to workers, and even when it was, the absence of a standard application form until 1972 made it difficult for workers to determine what was needed. Further delays were encountered after an affirmative finding by the Department of Labor, since individuals had to be personally certified by the state employment agencies. Because the information required was different from that normally required for unemployment compensation eligibility, the process would normally be delayed even further as the agencies searched for information.

To some extent, these delays have been minimized in the 1974 TAA program. Investigation is required only by the Department of Labor, and the personal eligibility requirements now require information that is readily available to the state agencies. Despite these changes, delays still exist and will continue to exist. For example, while the Department of Labor was initially able to rule on petitions for eligibility within sixty days, in the July-September quarter of 1976 only 6 percent of the petitions were ruled on in this time, and over 50 percent took longer than ninety days. While some of this delay is due to the sudden increase in the number of petitions, delays are inherent in any program that has restricted eligibility. It follows, therefore, that if the TAA program is to be differentiated from regular unemployment insurance (UI), delays in benefits of one to three months will occur.

Benefit Adequacy. The most frequent charge against the TAA program is that the benefits provided are inadequate—they do not foster a rapid movement to alternative employment, and they do not compensate the worker for losses incurred. Judgment on this issue must be mixed. On the rapid movement to alternative employment there is ample evidence that the TAA program either has no effect or encourages individuals to remain unemployed longer.[10] Compensation for losses incurred is a different matter. Workers who are permanently separated from their jobs incur large losses in earnings when reemployed, and many do not return to employment at all. For these workers the TAA program provides only short-term income support. However, under the 1974 TAA program, permanent job losers are only a fraction—perhaps a small fraction—of all TAA recipients.[11] For individuals who are on temporary layoff, the TAA program provides substantial compensation, and in some cases overcompensates, for lost earnings. As an example, consider the case of an individual separated in June 1976. Assuming that the individual was earning the average in manufacturing, $208.06 per week, his trade readjustment allowance would be $145.65. This appears to be a substantial difference, but due to the nontaxable nature of these benefits, the weekly difference is only $16.60.[12] Thus, a year's unemployment would mean a difference of only $863 in net income. In multiple-earner families this loss is less and if the member with the lower earnings receives adjustment-assistance benefits may even become a net gain.

This example points out a central problem with the TAA program. Since the major feature of TAA is the payment of unemployment compensation at a higher rate and for a longer period than regular UI programs, it is most successful in aiding those who need assistance least—those on short-term layoff. Indeed, the program can be criticized only because such payments, by linking benefits to unemployment status, implicitly encourage longer spells of unemployment. But for workers who are permanently displaced and who therefore incur the greatest losses, the program offers only short-term support and has little or no effect on subsequent earnings.[13]

Differential Treatment of Trade-impacted Workers. An issue that frequently arises in discussions of adjustment assistance is why individuals who have lost jobs due to imports should be treated differently from other unemployed individuals. Jobs are continuously being lost, and new ones created, due to many factors—technological change, shifting patterns of taste, population change, and so on. Workers who lose jobs for reasons other than increased trade face the same problems as trade-impacted workers, so the argument goes, and equity would dictate that they be treated similarly. Arguments in support of differential treatment have usually been based on the idea that the government through its policy decisions on tariffs and quotas was in part responsible for the unemployment of trade-impacted workers and therefore was obliged to respond differently. While this argument is not universally accepted, it is the premise upon which the TAA program is based. Implicit in it is the view that all other sources of unemployment are, in some sense, risks of the marketplace that workers must bear. If one accepts this argument, eligibility for the TAA program under the 1962 act follows naturally: benefits were to be provided to individuals whose unemployment was linked to tariff *concessions.* But the 1974 program has removed this link; variation in imports due to any reason can qualify individuals for adjustment assistance. The elimination of this direct relationship makes it difficult to justify the existence of adjustment assistance in its present form and has important implications for the size of the TAA program and the type of individuals who receive benefits. Whereas under the 1962 program recipients of TAA benefits were almost entirely workers who had been prematurely separated from their jobs, under the present program workers who are on short-term layoff and who expect to return to their jobs with no loss of earnings can now receive TAA benefits.[14] Although experience with the TAA program under the 1974 act is limited, what evidence does exist suggests that a profound change has occurred due to severing the link to trade concessions. From April 1975 to September 1976, a total of 1,075 petitions for adjustment assistance was filed with and investigated by the Department of Labor. Of these 435 were certified and 160 were pending by September 30. More than 105,000 workers were receiving payments under the act in the first eighteen months compared with the 54,000 who received benefits under the previous program in five years.[15]

The "type" of trade-impacted worker has also changed. The automobile industry now accounts for the largest number of TAA recipients, and the primary and fabricated metals industries are not far behind. Also, most TAA recipients return to the previous employer, according to the Department of Labor, which is considerably different from the situation under the old program when 70 percent did not find employment even in the same industry.[16]

The blurring of the distinction between adjustment assistance and unemployment compensation raises, as we noted above, questions of equity. Without a linkage to tariff or quota reductions, decisions about eligibility for TAA have a certain arbitrariness. Thus, if imports of foreign cars increase, employees who manufacture bumpers for an automobile manufacturer may be eligible for TAA benefits, but if the bumpers were purchased from a firm that did not make automobiles, its employees would not be eligible for benefits.[17] Similarly, individuals performing service operations, but not the actual manufacture of a product, are not eligible. Further examples could be given, but the point is clear: without direct connection to tariff reductions, an adjustment-assistance program can be limited only by arbitrary restrictions on eligibility. The consequences of such arbitrariness are inevitable. Workers perceive the TAA program as being unfair, and receipt of benefits is regarded as a political matter. Public opinion for programs that provide benefits in arbitrary fashion is unlikely to develop.

In summary, both previous and present adjustment-assistance programs have had critical flaws that have reduced their usefulness. The administrative structure of the 1962 program resulted in lengthy delays in benefit receipt, which severely limited the value of the benefits. Although the procedures were streamlined in the 1974 act, the increase in the number of cases has resulted in lags that are still substantial. One would have to conclude that the present form of adjustment assistance is not readily adaptable to speedy and effective administration.

A judgment about the adequacy of benefits under the adjustment-assistance program must necessarily be mixed. For individuals who are permanently separated from their jobs, the program offers little aid. Adjustment allowances will provide short-term compensation with relatively small financial loss. However, the real loss that these individuals suffered was in their reemployment earnings, if they found jobs at all, and no part of the adjustment program was adequate to prevent this loss. Partly by design—neither the 1962 nor the 1974 programs were designed to compensate workers for financial loss—and partly due to ineffective programs—for example, training—the adjustment-assistance programs have not been able adequately to minimize the burden of adjustment borne by those who are permanently separated from employment. For those workers who are only temporarily unemployed, mostly those covered under the 1974 act, the TAA program provides adequate and in some cases more than adequate compensation. The losses experienced by such workers are both relatively and absolutely small compared with those experienced by permanent separations.

Finally, although the concept of adjustment assistance has been a basic part of U.S. trade policy since 1962, the changed conditions of eligibility for TAA benefits under the 1974 act significantly weaken the rationale for providing such benefits. As the distinction between the Trade Adjustment Assistance program and regular unemployment compensation diminishes, the purpose of adjustment assistance becomes lost.

III. ALTERNATIVE APPROACHES TO ADJUSTMENT ASSISTANCE

The previous sections reviewed problems that beset the current adjustment-assistance program. Some of these problems can be eliminated by minor changes, but the majority seem resolvable only by significant changes in the structure and orientation of the existing program. In considering alternative forms of assistance, a natural reference is the experiences of other countries with similar problems. In the first part of this section we review the labor-market solutions employed by the major trading partners of the United States. Although this information is illuminating, it must be viewed in perspective. Institutions, particularly labor-market institutions, vary widely across countries, and thus what works in one country may not succeed in another. Nonetheless, cross-country comparison can be useful in suggesting the possible elements of an adjustment-assistance program. In the second part of this section we use the insights gained from this review and the discussion of the previous section to outline an alternative adjustment-assistance program.

ADJUSTMENT ASSISTANCE IN OTHER COUNTRIES [18]

An examination of the adjustment-assistance effects of other countries reveals a most interesting fact: among the major trading partners of the United States—Canada, the United Kingdom, West Germany, Japan, and Sweden—only the United States has a separate program designed to aid workers displaced by foreign trade. There are Trade Adjustment Assistance programs in other countries—for example, Canada and West Germany—but they are designed to provide technical and financial help to firms. What assistance is provided to workers comes from general programs, or, in a few cases, from ad hoc programs restricted to a specific industry. In essence, trade-displaced workers in other countries receive the local equivalent of unemployment insurance in the United States. These "unemployment insurance" programs are similar to that of the United States in that they emphasize cash payments, but they also contain other benefits aimed at relocating or retraining workers. Canada, under the Manpower Mobility Assistance program, pays job-search allowances, relocation expenses up to $1,000, and will provide up to $1,500 if an unemployed worker sells a house and moves to a new locality. Job training is also available through the Technical and Vocational Training Assistance Act.

In Great Britain, unemployment compensation is paid under

the Redundancy Payments Act of 1965, based on age and experience with a particular firm. Conditional upon having two years of experience, workers aged eighteen to twenty are entitled to one half of one week's pay for each year of experience; those aged twenty-one to thirty-nine are entitled to one week's pay, and workers over forty are entitled to one and one-half week's pay for each year of experience.[19] Training is provided by the Industrial Training Act of 1964, with the training being provided by the firm that hires the worker. The costs of training are paid for by taxes on the firms.

Sweden offers similar incentives for workers to relocate. Unemployment benefits are available, as are job-training programs; relocation expenses; and, of particular importance given Sweden's chronic housing problem, preferential housing treatment.

Limited assistance is available in West Germany and Japan basically due to the peculair labor-market institutions in these countries. Both economies have experienced strong growth since the 1950s and except for brief periods have encountered more labor shortages than surpluses. This experience has led to the development of the institution of lifetime employment—*shūshin koyō*—in Japan, and, in West Germany, a reliance upon immigrant labor from southern Europe. Fluctuations in employment consequently have not had an impact on most workers in the past. There have been exceptions to be sure—coal mining during the late 1950s and early 1960s experienced significant declines in employment due to government-directed rationalization—but these have been isolated cases, and little political support for adjustment assistance has developed.

The rationalization of the coal and steel industries in the Common Market countries provides an interesting exception to the general pattern of adjustment assistance in other countries. In this case, it was explicitly recognized by the individual countries that rationalization of these industries would dislocate many individuals and thereby generate political problems. In response, the European Community adopted an adjustment-assistance program that was quite similar to the TAA program in the United States. It differed in one respect, in that it explicitly attempted to minimize the earnings losses suffered after new employment had been found. The program authorized compensation of individuals at up to 90 percent of previous earnings for fifteen months after displacement. Thus, if an individual could find employment at only 75 percent of previous earnings, the program would pay an additional 15 percent. No evaluation is available, at least in English, of the effects of this program on unemployment patterns or subsequent earnings, but it seems likely that this novel approach must have had some effect.

This review of the adjustment-assistance policies of other countries provides an interesting comparison with U.S. efforts. Although other countries do not have separate programs for workers, the services provided under general programs are similar to those provided under TAA. This is hardly surprising, since the services provided under TAA in the United States are similar to those available under unemployment insurance; the only difference is the slightly more liberal financial benefits and relocation allowances. Not surprising also is that, with the possible exception of Sweden, there is no strong evidence that such programs have much effect. Indeed, this brief review of alternative adjustment practices suggests that the major factor that minimizes the adjustment costs of worker dislocation is the level of aggregate demand. In countries experiencing strong economic growth, the reabsorption of displaced workers is swift and, although information on earnings losses is minimal, there do not appear to be great costs involved in transferring workers to new jobs. This is consistent with the views expressed in the Trade Expansion Act of 1962—adjustment assistance was to be only a minor aid in offsetting the costs of adjustment; a strong economy would be the major factor in minimizing adjustment costs. The experience of the last decade has taught us that, at least in the mature industrial economies, this precondition is not always fulfilled.

AN ALTERNATIVE APPROACH TO TRADE ADJUSTMENT ASSISTANCE

Having reviewed the major aspects of adjustment-assistance programs in the United States and other countries, we can inquire what features would be desirable in a future adjustment-assistance program. The first issue is: Who should receive TAA benefits? In the original TAA program and in most special programs in other countries, eligibility for adjustment assistance was tied to a specific action by the federal government—usually changing tariffs or quotas. Subsequent developments in the 1974 Trade Act led to a greatly expanded eligibility criterion: variations in impacts for any reason could trigger adjustment assistance. The expanded eligibility results in two classes of beneficiaries—those who are permanently separated from employment due to imports, and those who are on temporary layoff and who, therefore, incur only minor losses. [20] The question is: Should both types of individuals receive TAA benefits? The arguments in favor of a broad-based program of adjustment assistance[21] are implicitly based upon the arguments that it is arbitrary to single out one source of government action (e.g., lowering tariffs or quotas) as being deserving of assistance, and ignore other actions (e.g., tax incentives that lead to an [artificial] advantage for overseas production), and that the cost of not distinguishing among recipients is, apart from the obviously larger beneficiary population, small or nonexistent. Both arguments ignore crucial aspects of labor-market behavior. First, the desirability of linking adjustment assistance to some specific action of the government is not related to any concept of merit or causation; rather it is an attempt to identify, in the most efficient manner, those individuals who suffer losses greater than can reasonably be remedied through existing labor-market institutions, such as unemployment insurance. If linking adjustment assistance to tariff changes does not adequately identify those who are particularly injured, then some other criterion can be chosen. Note that one cannot claim that any method is more discriminatory than another. All programs that provide benefits to a subset of the population are inherently discriminatory. The only question one can ask, given a collective desire to direct benefits to workers adversely affected by trade, is whether the eligibility criteria of the program direct benefits to those most severely affected. From this consideration, and the fact that workers on temporary layoff incur little or no loss of earnings upon reemployment, and are covered by regular unemployment insurance during the interim, there appears to be no reason that would support providing benefits at a higher rate to workers whose layoffs were due to increased imports. Indeed, fundamental questions of equity would arise if workers who were otherwise identical and who incurred five weeks of layoff were compensated at different rates. For workers who have been permanently separated from previous employment, the case for adjustment assistance is much stronger, particularly so given the large losses in earnings they incur.

The argument that the provision of adjustment assistance to a broader class of workers will not occasion any indirect costs—that is, the costs of such a program will be higher only due to the expanded population base—ignores the fundamental role wage differentials play in the labor market. In the absence of such benefits, workers would be led not to enter industries that are losing or have lost part of their comparative advantage or, if already employed, would consider leaving the industry in response to the fluctuations in income occasioned by temporary layoffs. But if these fluctuations are eliminated or substantially lessened, as appears to be the case under the current program, the incentive to adjust is lessened. Consequently, the result may be an eventual large mass layoff that labor markets adjust to only with difficulty and with significant lags rather than a series of smaller adjustments that may involve substantially smaller costs.

Both of these considerations argue for a restriction of adjustment-assistance benefits to those workers who are most seriously injured—those who are permanently separated from their jobs. The thrust of the argument would suggest, however, that *all* workers, without regard to the proximate cause of unemployment, should be so aided. In other words, it is in the spirit of these arguments that the word "trade" be dropped from the TAA program and eligibility opened to all workers involved in, say, plant closings. While this has a strong appeal in terms of consistency, there are valid reasons for continuing a modified form of the present program. It is easier both to monitor and to modify a program that has an easily identifiable recipient base, and there may well exist administrative economies as well. It seems clear, however, that the TAA program could serve as a prototype for other programs.

Assuming an eligible population for adjustment assistance that is restricted to those who are permanently separated from previous employment, the question becomes: What elements should form the basis of the TAA program? The problem these individuals face is clearly one of inadequate job opportunities. Elimination of their previous jobs has resulted in a reduction in specific human capital, the effects of which persist for several periods. In practice, it takes a while for individuals to realize that some fraction of their previous productivity was firm-specific and that their value to another firm is less, often substantially. Existing programs do little to change this situation, since employment is not encouraged by subsidizing unemployment, and job-training programs do not in themselves provide jobs. One solution to this problem, which has been used in Great Britain and Sweden, is to provide public works programs. But this is a very blunt weapon, and one that takes time to organize. Furthermore, since the locus of job displacements is continually changing, the number of workers in any one area may be too small for such a program to adequately use the talents available. Thus, while such a program will provide jobs, it may not compensate individuals adequately. Moreover, timely receipt of benefits is unlikely under such a program unless it is functioning as part of a larger public employment program.

Currently proposals are pending in Congress for an overhaul of the welfare program. These proposals, if enacted, are likely to involve an expanded public sector jobs program. Reports indicate, however, that the public sector jobs program will, if enacted, pay wages at the minimum wage level. For most trade-displaced workers even a 25 percent reduction would not reduce their earnings to the minimum wage level, and thus such programs are not likely to have much of an effect on these individuals.

Since the major loss suffered by trade-displaced workers is the precipitous reduction in earnings upon reemployment (which partially accounts for the long spell of unemployment), the most direct way to deal with the problem is to provide a wage subsidy. This, in essence, was the approach of the European Community in dealing with the rationalization of the coal and steel industries, and is similar in principle to the investment tax credit. While the concept of a wage-subsidy plan is clear, there are a number of details which must be treated carefully if the program is to reduce both the amount of unemployment suffered by trade-impacted workers and the earnings loss attendant to reemployment.

First, the wage subsidy should be directed toward eliminating the average loss suffered by individuals. Available information indicates that a subsidy of 20 percent for about three years would eliminate the average loss. Further refinements could be made, such as a different subsidy rate—say, 25 percent—for workers over sixty, or for a rate that declined over time. Once a particular subsidy rate has been decided upon, the question of how to pay it arises. Direct payment to certified individuals seems the most obvious and direct method, but the method provides no incentive for firms to expand employment. In effect, a wage-subsidy paid directly to the worker becomes a generalized transfer payment that occurs independently of the worker's employment status. Conditioning the amount of the subsidy on either previous earnings or reemployment earnings would provide additional incentives for workers to remain unemployed and search longer for higher-paying jobs, thereby increasing their measured unemployment rates. If, however, the subsidy is paid directly to the employer, then the incentives of the worker are not adversely affected and the number of jobs open to the worker will be expanded. In this case, the effect of a wage subsidy paid to the employer leads to shorter durations of unemployment and greater expected earnings upon reemployment.[22]

Although the administrative details of the process would have to be determined, one obvious method would be to issue eligibility cards to all certified workers, which could then be presented to firms during employment interviews. An employer who hires a trade-impacted worker would then be allowed to deduct the subsidy rate—20 percent of actual earnings—from his business income taxes. Thus, a wage subsidy paid in this manner becomes, in essence, a labor tax credit.

Although a wage-subsidy program appears desirable because of its effects on unemployment and earnings, there are several areas in which a wage-subsidy program will differ significantly from current and previous adjustment-assistance efforts. A wage subsidy paid to employers will not, for example, provide benefits to those individuals who do not become reemployed. For those individuals who voluntarily choose not to work—whether due to an optimal timing of the retirement decision or to a desire to, perhaps temporarily, engage in nonmarket activity such as raising a family—there is no real injury due to trade and thus the appropriate assistance is being provided. The option of working is, of course, always available to these individuals. It may be argued, however, that not all individuals who do not find work are voluntary withdrawals from the labor force. In other words, there may exist some areas in which there exists a shortage of job openings. The empirical magnitude of this fraction of labor force withdrawals is a matter of considerable debate; however, the wage-subsidy program can be made flexible enough to provide greater incentives for employment in unusual cases. For example, the wage subsidy could be increased in areas of particularly high unemployment levels, or it could be made dependent upon the workers' length of unemployment. With sufficient flexibility allowed for in the determination of the wage subsidy, there is no reason to believe that this approach would provide lower benefits to workers than the previous approaches.

One area in which complexities arise is that of determining eligibility. If eligibility is not defined strictly, then it is possible that a wage-subsidy program could create incentives for firms to lay off workers and rehire them at subsidized wage rates. If benefits are available to individuals on temporary layoff, it is obvious that a wage subsidy creates incentives for firms to lay off workers, claim injury due to imports, and then benefit from lower wage costs. Even when there are permanent job losses, not all firms or plants completely cease operations, and so in these cases there is also an incentive for firms to lay off more workers than they otherwise would, and to eventually hire them back.

There are two ways to eliminate this problem. One is to have a very careful and intensive examination of the existence of trade impact in each case. Precise delineation of which products are affected and which workers were engaged in producing them would be needed. To pursue this route, however, would inevitably lead to the same problems that occurred under the 1962 act; the investigatory lag would result in benefits being delayed, thus reducing their usefulness.

An alternative approach is to limit the applicability of the subsidy to individuals who change employers. This will remove the incentives for firms to place more workers on temporary layoff and will avoid subsidizing firms that would otherwise be unable to compete in a specific product class. Although this requirement seems discriminatory, there is a strong rationale for it: the substantial loss in earnings which trade-impacted workers suffer. Furthermore, if wage subsidies were available to impacted firms, there would not be any incentive to reallocate production to products in which they have a comparative advantage.

In terms of the workers' well-being, the appearance of discrimination among workers is mostly illusory. Since each eligible worker has the option of gaining employment at a different firm, the fact that some may return to their previous employer and not receive any direct benefits from the wage-subsidy program is merely indicative that their value of the return option exceeded the alternative of alternative employment. Firms that have been adversely affected by trade may, indeed, feel that a wage-subsidy plan limited to new hires from other trade-impacted firms is discriminatory, but again it is not. All firms have the option of hiring new employees who are eligible for the wage subsidy. To allow the wage subsidy to apply to previously employed workers would both overcompensate workers (since firm-specific human capital will not have been lost) and conflict with the basic goal of trade adjustment—reallocating workers to jobs in which the United States possesses a comparative advantage.

Finally, we note that a wage-subsidy program, despite its potential benefits, has one important political drawback: it lacks visibility to those who are most immediately concerned. A program that provides higher monetary benefits or public service jobs to affected workers provides very tangible evidence of political action. Dollars paid or public sector jobs filled can be easily counted, and although such actions may create opposition among some parts of a politician's constituency, such opposition is weak relative to the political demand for benefits. A wage-subsidy program, even if it creates more jobs and generates higher reemployment earnings, does so in a manner for which it is not easy for a politician to claim credit. Thus, it is obvious that an essential element for the success of such a program is a careful monitoring of the reemployment experiences of trade-impacted workers in order to document the efficiency of such a program.

To summarize, then, a wage-subsidy program, coupled with regular unemployment insurance benefits, is proposed as an alternative to the existing TAA program. The major advantage of this approach is that a wage-subsidy program, in contrast to income-maintenance programs that have characterized previous adjustment-assistance programs, provides direct incentives for job creation and thereby for minimizing unemployment among trade-impacted workers. Moreover, as we have outlined it, a wage-subsidy program will have a direct effect upon earnings subsequent to reemployment. Finally, the administrative complexity and cost of operating such a program appear no larger than current efforts. Whether the direct budgetary costs of operating such a program are comparable is a question to which we now turn.

IV. THE BUDGET COSTS OF TRADE ADJUSTMENT ASSISTANCE

A major consideration in the choice of an adjustment-assistance program is the direct budget cost of such programs. All else the same, the program that has the least cost will be the socially most desirable one. In the preceding section we argued that a wage-subsidy program could provide superior benefits to trade-impacted workers; it remains to be shown whether this can be achieved at a reasonable cost. In this section we compute the cost of providing adjustment assistance under three possible programs. To provide an appreciation of the scale of adjustment-assistance programs, we use these estimates to calculate the budget costs that would occur under several of the tariff policies considered by Deardorff, Stern, and Greene.[23]

The average cost of adjustment assistance per recipient can be broken into three components:

a) *unemployment compensation*—which depends upon the benefit rate, previous earnings, and the length of time unemployed;

b) *training and counseling services*—which depend on the fraction who enroll in these programs; and

c) *wage subsidy*—which depends upon the subsidy rate and reemployment earnings.

We consider three programs: program 1—identical to the current TAA program; program 2—all features of the current program are retained and a wage subsidy of 20 percent for three years is added; and program 3—the current TAA program is supplanted by a three-year wage-subsidy program with the subsidy rate declining from 20 to 15 percent, and finally to 10 percent in the last year. Individuals are still eligible for unemployment compensation.[24] The parameters upon which these calculations are based are contained in Table 4.3, and the resulting average cost estimates are given in Table 4.4.

The results in Table 4.4. indicate that a wage-subsidy program such as we have suggested costs the same per worker as the current program; wage-subsidy payments under program 3 turn out to be roughly the same as the extra unemployment benefits available under the current program. The distribution of benefits will be different, however, since wage subsidies will accrue only to those who become reemployed. Under this program there will be more individuals who find employment, so that the net distributive effect will be unclear. Finally, note that the combination of the current TAA program with a wage subsidy results in almost a doubling of the average cost. In essence, the

TABLE 4.3

SUMMARY OF PARAMETERS USED IN CALCULATING THE AVERAGE COST OF TAA BENEFITS

	Program 1	Program 2	Program 3
w = pretax weekly earnings before separation of reemployed TAA recipients (in 1976 dollars)	$226.8	$223.7	$223.7
w' = pretax weekly earnings before separation of TAA recipients who do not become reemployed	$214.6	$217.6	$217.6
D = weeks of compensable unemployment* for reemployed TAA recipients	34.2	34.2	34.2
F = proportion of trade-impacted workers who find reemployment	.60	.71	.72
B = proportion of trade-impacted workers who enroll in job-training programs	.13	.13	.02
r = average training cost per enrollee	$1,489.00	$1,489.00	$1,489.00
S = average amount of job search and relocation allowance per TAA recipient	$100.00	$100.00	$100.00
α = proportion of trade-impacted workers eligible for assistance	.8	.8	.8

SOURCE: Computed from information in Neumann, *An Evaluation*, and simulations with the employment model in Kiefer and Neumann. Data are from TAA recipients during the period 1969–73, updated to current.

TABLE 4.4

AVERAGE COST OF THREE TAA PROGRAMS,
PER INDIVIDUAL

	Unemployment Compensation	+	Training and Job Search	+	Wage Subsidy	=	Total
Program 1	6,383	+	294	+	0	=	$6,677
Program 2	6,099	+	294	+	4,955	=	$11,348
Program 3	2,481	+	294	+	3,769	=	$6,544

higher unemployment benefits induce individuals to remain unemployed longer, which therefore increases the cost of the
program.

ADJUSTMENT-ASSISTANCE COSTS OF ALTERNATIVE TRADE POLICIES

To provide an indication of the magnitude of an adjustment-
assistance program, we compute the costs of six tariff-policy
options, considered by Deardorff, Stern, and Greene. The six
policies considered are those in which U.S. tariffs are reduced
from current levels. Table 4.5 contains the estimated employment effects for the traded-goods sectors, ISIC industries 1, 310-
390. Aggregate costs for each of the three adjustment-assistance
programs are given in Table 4.6.[25]

Three estimates imply that the costs of providing adjustments
assistance would range in the aggregate from $43 million to $287
million. Compared with TAA expenditures of $170.5 million in
1976, these amounts do not look particularly large. However,
these estimates may understate the number of workers eligible
for adjustment assistance, since they are based on net displacements from an industry. It is difficult to assess the magnitude of
this bias. An interesting feature of these estimates is that, as
tariff policy varies, 50 to 75 percent of the adjustment-assistance
costs are incurred in five industries-ISIC-1, 310 to 323. This
suggests that a geographical concentration of displaced workers
is likely to occur in the future, and correspondingly, the need for
an effective adjustment-assistance program will be as evident as
before.

TABLE 4.5

U.S. EMPLOYMENT LOSSES BY INDUSTRY
UNDER SIX TARIFF POLICIES:
ISIC INDUSTRIES 1, 310–390

Policy	2	3	4	5	6	9
1	−3.247	−6.495	−1.480	−1.426	−1.485	−4.30
310	−2.231	−4.462	−1.049	−1.263	−0.854	−3.394
321	−1.034	−2.068	−1.031	−0.279	−1.222	−
322	−1.617	−3.233	−0.560	−1.876	−0.412	−2.545
323	−0.408	−0.815	−0.381	−	−0.427	−0.080
324	−	−	−	−	−0.234	−
331	−	−	−0.204	−	−0.392	−
332	−	−	−	−	−	−
341	−	−	−0.105	−	−0.162	−
342	−0.262	−0.524	−	−	−0.004	−0.781
35A	−	−	−	−	−	−
35B	−2.285	−4.569	−1.407	−0.240	−1.490	−1.341
355	−	−	−	−1.013	−	−
36A	−0.886	−1.771	−0.670	−	−0.921	−1.703
362	−	−	−	−	−	−
371	−0.178	−0.356	−0.443	−	−0.712	−
372	−0.512	−1.024	−0.650	−	−0.742	−
381	−	−	−	−	−	−
382	−	−	−	−	−	−
383	−	−	−	−	−	−
384	−	−	−	−0.467	−	−
38A	−	−	−	−	−	−
Σ Domestic Employment Losses	12.63	25.32	7.98	6.56	9.06	14.14

SOURCE: Computed from material provided by Deardorff, Stern, and Greene.

V. SUMMARY

In this study of trade adjustment-assistance policies in the United States, we have examined three questions: What types of assistance have been provided? How successful have these programs been? And what alternative could be considered in the future? The assistance provided to trade-impacted workers has been varied, but the trend has clearly been to rely upon specific programs of assistance.

TABLE 4.6

COSTS OF ADJUSTMENT ASSISTANCE
(millions of 1976 U.S. $)

Trade Policy	Program 1	Program 2	Program 3
2	84.6	143.8	82.9
3	169.0	287.2	165.6
4	53.2	90.4	52.2
5	43.8	74.6	43.0
6	60.4	102.6	59.2
9	94.3	160.3	92.5

SOURCE: Calculated from Tables 4.4 and 4.5.

In practice, these programs have met with little success in the United States, and related programs in other countries appear to have had similar results. The failures of these programs to minimize the burden of trade-related job losses can be attributed in part to diverse problems—benefit delay, inappropriate training opportunities, and so on—but the major defect was conceptual. As operated, the programs amounted to expanded unemployment insurance payments. In a labor market characterized by high demand, such programs may have been quite adequate, but in a situation where the closing of one firm has a significant impact on local demand, the result is a lack of jobs. More importantly, since workers' firm-specific knowledge is reduced in value, those who do find jobs suffer substantial earnings declines. The TAA program as operated under the 1962 act and the 1974 act is ill-equipped to deal with these problems. Although short-term income maintenance is provided by the TAA program at a fairly high rate, its effect on the reemployment situation facing most workers is minimal.

In order to minimize the costs borne by trade-displaced workers, an adjustment-assistance program must focus on increasing the employability of the displaced workers. Several options exist, but the nature of trade dislocations and the type of individuals affected render some possibilities infeasible. Retraining efforts have not been successful, basically because they have not been focused on the special problems of the trade-impacted worker, and it may be very difficult to provide the appropriate training. A public employment program could have some effect, but it is a very blunt instrument. A program of wage subsidies, paid to employers of trade-displaced workers, represents a possibility that can minimize the impact of job loss to individuals both by increasing employment opportunities and by eliminating part or all of the earnings loss at relatively low cost. Indeed, a wage subsidy coupled with regular employment insurance in lieu of the present TAA benefits is likely to be less expensive than the current program.

NOTES

1. S. Metzger, "Adjustment Assistance," in the U.S. Commission of International Trade and Investment Policy, *United States International Economic Policy in an Interdependent World* (Washington, D.C.: U.S. Government Printing Office, 1971), p. 320.

2. U.S. Commission on Foreign Economic Policy, *Report to the President and the Congress* (Washington, D.C.: U.S. Government Printing Office, 1954). Earlier versions of some of the ideas are credited to John Coleman of the Committee for a National Trade Policy, Meyer Kestenbaum of the Committee for Economic Development, and Stanley Ruttenberg of the (then) Congress of Industrial Organizations in R. Bauer, I. De Sola Pool, and Z. Dexter, *American Business and Public Policy* (New York: Atherton, 1963), pp. 34-35.

3. Public Law 87-794, sec. 301 (c), (2).

4. See J. Manley, "Adjustment Assistance: Experience under the Automotive Products Trade Act of 1965," *Harvard International Law Journal* (Spring 1969): 294-315.

5. The companies involved operated plants in both the United States and Canada, and the union, the UAW, also represented workers on both sides of the border. Neither party had an incentive, therefore, to press for strong actions such as escape-clause relief.

6. See C. Frank, *Foreign Trade and Domestic Aid* (The Brookings Institution, Washington, D.C., 1977) p. 57.

7. See Committee on Ways and Means, *Trade Reform*, 93d Cong., 1st sess., for the list of problems that business and organized labor found in the 1962 program.

8. See M. Bale, "Adjustment to Freer Trade: An Analysis of the Adjustment Assistance Provision of the Trade Expansion Act of 1962," Ph.D. dissertation, University of Wisconsin, 1973; J. McCarthy, *Trade Adjustment Assistance: A Case Study of the Shoe Industry in Massachusetts,* Federal Reserve Bank of Boston, Research Report No. 58, 1975; and G. Neumann, *An Evaluation of the Trade Adjustment Assis-*

tance Program, report submitted to the Bureau of International Affairs, U.S. Department of Labor, under contract number ILAB74-23.

9. Brechling provides strong evidence that quits within an industry respond sharply to declining employment opportunities. See F. P. Brechling, "A Time Series Analysis of Labor Turnover," in W. G. Dewald, ed., *The Impact of International Trade and Investment on Employment,* mimeographed (Washington, D.C.: U.S. Department of Labor, 1977).

10. See Neumann, *An Evaluation,* p. 34.

11. Henle, "Trade Adjustment Assistance," p. 44, quotes a Labor Department estimate that 90 percent of all TAA recipients are only temporarily laid off.

12. Assuming an average tax rate of 22 percent—13.2 federal, 5.85 FICA, and 3 percent state.

13. Because of the sharp earnings losses incurred by permanently separated workers, roughly 20 percent, the TAA program is likely to have a significant effect on duration. An individual who was earning $x per week receives $0.7x$ as TAA payments. If his best employment offer is $0.8x$, then he is indifferent between working and receiving benefits of $0.7x = (1 - t)\,0.8x$, where t is the average tax rate. This implies, with no value given to leisure, that workers facing a tax rate greater than 12.5 percent would always exhaust their benefits. More generally, if z denotes the expected percentage loss in earnings at reemployment, an individual will prefer working only if

$$t \le \frac{0.3 + z}{1 + z}$$

14. It is difficult to understand why all workers on layoff do not petition for TAA eligibility. The process has been streamlined to such a degree that the costs to an individual are small, and the potential gain, in terms of higher benefits, is large. The major costs are of course borne by the government.

15. See Henle, "Trade Adjustment Assistance."

16. Neumann, *An Evaluation,* p. 29.

17. The component parts issue was present under the 1962 act, but the issue arises frequently under the new act also.

18. This section draws extensively on material in chapter 9 of C. Frank, op. cit. 1977), pp. 124-147.

19. See C. Smith, *Redundancy Policies,* BIM Report No. 20, 1974, p.

20. We say only "minor" losses, since such individuals are eligible for various other income maintenance plans such as regular UI, and negotiated private agreements such as supplementary unemployment benefits.

21. See, e.g., Frank, pp. 124-147.

22. Evidence supporting this assertion is given in N. Kiefer and G.

Neumann, "Estimation of Wage Offer Distributions and Reservation Wages," in S. A. Lippman and J. McCall, eds., *Studies in the Theory of Search* (Amsterdam: North-Holland, 1979.) The essential idea is that a wage subsidy to the employer creates, via the conventional demand for labor argument, an incentive for employers to hire trade-impacted workers relative to other factors of production.

23. Alan V. Deardorff, Robert M. Stern, and Mark N. Greene, "The Implication of Alternative Trade Strategies for the United States," chapter 3 of this volume.

24. For consistency we attribute all unemployment payments as costs of the TAA program. This convention underscores the fact that we are calculating the budgetary and not the social costs of adjustment assistance.

25. Aggregate costs are simply the sum of industry costs, which can be found by multiplying the average program cost per recipient by the number of jobs lost in each industry.

Part III

COMMODITY POLICY

Chapter 5

INTERNATIONAL COMMODITY MANAGEMENT AS A POLICY PROBLEM FOR THE UNITED STATES: THE GRAINS CASE

WILLARD W. COCHRANE

Professor of Agricultural Economics
University of Minnesota

I. INTRODUCTION*

Recent historical developments in world food and agriculture by geographic areas, by category, of development, and by principal economic activity (e.g., production, trade) have been de-

*The original draft of this chapter was written in the Summer of 1977. With the recent collapse of the negotiations over establishing an international system of grain reserves, the author thinks the U.S. may have to place greater emphasis on *bilateral* agreements as a substitute for *multilateral* agreements. The author, nevertheless, still prefers the policy package presented here as a long-run approach to international grains management.

scribed in numerous publications and are regularly reported upon.[1] Thus, a background statement fully describing developments in world food and agriculture for the period 1960-75 will not be presented here. But a word needs to be said about the hectic 1970s. The world market for grains began to tighten in 1970-71. To this tightening world market situation for the grains, add the facts of (1) a poor grain crop in the USSR in 1972, and (2) the decision by the Soviets to enter the world market and acquire supplies of grain to offset their domestic crop loss. Add, further, a poor grain crop in much of South and Southeast Asia in 1972 and efforts on the part of those countries to acquire grain supplies in the world markets. In this context, the United States and other exporters increased their exports of grain dramatically and reduced their carryover stocks to near-pipeline levels. In this state of reduced stocks, a great fear developed in world grain markets that some unexpected event might occur to further worsen the supply situation. Given the state of fear and uncertainty in early 1973, importing nations and private handlers and processors of grain all tried to improve their stock positions by acquiring additional supplies in the market. The result was a wild scramble for supplies in the summer of 1973, with grain prices shooting skyward.[2] The shortfall in world grain production in 1972 was followed by a good crop in 1973 and then another poor crop in 1974. These variations in world grain production induced sharp and wide fluctuations in world grain prices during these years.

Crops were uniformly good around the world in 1976, and indications for 1977 suggest another set of bountiful crops around the world. The crisis conditions of 1972-74 have thus come to an end, and stocks of grain are being built up in such diverse areas as India and North America. The years 1976-77 may be viewed as transition years. But transition to what? Transition to a chronic surplus situation once again? Or a transition interval between periods of food shortage? A great veil of uncertainty hangs over the world food and agricultural situation in 1977.

As the experts analyze past trends, weigh the imponderables and project into the future, a wide range of possible food and agricultural situations emerges for the world over the next twenty years. Some of the experts are terribly pessimistic, predicting famine and chaos for much of the less developed world.[3] Some are modestly pessimistic, suggesting the likelihood of a sustained increase in the real price of food.[4] Some are modestly optimistic, arguing that there will be food enough to feed the expanding populations in the less developed world if all the nations, rich and poor, cooperate in dealing with the problem.[5] And some are highly optimistic, predicting an increase in world food production that outpaces increases in demand.[6] *There is no consensus among the experts with regard to the probable long-run food and agricultural situation in the world.*

There is, however, considerable agreement among the experts that the world will be plagued by short-run flucuations in the production of grains, which lead in turn to wide, sharp, and unpredictable fluctuations in world grain prices. The reasoning runs as follows:

1. The world demand for *total* grains is highly price inelastic—possibly approaching -0.1. The export demand confronting a nation like Australia may exhibit greater elasticity than -0.1 for the same reasons that the demand curve confronting a single firm is more elastic than that for the total industry. But the world demand for grains that confronts world supply is severely inelastic.

2. The world production of grains varies from trend by 1 to 3 percent per year as the result of variations in the weather, hence in crop-growing conditions. These annual variations in the weather are completely unpredictable.

3. The world is linked together by international trade in the grains, so that a shortfall in production in one area (say, the Soviet Union) is quickly reflected in the price of grain in those countries linked to the world market. But only a few countries maintain an open link to the world market, the United States being one of the principal ones. Thus, the full brunt of price movements in the grains in response to changes in world supply is absorbed by the United States, and much of the adjustment in resource use to the wide price movements in the grains must

take place in the United States. Stated differently, the United States *is* the world market for grains to which most countries maintain some kind of a government-regulated link.

What we have in the grains is thus an international market, *although a strange and imperfect one,* in which total grain production varies modestly from year to year, around trend, as the result of variations in the weather. These modest variations in production, given the severe inelasticity of demand for grain, result in turn in wide swings in grain prices, and since the variations in the weather are unpredictable, the fluctuations in grain prices are unpredictable. Resource adjustments to these wide, sharp, and unpredictable fluctuations in grain prices take place primarily in the United States, since it alone among the important trading nations maintains an open link to the world market.[7]

The author of this statement is one of those of a modest pessimistic persuasion who holds that the real price of grains, hence all food, is likely to rise over the long-run future. Further, I would argue that even if the probability of the real price of grains rising over the long-run future is only 50-50, the consequences to world society of such a development occurring are so adverse—so devastating—that the nations of the world should act in their policy formulation and execution as if a rise in the real price of grain over the long run were the most probable development. With regard to the short run, the author of this statement holds with complete certainty the view that unpredictable variations in the weather around the world will give rise to wide, sharp, and unpredictable fluctuations in world grain prices. This, in the view of this writer, is the prospective world situation for the grains in which a management policy for the grains by the United States must be formulated.

This statement is organized around the clusters of questions that were formulated in the development of this project. Those clusters of questions are as follows:

a. Can we specify a plausible range of alternative buffer stock levels for grains (food and feed) that would meet specific price-stabilization targets? What would be the cost of financing these different buffer-stock levels? What cooperation can we expect from the Europeans, Japanese, Soviets and other wealthy countries in financing these buffer stocks? Is it realistic for the United States to base its policy upon cooperation and cofinancing?

b. Is the current large buildup of wheat reserves a temporary phenomenon? Or is it a long-term phenomenon? What statements can be made about likely future price relationships between feed and food grains? Are there specific guidelines that could be recommended now for American policy formation purposes which would be useful for determining the long-term division of acreage inside the United States for feed and food grains?

c. What preliminary conclusions can be drawn now about the likely long-term effect on the demand for U.S. grain exports of increased agricultural productivity in the LDCs? What is the range of the estimates for LDC agricultural productivity increases (by world region and by major commodity—rice, wheat, corn, and soybeans)? What assumptions about LDC increases in protein consumption and meat consumption are behind these estimates? Given this range of estimates, what effect will alternative levels of LDC performance have on the need for short-term buffer stocks of the kind discussed above?

Insofar as it is possible, the specific questions noted above will be answered. Where firm answers are not possible, the subject area to which the questions apply will be discussed. Finally, a section dealing with commodity management policy recommendations is included.

II. BUFFER STOCKS FOR GRAINS

Scott Steele, of the U.S. Department of Agriculture, argues that an international reserve system for all grains that totaled 60 to 70 million tons (over and above pipeline stocks) would have covered 95 percent of the shortfalls in production from trend during the period 1950-75.[8] A study conducted at the University of Minnesota presents evidence to indicate that the world price of grain could be held within a range of plus or minus 10 percent of a constant world equilibrium price some 85 percent of the time in the years ahead with a stock that averaged some 60 million tons if variations in production were similar to those of the period 1950-73.[9] Other studies of world grain price fluctuations and buffer-stock requirements have produced similar estimates of buffer-stock requirements. Thus, there is widespread agreement that an international system of grain reserves (over and above pipeline stocks) that averaged 60 to 80 million tons would even out supplies between crop seasons and dampen down world grain price fluctuations to an acceptable range and level of probability—to, say, a range of plus or minus 15 percent of the world equilibrium price some 90 percent of the time. An international system of grain reserves is feasible in physical terms.

The storage costs of a ton of grain per year ran between $8 and $9 in the United States in 1976. Thus, the storage costs of an international grain reserve that averaged 70 million tons in U.S. prices would currently approximate $600 million per year. To this must be added the acquisition costs of the grain for each year, and from this must be subtracted the sales receipts of the grain for each year in order to obtain a measure of the total annual cost of a reserve-stock program. The acquisition cost of 70 million tons of grain might approximate $7 billion as of 1977 (30 million tons of wheat at a price of $105 per ton, and 40 million tons of corn at $94 per ton).

If the target stabilization price over time held constant and national reserve stock agencies consistently acquired grain at prices below the stabilization target price and released grain at prices above the stabilization target price, the reserve-stock agencies should make a profit on their merchandising operations, and this profit would offset the annual storage costs— perhaps only partially, or perhaps more than offsetting them; in the latter event the whole reserve-stock operation would be turned into a profitable one.

If, however, the stabilization target price trended downward over time, the cost picture would be altered considerably.[10] In such a course of events, the national reserve-stock agencies would in a preponderance of years be required to acquire stocks to support prices, and there would be few opportunities to sell grain at or above the stabilization target price. In this type of situation, stocks would tend to accumulate continuously unless a limit were placed on the accumulation of stocks, and storage costs would increase with the stocks. Also, the opportunity to sell stocks at a profit would be limited severely. Thus, the total costs of a reserve-stock operation in this type of situation could be expected to increase continuously and at some point become prohibitive to the national societies involved. This is the type of situation that confronted grain-exporting nations in the 1950s and 1960s.

If, on the other hand, the stabilization target price trended upward over time, the grain-reserve operation could be highly profitable—highly profitable, that is, as long as it lasted. In this situation the national reserve-stock agencies would be required to release stocks in the preponderance of years in attempts to hold market prices at the upper price boundary of the stabilization range. Thus, the storage costs of these agencies would be reduced as stocks were deaccumulated, and profits on merchandising operations would be large. But such an operation, profitable though it might be, would come to an end as the reserve-stock agencies ran out of stocks. And at this point, the international system of grain reserves would have failed, as it would no longer have the capacity to hold market prices at the upper boundary of the price-stabilization range. In this case, high profits do not spell success.

The question now arises: What should be the role of the United States in a system of international grain reserves? As we shall see, there is no easy, simple answer to this question. First, there is the question: Does the United States want a grain-reserve program at all? It is probably the case that most urban consumers in the United States would support the idea of a grain-reserve program for the United States *if they understood the issues.* But they don't; hence they have no position on the question. A few consumer groups strongly support the idea of a grain reserve for the United States, but their political strength is not great. On the other hand, there is considerable opposition to a grain reserve for the United States, and it is highly vocal. Grain producers generally like the idea of a support price, but they are strongly opposed to any kind of a ceiling over their product prices. The grain trade is generally opposed to any kind of intervention in the market, and individual traders find all kinds of reasons why a reserve-stock program in the grains would not work satisfactorily. Theoretical economists using consumer-surplus and producer-surplus concepts most often deduce that the welfare of society would be reduced by the operation of a reserve-stock program for the grains.[11] Thus, there is a formidable array of opposition to the idea of a grain-reserve program in the United States.

Given these very real and powerful political pressures, what is the position of the Carter administration on grain reserves? Secretary Berglund, before the Third Ministerial Meeting of the World Food Council, had this to say:

> But food security is not the sole obligation of the United States or a few nations. The world should not want its food security to rest in the hands of a few nations. Responsibility for world food security must be shared widely. Therefore, the United States hopes the International Wheat Council soon can lay the foundation for negotiations of an agreement which would include a coordinated system of nationally-held reserve stocks. We believe a world food security system should include these features: First, a reserve stock mechanism must be designed to reduce wide fluctuations around the long-run trend in market prices. We are willing to consider price indicators to trigger reserve actions. Second, the cost of reserve stocks must be shared among both exporting and importing nations. Special provisions should be made to assist poor nations in meeting their share and third, we must prevent interruptions in trade for grains which prevent adjustments in consumption and production in times of extreme surplus and scarcity.[12]

In short, the United States is willing to talk about a meaningful international system of grain reserves, and its role in that system. Further, Secretary Berglund stated at the same meeting of the World Food Council that "We will make every effort to maintain our level of food aid at a fair share of the World Food Conference target of 10 million tons." This is important for two reasons. First, it recognizes the need for food aid to the poorest of poor, for whom grain price stabilization has little meaning, since they are too poor to purchase grain in commercial markets. Second, it recognizes the willingness of the United States to participate in programs outside a system of grain reserves to help feed these people.

The position of the Carter administration with regard to a grain-reserve program was further developed in a statement released in late August 1977. That statement reads in part as follows:

Strategic grain reserves will be acquired in four separate actions:

First, the Administration will seek Congressional approval to create a special International Emergency Food Reserve of up to 6 million tons. This reserve could only be released for noncommercial food aid for world nutrition assistance and to meet United States' obligations under a proposed international reserves agreement.

Second, the farmer-owned wheat and rice reserve program announced by the Secretary in April, 1977 will be expanded to include feed grains. A feed grain reserve of 17 to 19 million metric tons is planned. The minimum release price for feed grains is expected to be equal to 125 percent of the loan ($2.50 for corn); the loans are expected to be called when the price reaches 140 percent of the loan ($2.80 for corn).

Third, the food grain (wheat and rice) reserve program announced in April, 1977, at least 300 million bushels of wheat (8.16 million tons) and 13.2 million hundred-weight of rice (600,000 tons) will be held off the market until the price exceeds 140 percent of loan levels, and loans can be called when prices exceed 175 percent of loan levels.

Fourth, some 1975-crop rice and 1976-crop wheat has or will be turned over to the Government when CCC price support loans mature in coming months. This grain will also become part of the overall grain reserve.[13]

In support of the above action the administration pointed out that world grain stocks have risen dramatically in the past year while grain prices have become severely depressed but that this situation could change abruptly. Thus, the administration argued that if we as a nation are to rebuild our stocks in a way that will help us avoid a repeat of the severe shortages and extreme price fluctuations that occurred in the period 1972-75, this is the time to do it. This is the time to do it at least cost to the taxpayer and with greatest benefit to the farmer.

This same White House release announced a 20 percent set-aside for wheat to become effective for the 1978 crop. The Carter administration is clearly of the view that the creation of a buffer stock in 1977-78 will not adequately deal with the emerging surplus conditions in the grains, particularly in wheat. For the short term, at least, the Carter administration is turning to that often used device in the past, namely, production control.

Having made the decision to build a limited grain reserve of some 30 to 35 million tons, the Carter administration plans to attempt to negotiate an international system of nationally held grain reserves. What might we expect from the negotiations in the International Wheat Council or perhaps a special international conference on grain reserves? We know that several countries are building grain reserves. The Soviets are building reserves. India is building reserves. The United States is accumulating stocks and is now committed to a limited grain-reserve program. The Japanese are looking for ways to assure a sustained flow of grain imports into their country. But we also know that price-stabilization objectives of the EEC countries are greatly different from those of the United States. The pricing objectives of the Japanese for the grains are different from the United States and the EEC countries. And the great state trading nations have a strong preference for secret bilateral deals. Thus, in the judgment of this writer, it seems highly unlikely that an international negotiating conference on grain reserves could reach any agreement on price-stabilization objectives—price-stabilization targets and stabilization ranges—or on any international formula for financing the holding of reserve stocks at this time. But an international negotiating conference on grain reserves might get commitments from some of the leading grain-trading nations, both importers and exporters, with regard to the target size of a grain reserve that they would be willing to build and operate. Given the commitment of the United States to building and operating a grain reserve that averaged 30 million tons, there might then be a chance of getting the EEC countries, Japan, India, Canada, and Australia to commit themselves to the carrying of grain reserves that would bring the international system of grain reserves up to 60 or 70 million tons. This, with what the Soviets might be expected to carry without commitment, but in their own selfish interest, would amount to a respectable international grain reserve. The commitment of the Soviet Union and other importing nations to carrying a legitimate grain reserve might be achieved more readily through the negotiation and renegotiation of long-term bilateral agreements by the United States with each of those countries. But such a policy step on the part of the United States would represent a departure from its traditional position of favoring free and open markets.

It is one thing, however, to get some, or most, or all of the leading grain-trading nations to commit themselves to build and operate a grain reserve of a given target size, and quite another to get all of those national programs harmonized with respect to stabilization objectives, acquisition and release decision rules and some sharing of the financing burdens. What might emerge from an international negotiating conference is a set of uncoordinated national grain-reserve programs. If such should be the case, a decade or two might be spent in harmonizing those individual country plans into an international system of grain reserves.

If the development described above should be realized, which in the judgment of this writer is the best that is likely to be realized, what should be the policy response of the United

States? First, it should be recognized that, although the development described above is far from ideal, it is not all bad. A
reserve, say, of 10 to 15 million tons of grain held by the Indian
government would in the event of a shortfall in production in
India obviously be used before that country purchased grain in
the commercial market. The deployment of the grain reserve by
India, regardless of the specific decision rules followed, would
have the effect of moderating the demand for grain in the world
commercial market and thus have the effect of moderating the
price response in the international commercial market to the
production shortfall in India. The existence and use of uncoordinated national grain reserves could not help but serve to
dampen down world grain price fluctuations, although the uncoordinated use of those reserves could well lead to individual
country marketing problems and to trade distortions.

In this context it would seem reasonable for the United States
to operate an efficient grain-reserve program of limited size—30
to 35 million tons as the average size—in which the price-stabilization objectives of the program are consistent with: (1) the
international trade objectives of the United States, and (2) the
domestic food and agricultural policy of the United States. If
these sets of objectives are in conflict, then all sorts of problems
will arise with regard to the formulation of a satisfactory set of
price-stabilization objectives for the United States. One reasonable solution to this problem takes the following form. Seek to
stabilize domestic and world grain prices around the concept of
the long-run *world* equilibrium price.[14] The target stabilization
price for any given year would be the estimate of the long-run
equilibrium price for that year. The domestic price support for
any grain would be equal to the lower boundary of the price-
stabilization range in the grain-reserve program. Such a set of
programmatic actions would result in: (1) a pure concept of
price stabilization in which no effort is made to push the level of
grain prices up or down; (2) an internal level of price support
that is consistent with the stabilization-price objective in that the
level of domestic price support is equal to the lower boundary of
the price-stabilization range; and (3) a set of pricing arrangements that are conducive to free and expanded trade.

But if the United States does not realize that cooperation from its trading partners, what then? First, *the United States cannot expect to stabilize its internal grain price level through the stabilization of the world price level.* Second, if the United States is desirous of stabilizing its internal grain price level, it must take additional steps to do so. What will those additional steps involve? They will involve: (1) the pursuit of an export policy that limits grain exports from the United States when the world price of grains is rising; and (2) the employment of production controls and import restrictions when the world price of grains is falling. The effect of each of these commodity management policies is to insulate the domestic agricultural economy from the world economy and thereby effect an adjustment of supplies to demand in the domestic market in ways that will minimize market price fluctuations around the target stabilization price. The pursuit and achievement of price stabilization in the domestic market in this case is achieved at the expense of free and expanded trade.

In summary, the United States is confronted with a complex set of issues with respect to grain price stabilization and grain reserves. First, there is the question of how much importance the national society attaches to price stabilization in the grains, hence to food generally. The answer to this question is by no means settled as of the summer of 1977. Second, if the answer to the above question is found to be in the affirmative, how important is it that the price-stabilization objective for the grains be achieved in ways that are supportive of free and expanded trade? If the free and expanded trade objective is important, then the stabilization of grain prices domestically must be achieved through the stabilization of *world* grain prices. This requirement means in turn that a grain-reserve operation, either a single operation or a system of national operations, be established with the capacity to even out world supplies between crop years and moderate to an acceptable degree world grain price fluctuations. An international grain reserve that averaged 70 million tons might well be involved in such an operation. Third, if the United States could persuade the leading grain-trading nations to build and operate such a system of grain reserves, the future would look bright for the United States. But what if it cannot persuade the leading grain-trading nations to build and operate such a system of reserves? What does the United States do then? Does it attempt to build and operate a grain reserve that averages 70 million tons in size unilaterally? Probably not, for several reasons: cost, monopoly position, pride. Fourth, should the United States consider building and operating a limited grain reserve of, say, 30 million tons' capacity? The answer to this question seems to be that it intends to do so. But it must recognize first that such a reserve program has a limited capacity to stabilize world grain prices, and second that the achievement of an acceptable degree of price stabilization in the world is dependent upon the receipt of help from other national grain-reserve programs. But if that help is not forthcoming and the United States is still desirous of achieving a stable domestic grain price level, then it must be prepared to take additional steps: to limit exports in periods of world shortage and to control production and restrict imports in periods of world surplus. Fifth, in such an event, the United States will have decided to forsake the policy path of free and expanded trade in its pursuit of the policy objective, a stable domestic grain price level. And for a nation that must export some 40 percent of the grain it produces, the achivement of domestic price stabilization at the expense of strong and favorable trading relations could have disastrous consequences.

The clean commodity management policy avenues for the United States involve either giving up the grain price stabilization objective completely or operating a grain-reserve program unilaterally with the capacity to stabilize world grain prices. But each of these nice clean policy avenues seems to produce economic and social consequences that are unacceptable to the American people. The American people seem likely to opt for some course of action in between. In such an event, the issues become extremely complex, and the lines of action and their consequences become exceedingly messy. But the issues and the various courses of action can be sorted out and analyzed, as we have tried to do in this paper. And this in turn should help

Americans decide what it is that they really want to try to do in this area.

III. ISSUES OF WHEAT FEED-GRAIN RELATIONSHIPS

The position one takes with regard to the current buildup of wheat stocks as to whether it is a temporary or long-term buildup depends upon one's long-term outlook on the world grain supply situation. As was made clear in the introduction to this chapter, there is a wide difference of opinion among the experts regarding the long-run supply situation for the grains. Nonetheless, some important points can be made regarding wheat supply-price behavior that bear on wheat commodity management policy.

Much of the wheat of the world is produced in low-rainfall, high-risk production areas. This is particularly true of wheat production in North America and the Soviet Union (the relatively high degree of variability in production in these two areas may be viewed in Figure 5-A). Thus it is not uncommon in wheat production to have a series of high-yielding years followed by a series of poor-yielding years, resulting in significant variation in total wheat production. But these variations in wheat production do not follow any observable pattern or periodicity. With the present state of knowledge, they are completely unpredictable.

It is further the case that the price elasticity of the world demand for wheat is extremely inelastic.[15] Given this extreme price inelasticity of demand for wheat, any small change in supply or the rate of growth in supply must result in a wide swing in the price of wheat. In short, wheat is a very unstable commodity, swinging easily and readily back and forth from a shortage to a surplus condition. And the current buildup of wheat stocks could be representative of one of those short swings, which in this case results from two very good wheat crops in a row around the world.

It should be further recognized that the world production of wheat on a trend basis has been growing rapidly. For the fifteen-

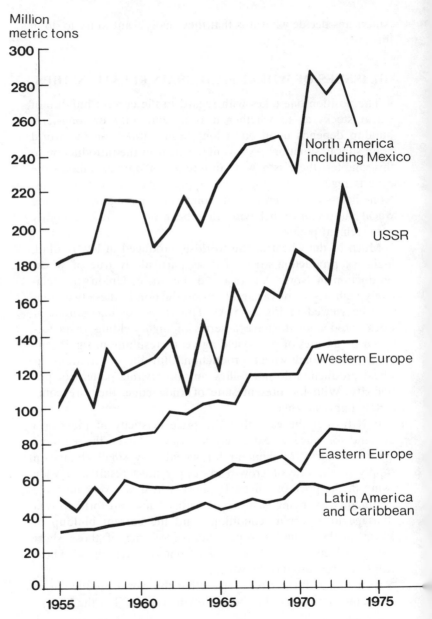

Fig. 5-A. Cereal production in major regions of the world, 1955 to 1974.

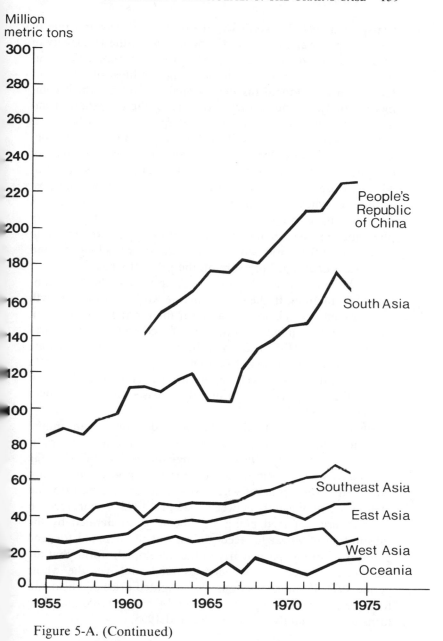

Figure 5-A. (Continued)

year period 1960-75, world wheat production grew at a rate of 3.1 percent per annum. A study undertaken at the University of Minnesota shows that if this rate of growth in production continues to 1995 and the subsitutional possibilities of wheat for feed grain are ignored (as they sometimes are in wheat commodity analyses, and as they often are in the operation of national price-support programs), then the real price of wheat over the long period 1975-95 will decline importantly.[16] With medium rates of world population growth, the income elasticity of demand for wheat is not strong enough to cause the real price of wheat to rise. Ignoring for the moment the substitutional possibilities of wheat for feed grains, the Minnesota study suggests that the current buildup of stock of wheat is not a temporary phenomenon. We should expect world supplies of wheat to press against the world demand for wheat over the long run and so create a downward pressure on the price of wheat.

But the long-run supply-price situation for feed grains is considerably different. In the first place, the world historical growth rate for feed grains is somewhat lower than in the case of wheat. The rate of growth in the production of feed grains for the world for the period 1960-75 is 2.7 percent per annum. Given this rate of growth in production, UN trend projections in per capita income, and the relatively high income elasticities for feed grains, the real price of feed grains increases significantly over the period 1975-95.

When we let wheat substitute for feed grains as an animal feed, the supply-price picture for wheat and feed grains is changed importantly. Over the long-run period 1975-95, the low-priced wheat is substituted for the high-priced feed grains, causing the world price of wheat to stop its decline by 1985 and then to rise significantly between 1985 and 1995. The increase in the real price of feed grains is, of course, moderated by the substitution of wheat for feed grains; but the demand for feed grains is so strong, particularly in the developed, world, that the real price of feed grains increases modestly over the whole period 1975-95. In this analysis, the weighted price of wheat and feed grains declines slightly between 1975 and 1985, and then turns up importantly between 1985 and 1995.

The Minnesota study makes clear the different behavioral characteristics of wheat and feed grains. Wheat is characterized by a relatively slow-growing world demand and an extremely price inelastic demand. Thus, its price tends to lag behind the price of feed grains on a trend basis. But in the short run, wheat is a highly volatile commodity, shifting quickly from shortage to surplus and back again. Feed grains are characterized, on the other hand, by a relatively rapidly growing world demand, fueled to an important degree by rising real incomes in the developed world and a somewhat more price elastic demand. Thus, the price of feed grains is likely to remain strong over the long-run period 1975-95, and the price of feed grains fluctuates less than the price of wheat as livestock feeding rates are adjusted to movements in the price of feed grains. But if wheat is allowed to substitute freely for feed grains in national markets, wheat prices will tend to follow feed grain prices over the long run, 1975-95.

Since wheat in the United States is produced in one well-defined area and corn and soybeans in another, although there is some substitution at the extensive margin,[17] it would be a mistake to try to dictate through government plans and programs any long-term division of total acreage for use as wheat and feed grains. Wheat can be used as a feed, and sorghum can substitute for wheat in some producing areas. This being the case, the support price for wheat in the United States should be set no higher than the support price for corn than the feeding value of wheat is over corn. With such a commodity-pricing policy, wheat would be substituted for corn as a livestock feed whenever it became surplus and its price fell to a level where it could economically be substituted for corn. This would put an effective floor under the market price of wheat, cause it to move into consumption whenever it became surplus, and cause the prices of wheat and feed grains to move through time in a roughly parallel fashion.

The United States is close to such a commodity price policy at the present time. But the EEC countries, and Japan with respect to rice, hold the prices of food grain far above the price of feed grains, thus inducing the buildup of large surplus stocks of food grains from time to time. Such surplus stocks are in turn exported with the use of export subsidies. When the world is chronically short on grains, as was the case from 1972 to 1975, such commodity-pricing policies cause no great difficulty. But when world supplies of grain are in rough balance with demand, as has been the case in 1975-77, or when the world is plagued with chronic grain surpluses as it was from 1954 to 1970, then such internal commodity-pricing policies must lead to the use of all kinds of export subsidy arrangements, which in turn lead to retaliatory actions and trade wars. In sum, we should expect wheat prices to oscillate around feed-grain prices over the long-run future. But if we follow a sane price policy with respect to wheat, the market price of wheat should follow the market price of feed grains rather closely.

The above discussion of the long-term price prospects for wheat and feed grains is based on the assumption that rates of growth in production will be the same in the long-run future as they were in the long-run past. But is that a realistic assumption, in light of the increased scarcity of most farm-production inputs? It is my thesis that if research, investment, trade, and domestic price policies in food and agriculture in countries around the world in the period 1975-2000 are not greatly different from those of the early 1970s then: (1) the supply of all grains is going to lag behind the demand for all grains; and (2) the real price of grains will trend upward over the long period 1975-2000.[18] When I look at the various forces that will come to bear in the production and utilization of grain around the world over the next twenty-five years, then it seems to me that the world crossed a great watershed in the 1970s in the production and utilization of grain and that this crossing will be reflected in an increase in the real price of grains in the years to come.

The argument that the real price of grain will rise over the long period 1975-2000 rests on several strands of thought. Three strands are considered here: supply factors, demand factors, and conjectural factors.

Supply Factors. Total cultivated land in the world is a small percentage of the total land mass—some 11 percent. But this does not mean that the arable land in the world can easily or readily be expanded. It is estimated that the total potentially arable land in the world amounts to about 24 percent of the total land mass.[19] But much, if not most, of this land can be made arable only at considerable cost—costs required for draining, clearing, leveling, or terracing to transform nonarable land into arable land. Further, the land so transformed is very likely to be less productive than land already in cultivation. If this were not the case, investment would already have been made in the land to convert it to an arable status. This means that the supply function for arable land has slope (that is, additional amounts of arable land will be supplied only at increasingly higher arable land prices). And for most of the developed world and the less developed regions of Asia, the supply function of arable land is highly inelastic. It may be that the supply of arable land in Africa and South America is elastic, but, because of development costs, even in those areas the supply function must be positively inclined.

The line of reasoning presented above with respect to land holds with even greater force with respect to water available for irrigation. Water has become an exceedingly scarce resource around the world. This is not to say that water available for irrigation cannot be increased in supply. It can, but only at considerable cost—costs required to pump water from greater depths, to transport water greater distances, to impound water in less efficient ponds and reservoirs, and to move water through or around natural barriers. This means as a generalization that the supply curve for water for irrigation is positively inclined, and in many areas it is steeply inclined.

The public recognition of the limited oil reserves in the world relative to demand in the early 1970s, the skyrocketing prices of petroleum products, and the general and significant increase in energy prices had a direct and adverse effect on agricultural production. The prices of all non-farm-produced inputs that are dependent on energy in their production (e.g., machinery, nitrogenous fertilizer) rose significantly, as did the prices of direct energy inputs (e.g., electricity, gasoline). This, of course, increased the cost of producing agricultural products in the

1970s. In the long run, the prices of agricultural products must increase sufficiently to cover the higher costs of energy, direct and indirect, to agricultural producers. Further, most signs point to a long-run increase in the cost of energy to users, not to a decrease. Thus, the growing scarcity of that easy-to-use source of energy, petroleum, in particular, and the rising cost of energy, generally, must be viewed as additional deterrents to the rate of growth in agricultural production around the world.

It is the interaction of the growing scarcities of land, water, and energy that operates as an important drag to increased production. Higher-priced energy will be required in ever larger amounts to bring about an increase in total agricultural production where dwindling supplies of water must be pumped and moved to new lands that have been leveled and diked to produce crops that make heavy use of fertilizer. The whole process is technically feasible, but it can take place only at higher and higher costs, and hence at higher and higher product prices. This is the meaning of the increased scarcity of conventional resources that confronts producers of agricultural products, whether in the United States, India, or Brazil.

Demand Factors. Short of some demographic miracle, or the general onset of Malthusian controls, the population of the world is expected to increase about 60 percent between 1975 and 2000, and perhaps by as much as 80 percent by the year 2000. It is sometimes observed that most of this increase in population will occur in the less developed world, with the direct or indirect implication that the surplus-food-producing developed world will not help feed the food-deficit less developed world. This could be the way the tightening food situation in the world is resolved; the developed world holds down the real cost of food to its consumers by restricting food-aid shipments, while the Malthusian controls of starvation and increased death rates among the very young and very poor take over in the less developed world. But this, in the view of this writer, at least in its crudest form, will not be the course of world developments. Strong but not always effective efforts will be made in the less developed world to keep the rate of growth in food production from lagging behind population growth in those areas. And sincere but not always wise efforts will be made in the developed world to assist the less developed regions in meeting their increased food requirements. These efforts will include economic assistance, technical assistance, and food aid.

Whether all of these efforts will prove successful in meeting the food requirements of a world population that has increased 60 percent by the year 2000 remains to be seen. But the important point to be made here is that those efforts will exert a strong pull, or a strong demand, on the scarce productive resources described in the previous section. This strong pull will operate to increase the prices of those inputs: it must, to induce them to move into the agricultural productive system. And to cover the increased costs of production resulting from the higher input prices, in the long run the real price of the product must rise. This is the way a major increase in the world population will operate to create an upward movement in the real price of food.

But if economic development takes place in the less developed world in the future at the pace that the political leaders of that world hope and expect it will, then the increase in the demand for resources will be extraordinarily great. Nathan Keyfitz estimates that every individual who moves out of the poverty class and into the middle class in the less developed world increases the demand on resources by five times.[21] This same phenomenon occurs with respect to food. In the early stages of development, the income elasticity of food (read "grain") is very high, probably approaching 0.8. Thus, John Mellor argues that a growth of per capita income of 2 percent per year in less developed countries where the rate of population growth is 3 percent per year and the income elasticity of food is 0.8 results in a rate of growth in the demand for food (read "grains") of over 4.5 percent per year.[22] In short, rapid population growth and a moderate rate of per capita income growth lead to an explosion in the demand for food (read "grains") from the less developed world.

This, however, is not the end of the demand story. Developments in the developed world seem likely to create a further upward pressure on food prices. Rising real incomes in Japan,

Western Europe, Eastern Europe, the Soviet Union, and in certain newly rich areas have resulted in important increases in the per capita consumption of animal products—particularly meat. But typically those areas cannot produce all of the raw products out of which to produce the animal products they require, namely, feed grains and oil meals. Thus, these regions have turned increasingly to North America for the needed raw materials of animal production (see Table 5.1).

If the real incomes of people in the developed world continue to increase with economic development, we must expect: (1) the per capita consumption of animal products in the developed countries involved to increase; and (2) the imports of grain and oil meals into numerous developed countries from North America to continue to increase. This means that in the future developed nations will be competing strongly with the nations of the less developed world, *as they are now,* for surplus grains of North America and possibly Australia. This element of foreign demand, when added to world population growth, must result in an extraordinary strong total world demand for grains in the period 1975-2000. This strong total demand interacting with a lagging supply could create a persistent upward pressure on the world price of grains over the long-run future.

a. Conjectural Factors. The confirmed optimists will argue that the economic force of the physical-resource scarcities discussed above will be overcome by research, technological development, and farm technological advance. This may turn out to be the case. At this writing, it is impossible either to prove or disprove this argument. But there are bits and pieces of evidence that should give proponents of this argument some pause. First, farm technological advance and the resulting rate of increase in agricultural productivity have been uneven and inconsistent in the United States in the 1970s. The "green revolution" and the resultant increase in yields per acre in South and Southeast Asia have slowed down and leveled off in the 1970s. Thus, in both the developed and less developed worlds, that great force of the 1950s and 1960s, farm technological advance, is sputtering in the 1970s.

TABLE 5.1

PATTERN OF WORLD GRAIN TRADE, SELECTED YEARS, 1934-76
(annual average net exports [+] or net imports [−] in million metric tons)

Region	1934-38 [a]	1954-56 [a]	1960-62 [b]	1968-70 [b]	1972 [b]	1973 [b]	1974 [b]	1975 [b]	1976 [b]
USA	5	13	31	34	67	75	62	78	77
Canada		9	10	11	19	13	13	17	17
Western Europe	−24	−21	−26	−22	−18	−22	−20	−16	−31
Australia and New Zealand	3	3	6	9	7	7	11	11	12
Eastern Europe	5	−4	−7	−6	−7	−5	−8	−7	−12
USSR		2	7	6	−20	−5	0	−25	−7
Africa and Mideast	1	0	−4	−7	−5	−12	−12	−10	−13
People's Republic of China	2	1	−5	−4	−6	−8	−6	−2	−4
Japan		−4	−5	−14	−18	−20	−19	−19	−21
Other Asia		−2	−7	−9	−13	−15	−17	−18	−13
Latin America	9	2	1	5	−3	−4	0	−2	3
Total Exports [c]	25	30	55	65	93	95	86	106	109

SOURCE: U.S. Department of Agriculture.

[a] Calendar year.

[b] Year beginning July 1 except 1960-62 and 1968-70 for Argentina, Brazil, Australia, and New Zealand, where the year begins the following December or January.

[c] Total imports and total exports do not balance because of variations in reporting periods and different marketing years.

Second, although much research in agricultural production is taking place around the world and continuous improvements in agricultural production practices and technologies are being made, there does not appear to be any production development in the offing comparable to the revolution in corn production in the United States from 1935 to 1965, or to the revolution in wheat production in Asia in the 1960s. With respect to agricultural production developments, we appear to be in a period of refinements, not major breakthroughs.

Third, world grain production lagged behind world grain consumption in the 1960s—a decade of great technological development and rapid farm technological advance.[23] To cope with this lag in world grain production and growing resource scarcities, research, technological development, and farm technological advance must be more pervasive and more effective in the 1970s, 1980s, and 1990s than they were in the 1960s. And this is one possible outcome. But in the judgment of this writer, the odds are strongly against such an outcome. We will have farm technological advance in the 1970s, 1980s, and 1990s and the resulting increases in agricultural productivity, *but such technological advances and such increases in productivity are not likely to be great enough to: (1) meet the rapidly expanding demand for the grains around the world: and (2) compensate for the growing scarcities of conventional resources—land, water, and energy.*

Finally, there is that great conjectural factor, the weather. Various arguments are being developed and advanced by the climatologists that the climate is changing, and adversely so for crop production in the Northern Hemisphere. One argument states that the Northern Hemisphere has been slowly cooling since the 1940s. This cooling trend affects the flow and direction of wind currents in such ways as to make the monsoon areas of the world drier and growing conditions in steppe areas such as the American plains more variable and uncertain. Another argument states that the climate is warming as a result of increased CO_2 in the atmosphere—this is the "greenhouse" effect. And there are still other arguments. But the effect of each, if it is realized, is to change crop-growing conditions and create problems for producers of food.[24]

Which of these arguments proves to be correct and to what extent remains to be seen. But they do suggest that crop-growing conditions around the world are not likely to be any better over the next twenty-five years than they were during the past twenty-five years, and there is a possibility that they will be worse—perhaps much worse, perhaps only a little worse. In any event, the arguments being advanced by prominent climatologists do not give comfort to agricultural experts who argue that the rapidly growing world food requirements will be easily and readily met by increased food production. To the contrary, they suggest one more important cause for concern with regard to the future food supply-demand balance for the world.

In summary, it is argued here that it is most probable (although not certain) that the long-run trend in the real price of grains in the world will be upward. All the important forces that will be at work over the next twenty-five years would seem (as of 1977) to point in this direction. This view of the long-run future is similar to the views advanced by the English classical economists of the nineteenth century.[25] The opening up of the great grain basket in North America in the nineteenth century and the technological revolution in agriculture in the twentieth century threw off the timing of their argument by a hundred years or more. But the finite world, it is argued here, once more is closing in upon the expanding number of consumers and the expanding wants of those consumers.

IV. AGRICULTURAL PRODUCTIVITY

Cereal-production growth rates by region and by different periods and assumptions are presented in Table 5.2; production growth rates by individual grains are presented in Table 5.3. These production growth rates were computed by the International Food Policy Research Institute from data obtained from the U.S. Department of Agriculture.[26] The cereal-production growth rates presented in column 2 of Table 5.2 are for the period 1967-74; this was an unusual period—one of great productivity increases in the early part of the period in some LDCs and one of low yields in the later part of the period as the result

TABLE 5.2

GROWTH RATES: POPULATION AND CEREAL PRODUCTION
(percent per annum compounded)

Country/Region	Population 1975–85	Cereal Production		
		1967–74	*1960–74*[a]	*Required to Meet Deficit by 1985/86*[b]
Asia High Income	2.31	.99	2.20	11.31
Asia Low Income:				
India	2.46	1.96	2.59	3.32
Bangladesh	2.88	.41	1.21	4.47
Pakistan	3.26	4.92	5.47	3.91[c]
Indonesia	2.56	4.11	2.74	5.78
Philippines	3.17	3.07	3.63	5.38
Thailand	3.20	3.69	3.71	.65[c]
Other Asia	2.30	.97	1.23	2.60
Total Asia Low Income	2.63	2.01	2.44	3.54
TOTAL ASIA	2.61	1.95	2.42	4.16
N. Africa/Mideast OPEC	3.28	–.98	2.00	7.91
N. Africa/Mideast Non-OPEC:				
Egypt	2.31	1.92	2.54	5.68
Turkey	2.63	–.69	1.62	2.70
N. Africa/Mideast High Income	3.10	6.69	4.17	6.37
N. Africa/Mideast Low Income	2.99	.76	1.43	3.89
Total N. Africa/Mideast Non-OPEC	2.77	1.46	2.23	4.36

TOTAL N. AFRICA/MIDEAST	2.93	.90	2.18	5.26
Nigeria	2.99	.58	-0.09	6.82
Sub-Sahara High Income	2.76	1.86	2.76	4.46
Sub-Sahara Low Income	2.82	-.33	1.85	3.56
TOTAL SUB-SAHARA	2.88	.32	1.54	4.55
Mexico	3.41	.53	4.32	5.25
Other Mid-American/Caribbean	2.64	2.32	2.69	9.43
Argentina	1.21	2.67	3.28	.98 [c]
Brazil	2.82	3.15	3.94	3.71 [c]
Venezuela	2.93	-2.85	3.20	16.52
Ecuador	3.17	-4.43	.69	11.31
Other Latin America	2.70	2.03	1.87	6.64
TOTAL LATIN AMERICA	2.79	2.23	3.48	3.57
TOTAL DEVELOPING MKT. ECON.	2.71	1.69	2.50	4.25

SOURCE: *Meeting Food Needs in the Developing World*, IFPRI, Research Report No. 1, Washington, D.C., February 1976.

[a] Used for projecting production to 195/86.

[b] Rate required from 1974 trend value of production to meet 1985/86 high consumption.

[c] Exporting country in 1985/86.

171

TABLE 5.3

PRODUCTION GROWTH RATES FOR CEREALS,
DEVELOPING MARKET ECONOMIES, BY REGIONS
(percent per annum)

Region	1960/74				
	Rice	Wheat	Coarse Grains	Millets	All Cereals
Asia	1.98	6.89	1.47	1.65	2.42
	(1.70)	(8.23)	(−0.19)	(−1.17)	(1.95)
North Africa/	(3.36)	2.82	1.23	0.28	2.18
Middle East	(−0.93)	(1.97)	(−0.08)	(−5.38)	(0.90)
Sub-Sahara Africa	3.49	3.57	1.50	0.78	1.54
	(1.53)	(0.99)	(0.64)	(−0.73)	(0.32)
Latin America	3.30	1.28	4.17	−	3.49
	(2.30)	(0.80)	(2.60)	−	(2.23)
TOTAL DME	2.20	4.12	2.50	1.21	2.50
	(1.67)	(4.26)	(1.11)	(−0.93)	(1.69)

SOURCE: *Meeting Food Needs in the Developing World,* IFPRI, Research Report No. 1, Washington, D.C., February 1976.

NOTE: Figures in parentheses are rates for 1967/74.

of adverse weather. But except for wheat, rates of increase in cereal production are uniformly lower in the period 1967-74 than for the longer period 1960-74 (Table 5.3). The lower rates of production increase for all grains except wheat in the period 1967-74 suggest that many LDCs may have considerable difficulty in maintaining relatively high production growth rates in the long-run future unless strong and effective action is taken to maintain those rates.

Cereal-production growth rates for the period 1960-74 are presented in column 3 of Table 5.2. These more optimistic growth rates were used to project production to 1985-86 for less developed countries and regions shown in Table 5.2. Using these production growth rates, the International Food Policy Research Institute (IFPRI) concludes that the total cereal deficit for the total less developed, market-economy countries would increase to about 100 million tons of grain in 1985-86. This compares with a deficit of 45 million tons of grain in the food crisis year of 1974-75. And since the estimated deficit of 100 million tons is based on some very optimistic production growth trends, the estimated deficit could well prove conservative.

The cereal-production growth rates presented in column 4 of Table 5.2 are those rates required to satisfy the consumption requirements, or eliminate the deficit, in 1985-86 under a high-income growth assumption. On the basis of historical experience, the production growth rates presented in column 4 of Table 5.2 could not be met short of a miracle. Each of the LDCs listed in Table 5.2 will have to invest heavily in agriculture and irrigation and pursue wise and astute economic policies to sustain the rates of growth shown in column 3 of Table 5.2. Given the frailties of men and the internal discord in many less developed countries, rates of increase in cereal production somewhere between those rates shown in columns 2 and 3 in Table 5.2 seem most likely to be realized over the period 1975-86. This would mean a total annual cereal deficit for the less developed market economies of somewhere between 100 and 200 million tons of grain by the year 1985-86.

The IFPRI reassessed the long-term food prospects of the less developed world in the summer of 1977.[27] In this study food production and consumption in developing market economies are projected to 1990. Cereal production and its equivalent in other staples are projected to 1990 at the average annual rate of growth that obtained in the period 1960-75 (See Tables 5.2 and 5.3). On this basis it is estimated that the total grain deficit for these countries, which stood at 37 million tons in 1975, will increase to between 120 and 145 million tons by 1990, or by an amount that approaches the total volume of world grain trade in recent years. The estimated grain deficit for developing market economies obtained for 1990 in the 1977 study is not far different from the estimate obtained for 1985 in the 1976 study.

If the less developed market-economy countries of the world are confronted with a cereal deficit of between 100 and 200 million tons in the period 1985-90, how are they going to cope with that deficit? In part they may cope with it through increased hunger and starvation among their very poor and increased death rates among the very young and the very old. But in the main they will attempt to cope with the deficit through increasing their imports of grain. This will mean an increase in grain imports into the less developed world over 1974 of some 50 to 150 million tons of grains. Where will this grain come from? The trade data presented in Table 5.1 strongly suggest that it will come from North America. Over the past forty years the United States and Canada have become the preeminent exporters of grain in the world.

Thus it seems clear that if exports of grain into the less developed world increase greatly between 1975 and 1990 as the result of lagging agricultural productivity in that part of the world, almost all of that increase must come from North America. This will mean a very large increase in the export demand for grains produced in the United States and Canada and a consequent strong upward pressure on the price of grains in the United States and Canada. How much the price of grains would increase depends, of course, on the long-run supply response in the United States, Canada, and the rest of the world. But this is precisely the point at issue; this is the point on which there is wide disagreement among the experts. If, however, the thesis developed in this paper proves to be correct, the long-run rise in the price of grains would be significantly large.

It is sometimes argued that much of the increase in grain exports to the less developed world will be moved under some form of concessional sales (P.L. 480), and that, somehow, is different. It is different in terms of who pays for the grain exported. But it is not greatly different in terms of the effect on market price. A ton of grain sold under a concessional sales arrangement has the same general effect on the market as a ton of grain sold commercially. In both cases a ton of grain is removed from the supply available to the market, and the market is tightened by the removal of the ton of grain whether paid for by the American taxpayer or Indian consumers. The institutional separation of government-owned stocks and the commercial market may cause a delay in the price response in the commercial market to a ton of grain sold out of government stocks, but buyers and sellers of grain must, and ultimately will, take account of a decline in the volume of government-held stocks, hence upon total available supplies, in their trading operations.

The question is asked: Given the likely productivity developments in the less developed world, what is likely to happen to protein consumption and meat consumption of the average consumer in that part of the world? If the growth in cereal production ranges between the rates presented to columns 2 and 3 of Table 5.2, and the countries involved experience substantial increases in the size of their cereal deficits, we must expect the average per capita consumption of meat to decline, the average per capita consumption of protein to decline, and the average per capita consumption of calories to be held constant only through the greatest of efforts by the countries involved and the rich, developed nations of the West. Under the scenario sketched here the dietaries of the average person in the less developed world will not improve over the next ten years; they will worsen.[28]

Over this same period, and given present consumer aspirations, we must expect the per capita consumption of meat to increase throughout the Western developed world and Japan with rising per capita real incomes. Thus, a great and real conflict is posed: Will the rich, developed nations eat up the surplus of grain produced in the developed nations in the form of meat while death rates in the less developed world increase from increased hunger and starvation? This is a question to which the rich, developed nations will almost certainly be required to provide an answer in the decade ahead. And the question will be posed in its most acute form in the United States, as one of the richest nations in the world and certainly the greatest producer and exporter of grain.

The question is asked: What effect will the grain-production performance sketched above for the LDCs have on the need for a grain-reserve program? The answer to this question is straightforward. If a large part of the world is living in a chronic state of grain deficit, then any shortfall in production resulting from adverse weather will accentuate that deficit and create even greater hardship and human suffering. Given such a state of affairs, it is most important that the richer nations of the world maintain a system of grain reserves that averages some 70 million tons of grain in size. A system of grain reserves that averaged 70 million tons could play an important role in the world grain market evening out supplies between crop seasons, and thereby help all nations, particularly the very poor nations, cope with short-run shortfalls in production resulting from adverse weather and poor crops.

In this connection, it bears repeating that there are some people in Asia and Africa who are so poor that the operation of an international system of grain reserves has little or no meaning for them. They are too poor to enter the world market when and if their crops fail. To assist these people, the poorest of the poor, world society needs to maintain a permanent program of food assistance. The program size most often mentioned in the middle 1970s to meet the needs of these people is 10 million tons of grain per annum. Such a figure may be adequate for the 1970s, but the size of the program may need to grow to, say, 20 million tons per annum by the middle 1980s if rates of growth in cereal production are not greater than those suggested in this paper.

V. COMMODITY MANAGEMENT POLICY RECOMMENDATIONS

1. The government of the United States should recognize that: (1) although the average urban consumer is inarticulate with respect to his need for a grain-reserve program, he becomes angry and vocal when food prices rise sharply; (2) as the leading exponent of free trade and the largest supplier of grains to the international market, the United States is looked to by the free world as the guarantor of a stable, workable world market in the grains; and (3) the less developed countries look to the United States for grain supplies when they experience shortfalls in production, because it is almost the only place to look for such supplies. On the basis of these needs and responsibilities, the United States should initiate a limited grain reserve that *averages* no less than 30 million tons of grain in size. As of Septem-

ber 1977 the United States is committed to holding and operating a grain reserve of at least 30 million tons.

2. The United States should take the leadership in calling a conference in which each nation trading in the international grain market, both importers and exporters, commits itself to holding a grain reserve. The global average grain reserve target should be at least 70 million tons.

3. Recognizing that the price-stabilization goal of each nation holding a grain reserve is likely to differ to some degree from every other nation's, the United States should seek to establish a continuing international forum comparable to the GATT, but not the GATT, wherein the harmonization of country price-stabilization objectives for the grains could be discussed and efforts be made to resolve differences where those differences create serious trade problems.

4. In the management of its own grain reserves and in negotiations in the continuing international forum, the United States should seek to stabilize world grain prices around the concept of the long-run equilibrium price for each major grain category. The specifics of such a price-stabilization policy might take the following form:

a. Set the stabilization target price for each current year equal to the average world market price for the previous three years.

b. Establish a stabilization range around the target price of plus 20 percent and minus 10 percent. U.S. stocks would be acquired whenever market price fell to the lower limit of the range, and stocks would be released by an announced formula as the market price approached the upper limit.

5. The United States should do everything in its power to make such an international system of grain-reserve programs operate successfully because the successful operation of such a system of reserves should: (1) result in a reasonable degree of price stability in grain prices in world markets and in the United

States; and (2) expedite the movement toward free and open country markets in world grain trade.

6. But if or when the United States became convinced that the international system of grain reserves that had been established lacked the capacity to stabilize *world* grain prices, then it should formulate and announce a comprehensive export policy for the grains. The specifics of such a policy might take the following form:

a. The United States would announce to the world its domestic requirements, as well as the trade requirements of its regular foreign customers,[29] and indicate that those supply requirements will be protected by whatever management devices are required.

b. The United States would periodically, possibly every three months, announce the drawdowns in supply that have occurred and indicate the extent to which domestic requirements and those of regular foreign customers can be met without the imposition of export management devices.

c. Food aid exports to LDCs on concessional terms should be determined on the basis of the needs of developing countries, and the U.S. share of such needs should be built into the total protected requirements in point a.

d. Sales of grains and related commodities to state trading nations would be negotiated by the U.S. government with respect to the total volume of sales, range of prices, and other economic considerations such as transport subsidies.

e. If the worldwide shortage were of such magnitude and if free exports from the United States were so large as to cut into the requirements guaranteed under point a, then the United States would impose export controls, after properly informing world traders as indicated under point b. Exempt from these controls, of course, would be the already guaranteed exports to regular foreign purchasers and U.S. food-aid commitments. This would be the action of last resort, to protect and guarantee the domestic requirements and the requirements of foreign purchasers regularly dependent on the United States for supplies.

7. If the grain-reserve programs of the United States and its trading partners lack the capacity to stabilize world grain prices, or if domestic producers require assurance that domestic grain prices will be stabilized, then the following domestic programs should be in operation or on standby available to go into operation:

a. A price-support program available to all grain producers to be effectuated through the operation of non-recourse loans, where the loan rates are set each year at the lower boundary of the grain-reserve price-stabilization range.

b. Production-control programs to go into operation whenever the upper limit of the grain reserve has been reached (say, at 60 million tons where the reserve is programmed to average 30 million tons). Such production-control programs might, in a series of bountiful years, be required to stop the buildup of unwanted, surplus stocks.

8. The United States should provide financial support for the operation of a world food program designed to provide food aid to those countries and peoples too poor to benefit from the operation of grain-reserve programs. This program should be viewed as an aid program, and the need for it seems likely to grow over the long-run future.

9. If the thesis of the author of this paper is correct, namely, that the real price of grains will rise over the long-run future, or even if the probability of the thesis being correct is no more than a 50-50 proposition, then the United States should pursue a more resolute and a more effective set of policies and programs

in the future designed to assist the less developed nations to: (a) control their rate of population growth; and (b) increase their rate of growth in food production—particularly grain production. To this end the United States should:

a. Continue to provide generous financial support to the various UN agencies working in the areas of population control and food production. The programs of such agencies are sometimes ineffectual, but such internationally sponsored programs are absolutely essential to the minimization of Great Power rivalries.

b. Continue to provide generous financial support to the system of international research institutes for agricultural production. The United States should provide financial support to these international research centers *but not try to control or dictate their policies.* The model here should be the relationship of the U.S. government to the state agricultural experiment stations.

c. Find ways to improve and strengthen its bilateral technical-assistance programs in the areas of population control and agricultural production and marketing.

NOTES

1. See *The State of Food and Agriculture, 1975,* and earlier issues, UN Food and Agricultural Organization, Rome; and *The World Agricultural Situation,* December 1976, and earlier issues, U.S. Department of Agriculture, Economic Research Service, WAS-12, Washington, D.C.

2. For a review of this period see Willard W. Cochrane, *Feast or Famine: The Uncertain World of Food and Agriculture and Its Policy Implications for the United States,* National Planning Association, Report No. 136, February, 1974.

3. This position is developed at length in the two reports of the Club of Rome: Donella H. Meadows et al., *The Limits to Growth,* and Mihajlo Mesarovic and Eduard Pestel, *Mankind at the Turning Point.*

4. Willard W. Cochrane, "The Future of Farm Prices," *The New Rural America, The Annals of the American Academy of Political and Social Science,* January 1977.

5. This position is set forth in its most persuasive form by D. Gale Johnson in *World Food Problems and Prospects* (Washington, D.C.: American Enterprise Institute for Public Policy Research, 1975).

6. This position is most often expressed in the highly optimistic food-production targets of the national development plans of the various less developed countries.

7. D. Gale Johnson discusses this phenomenon in his pamphlet, *The Soviet Impact on World Grain Trade,* National Planning Association, Report No. 153, May 1977, pp. 38-39.

8. "Grain Reserves as a Solution to Unstable Markets," paper presented to the Society of Government Economists, Southern Economic Association Annual Conference, Atlanta, Georgia, November 18, 1976.

9. Willard W. Cochrane and Yigal Danin, *Reserve Stock Models: The World and the United States, 1975-85,* Technical Bulletin No. 305, Agricultural Experiment Station, University of Minnesota, 1976.

10. As stated in the introduction to this chapter, there is a wide difference of opinion among the experts regarding the long-term price prospects for the grains. The author of this statement is, however, of the view that the probability of grain prices, real grain prices, rising over the long-run future is much greater than the probability of grain prices declining. The argument in support of this conclusion is developed in the next section.

11. F. W. Waugh first developed the proposition that consumers facing random prices due to stochastic fluctuations in supply are better off than if price were stabilized at their means *(Quarterly Journal of Economics,* 58 [August 1944]: 602-614). The Waugh conclusion was based on the concept of consumer surplus. Using a similar argument, W. Y. Oi later demonstrated that firms having upward-sloping supply curves and facing random selling prices arising from stochastic shifts in demand would also lose from having those prices stabilized at their means *(Econometrica,* 29 [January 1961]: 58-64, 248). These and later arguments are summarized and discussed by Stephen J. Turnovsky in the article entitled "Price Expectations and Welfare Gains from Price Stabilization," *American Journal of Farm Economics,* 56 (November 1974): 706-716.

12. Address by Secretary of Agriculture Bob Bergland before the Third Ministerial Session of the World Food Council, Manila, the Philippines, June 20, 1977, U.S. Department of Agriculture Release 1682-77.

13. *World Food Security and Set-Aside Plans,* White House, Washington, D. C., August 29, 1977.

14. I grant that it is not easy to make this concept operational. But I also submit that if the concept cannot be made operational, then it is meaningless to talk about a true price-stabilization objective. I have argued many times in the past, and will argue here, that one reasonable method for approximating the long-term equilibrium price for one type of grain is to take an average of world market prices for that grain over a three-year period when world market prices are not riding on some international or large nation support-price program. The years 1974,

1975, and 1976 would qualify for such a period. Thus, I would suggest the stabilization target price for, say, wheat for 1977 should have been the average market prices for 1974, 1975, and 1976. And the stabilization target price for each succeeding year should be the average of world market prices in the previous three years. In other words, the target stabilization price for any given year would be a moving average of the previous three years. In each succeeding year, then, the stabilization target price would move in the direction dictated by the market but only at the pace permitted by the operation of the system of grain-reserve-stock programs.

15. See estimates of the price elasticity of demand presented in *World Demand Prospects for Grain in 1980 with Emphasis on Trade by the Less Developed Countries,* U.S. Department of Agriculture, Foreign Agricultural Economic Report No. 75, Economic Research Service, December 1971, pp. 27-37.

16. See William H. Meyers, "Long-Run Income Growth and World Grain Demand: An Econometric Analysis," Ph.D. disertation, University of Minnesota, March 1977.

17. On the high plains corn will rarely be substituted for wheat; corn yields too poorly under such low-rainfall conditions. Sorghum is sometimes substituted for wheat on the southern plains, and barley is sometimes substituted for wheat on the northern plains, but generally speaking, wheat is king on the high plains. Soft wheats and corn substitute for one another in the Eastern Corn Belt. But the demand for soft wheat is very limited; thus, the opportunity to substitute soft wheats for corn is limited.

18. This thesis, will, of course, be invalidated if the less developed countries invest more heavily in agriculture and pursue more effective population-control policies than they are presently doing, if the developed countries invest more in research and development in both energy and agriculture than they are presently doing, and if political stability is widely achieved around the world. But those "if" conditions are not presently being satisfied. Hence, I advance the thesis that I do.

19. *The World Food Problem,* a report of the President's Science Advisory Committee, vol. 2, White House, Washington D.C. May 1967, pp. 429-436.

20. These percentages were calculated from the medium variant projection published in *Selected World Demographic Indicators by Countries, 1980-2000,* Population Division, Department of Economic and Social Affairs of the United Nations Secretariat, ESA/P/WP55, May 23, 1975. The population estimates in this projection have been reduced modestly from earlier projections, and this, of course, reduces modestly the production task of world agriculture. Should rates of population growth decline still further, a point would be reached where the central argument of this part of the paper would become invalid.

But the requirement that world food production increase by 60 percent in twenty-five years remains a formidable one.

21. Nathan Keyfitz, "World Resources and the World Middle Class," *Scientific American,* 235, no. 1 (July 1976): 28-34.

22. John Mellor, *The Economics of Agricultural Development* (Ithaca, New York: Cornell University Press, 1966), pp. 73-79.

23. The counterargument may be made that production controls in the United States and Canada contributed to a lag in world grain production in the 1960s, and without those controls in operation it will be easier to overcome the lag in the 1970s. This is a reasonable argument, but the fact remains that the lag in grain production in the 1970s is not being overcome.

24. See Reid A. Bryson and Thomas J. Murray, *Climates of Hunger* (Madison: University of Wisconsin Press, 1977); and *A Program for Action,* Appendix A: "A Survey of Past Climates," Washington D.C.: National Academy of Sciences, 1975).

25. Benjamin Higgins, *Economic Development: Problems, Principles and Policies,* rev ed. (New York: Norton., 1968), chap. 3.

26. See the report, *Meeting Food Needs in the Developing World,* International Food Policy Research Institute, Research Report No. 1, Washington D.C., February 1976.

27. See Research Report No. 3, *Food Needs of Developing Countries: Projections of Production and Consumption to 1990,* (International Food Policy Research Institute, Washington, D.C., 1977)

28. For a full discussion of patterns of food consumption and dietary deficiencies in the less developed world see *Recent and Prospective Developments in Food Consumption: Some Policy Issues,* International Food Policy Research Institute, Research Report No. 2, July 1977.

29. Such amounts might be established on the basis of history, or through formal bilateral agreements.

Chapter 6

U.S. COMMODITY POLICY
AND THE TIN AGREEMENT

GORDON W. SMITH

Professor of Economics
Rice University

I. INTRODUCTION

In 1976, after a holdout of twenty years, the United States finally joined the International Tin Agreement (ITA). In good part this move was a political gesture, a sign that the United States was concerned with the plight of the raw-materials-exporting nations and willing to cooperate with them in reasonable producer-consumer arrangements to reduce market instability. Within the United States government it was generally believed that the potential economic gains (or losses) from membership would be small, but that the political payoff would be worth the effort.[1] The extent of such political benefits will depend on the American posture within the Tin Council (the governing body of the ITA), upon future U.S. tin stockpile disposal policies, and more generally upon the overall success of the Tin Agreement.

This paper explores the lines along which U.S. influence should be exercised in tin if the economic and political benefits are to be reasonably satisfactory. After a brief background section, I turn to a diagnosis of the shortcomings of both the ITA and U.S. stockpile practices in the past, drawing upon simulations of the Wharton (EFA) tin model. It will be shown that: (1) the ITA buffer stock was far too small to achieve reasonable stabilization targets; (2) although General Services Administration (GSA) stockpile sales were very important in mitigating upward price pressures during the times of shortage, their effectiveness was diminished by their longer-run unpredictability; (3) a more effective Tin Agreement would have required a buffer stock of a magnitude far too large to have been negotiated.

Although the past has not been particularly impressive, the future potential for effective stabilization is fairly high. With reasonable consumer contributions and some borrowing secured by warehouse warrants, the ITC buffer stock could be expanded to the levels required to stabilize prices within bands of ±15 percent around trend without recourse to disruptive export control. Furthermore, sales of U.S. surplus tin could be easily and explicitly coordinated within the ITA buffer stock. The main difficulty and principal source of conflict will be the proper determination of ceiling and floor prices to be defended. I argue that a ±15 percent band around trend would be an economically acceptable criterion toward which to strive. In practice, the determination of the appropriate trend prices is far from trivial, a fact that counsels against attempting to stabilize prices within much narrower ranges.[2]

In conclusion, I consider the economic importance—or lack of it—of stabilization to U.S. and producer nations.

II. BACKGROUND

MAJOR TRENDS

Primary tin, accounting for about 80 percent of total U.S. consumption, is virtually all imported, principally from Malaysia, Thailand, and Indonesia.[3] Import dependence seems destined to continue indefinitely, since the economic scope for recycling tin is not large, given current technology.[4] Indeed, U.S. production of secondary tin has actually been on a slight decline for twenty years in spite of fairly strong upward pressure on relative tin prices (see Table 6.1).[5]

TABLE 6.1
LME [a] SPOT PRICE OF TIN, 1955–1977
(1975 U.S. cents per lb.) [b]

1955	219		1960	222	
56	226		61	246	
57	210		62	249	
58	207		63	250	
59	225		64	338	
		Average: 217			Average: 261
1965	381		1970	316	
66	341		71	283	
67	315		72	280	
68	298		73	303	
69	315		74	420	
		Average: 330			Average: 320
1975	312				
1976	339				
1977 [c]	394				

SOURCE: K. Takeuchi, "Tin," mimeographed, World Bank Discussion Draft, 1977.

[a] London Metal Exchange (LME).
[b] Deflated by index of international inflation.
[c] Projection.

The single largest use of the metal both in the United States and worldwide is in tinplate, 90 percent of which in the United States goes into the container industry. Following in importance are solder, chemicals, and other end products as shown in Table 6.2.

Tin has been anything but a growth material. Total U.S. consumption *fell* from 1953 to 1974. More strikingly, U.S. consumption was actually lower in 1973 than in the Great Depression year of 1936! Consumption in the rest of the world has risen modestly in recent decades, but per capita consumption worldwide is definitely lower in the 1970s than it was fifty years before.[6]

This "sluggish" performance has multiple causes. First, tech-

TABLE 6.2
PRIMARY U.S. TIN CONSUMPTION BY FINISHED PRODUCTION, 1976 (metric tons)

Tinplate	20,766
Solder	13,506
Chemicals	4,718
Bronze and Brass	2,860
Tinning	2,284
Babbitt	1,832
White metal	2,093
Other	
Total	51,767

SOURCE: U.S. Bureau of the Mines.

nological changes have economized significantly on the use of tin. Some of the innovations have been mainly autonomous, that is to say, not closely tied to increases in the relative price of tin. Important examples of this type have been the development of frozen foods, which reduces the demand for cans; the two-piece drawn and ironed can, which eliminates the need for solder on the can's seam; aluminum beverage containers; microminiaturization of electrical circuits, which is reducing the need for solder. Other changes have been more directly price-related. Most obviously, as the relative price of tin has risen (see Table 6.1), there has been a reduction in the tin *content* of tinplate, solder, and some alloys. Sanitary tin containers typically use but one half of the tin they did twenty years ago.[7] The tin content in solder for car radiators has declined from 28 percent ten years ago to 13.8 percent today, and the solder in tin cans is now 1.5 percent tin compared with 5 percent ten years ago.[8]

The impact of higher prices on the tin content of tinplate is strong enough to detect econometrically. In the Wharton EFA tin model (1976) version),[9] the long-run price elasticity of tin metal used per ton of tinplate is -0.27 in the United States and -0.21 in Western Europe. Unfortunately, the effect of tin prices on U.S. and European consumption of tin for solder turns up statistically insignificant.

Ultimately, the upward relative price pressure, which has occurred in spite of these and other tin-saving innovations, must
be rooted in lagging production of the metal (see Table 6.3 for a
country breakdown). To what extent this development merely
reflects the inevitable exhaustion process of a natural resource or
instead is rooted in inefficient government policies in such countries as Malaysia and Bolivia cannot be resolved within the
scope of this paper. A few comments are in order, however,
since they bear upon the later discussion of ceiling and floor
prices.

TABLE 6.3

PRODUCTION OF TIN-IN-CONCENTRATES
ANNUAL AVERAGES, 1950-76
(metric tons)

	1950–54	1955–59	1960–64	1965–69	1970–76
Australia	1.758	2.161	2.878	5.884	10.182
Bolivia	32.504	29.367	22.749	28.674	29.559
Indonesia	34.093	27.628	17.830	14.992	22.492
Malaysia	58.842	52.594	58.232	71.512	70.607
Thailand	10.007	11.061	14.471	22.041	20.529
Other Western World	31.296	26.029	26.640	28.677	30.131
Total Western World	168.500	148.840	142.800	171.780	183.500

SOURCES: 1950–74, Wharton Econometric Forecasting Associates, Inc., *Forecasts
and Analysis of the Tin Market*, report to the General Services Administration,
Philadelphia, June 1976, 1975–76, International Tin Council.

Certainly, the real costs of production for the marginal producer, Bolivia, have risen steadily over the past twenty years.[10]
However, COMIBOL, the Bolivian state mining enterprise, has
served as a residual employer and is notorious for its operational
inefficiencies. Moreover, both Malaysia and Bolivia levy export
taxes, which at current International Tin Council (ITC) ceiling
prices ($4.55 per lb.) exceed 40 percent ad valorem at the mar-
gin.[11] Malaysia's "indigenization" policy[12] has also affected in
production adversely, especially in gravel pump mining. This
sector has accounted for about 50 percent of Malaysia's produc-

tion of tin-in-concentrates[13] in recent years and is dominated by Malaysians of Chinese background. Few new licenses have been issued for gravel pump mines recently, and their number has been declining,[14] partly because there have been few Malays with the capital and knowhow to enter the field. There is little doubt that a portion at least of the relatively higher prices has resulted from escalating taxes and particular social policies. One of the thornier issues facing the Tin Council is how these factors should be weighed, if at all, in setting floor and ceiling prices.

RECENT DEVELOPMENTS

The past five years have witnessed severe real price fluctuations in all currencies despite rather substantial ITA and GSA activity. The shortages of 1973-74 approximately doubled the real price of tin in most currencies [15] even though sales from the U.S. stockpile (43,000 tons) supplied more than 10 percent of world consumption over these two years. Prices fell back to previous levels during the following recession, and both export controls and ITC buffer-stock purchases were required to support floor prices. But in 1977 the basic shortage reasserted itself, the ITC buffer stock was exhausted early in the year, and as of this writing (December 1977), tin prices were above $6.00 per pound in New York, well in excess of the ITC ceiling level of $4.55 per pound in Penang. One difference from 1973-74 has been the absence of the GSA from the market: it has no authorization to sell.

An ominous note for tin producers in this situation is that continued scarcity and upward price pressures could spur the U.S. steel industry into an earlier perfection and introduction of blackplate for use in sanitary cans.[16] We will return to the point later in the paper.

III. THE INTERNATIONAL TIN AGREEMENT AND THE GSA [17]

Tin has a history of market regulation extending back into the 1920s. Since World War II the major nonmarket forces have been the ITA and the U.S. strategic stockpile administered by the GSA. This section examines the impact of each upon tin markets and analyzes the shortcomings of the ITA-GSA arrangement as it has existed until now.

The U.S. strategic stockpile of tin was formed mainly in the late 1940s and early 1950s in order to maintain normal consumption of the metal during a four-year war during which all foreign sources of the metal were cut off. At its peak, the GSA held over 350,000 metric tons of tin, more than enough to supply the Western world for two years at normal consumption rates. Since the early 1960s the strategic target has been reduced several times, and the GSA has sold more than 140,000 tons net, most of it at exceptionally high prices during 1963-66 and 1973-74. These sales were not made explicitly for stabilization purposes, since the GSA had no mandate to stabilize prices. However, diplomatic considerations—the desire not to offend tin-producing countries and to minimize "market disruption"— in effect concentrated GSA activity in periods of severe shortages,[18] much as would have occurred in fact with a wide-band buffer stock. And, of course, tin users pushed for sales from the stockpile as a means of filling production shortfalls.

The ITA has relied upon export controls and a buffer stock in its attempt to stabilize market prices between preestablished ceiling and floor levels. The authorized buffer stock has been small, rarely exceeding 20,000 tons, and the actual size was usually much less than that. Indeed, during the four years of greatest excess demand pressure, 1964-66 and 1974, the ITA held no tin at all. On the face of it, the buffer stock could not have been a very potent market force, and in fully 50 of the 222 months between the inception of the Tin Agreement and the end of 1974, average monthly prices were above ITA ceiling levels.[19]

The ITA was more successful in defending floor prices, which were penetrated only once, in September 1958. In part, this success (and the ITA's failure in defending its ceilings) arose from the fairly low levels at which floor and ceiling prices were fixed until recently.[20] But it must also be recognized that in its export quotas the ITA had an instrument which could defend prices against massive downward pressure, as it in fact did during 1957-60, when quotas were responsible for a decline of one third in tin production. In 1968, 1969, and 1973, quotas were so mild that large effects on market prices were precluded. The quotas of 1975-76 were somewhat more severe, and U.S. government estimates put the decline in production attributable to them at 10,000 to 15,000 tons,[21] significant but less than the 20,000 tons the ITA buffer stock purchased in 1974-75 in defense of the floor. Some evasion of the quotas has occurred, but never enough to substantially vitiate their impact.

Unfortunately, the administration of quotas was by no means always stabilizing. The 1973 controls were imposed in a time of incipient market shortages, while those of 1960, 1969,[22] and 1976 extended well beyond the period of downward market pressure, contributing significantly to later price run-ups.

One argument against export quotas is that while they might prevent penetration of floor prices, unlike buffer stocks they do nothing to defend the ceiling. Indeed, to the extent that quotas disrupt production and investment, as they did during the late 1950s, they may well contribute to upward price instability later in the cycle. It is true that if producers do not reduce output by the full amount of the export restriction, their stocks will increase, and these could well serve as a buffer against later demand pressures upon supply. Such has not usually occurred, however, with quotas under the Tin Agreement. Producers' stocks of tin were lower at the end of control periods than they were at their inception, except in 1975-76: [23] Export quotas under the ITA have typically acted as *production* quotas.

Simulations of the Wharton EFA world tin model (1974 version) for the period 1956-73 indicate that the ITA buffer stock had only a minor impact upon tin markets, as one would expect from the previous discussion. Far more important were the GSA's sales (see Table 6.4 and Figure 6-A), which reduced the variation in both prices and producer revenues, by perhaps threefold the effect of the ITA buffer stock. The true impact of export controls cannot be satisfactorily simulated with this model, but it was clearly substantial in 1957-60.[24]

The interaction of the ITA and GSA produced a loose, informal, and unique "commodity agreement" in which the GSA

TABLE 6.4

SIMULATIONS OF THE IMPACT OF
THE INTERNATIONAL TIN COUNCIL AND GSA STOCK
BEHAVIOR UPON THE TIN MARKET, 1956–73

Variable/simulation	No stock activity	ITC activity only	ITC and GSA stock activity
Average annual changes in real prices (absolute value) [a]	10.4%	9.4%	6.9%
Discounted total producer revenue (million 1967 $) [b]	5809.0	5812.7	5523.7
Standard error of the natural log of producer revenues around simulated trends [c]	0.280	0.266	0.200

[a] Annual average LME tin price deflated by U.N. index of dollar price of exports of developed countries, adjusted for changes in the £/$ exchange rate.

[b] Total revenues were discounted back to 1956, using a 5% real discount rate.

[c] Trend estimated for each simulation by ordinary least squares in semi-log form, 1956–73.

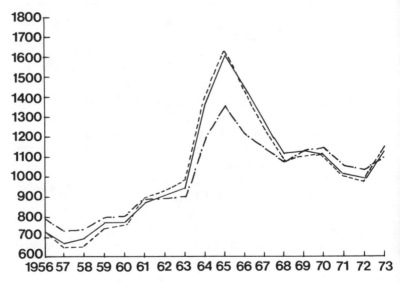

Fig. 6-A. Simulated behavior of deflated LME price (1963 U.K. £ per metric ton)

Legend: 1) If there were no buffer stock intervention: – – – –
2) If only the ITC buffer stock was used: ———
3) The actual historical data where both the GSA and ITC stockpiles were used: – . – . –

had primary responsibility for defending fairly high and unknown ceiling prices, whereas the ITA was engaged mainly in
defending fairly low but known floor prices. The effective band
between ceiling and floor prices was quite wide, perhaps ±20 to
25 percent around long-run trends, which is greater than usually
envisaged for commodity agreements.

To gain a better perspective on the requirements for a more
effective tin agreement than the ITA-GSA arrangement during
that period, it is useful to review another set of simulations.
They retain ITA export quotas as they were actually imposed
during 1956-74, but all stockpile activity must now be undertaken by the ITA itself. The ITA is assumed to have perfect
knowledge of long-term trend prices, which for the simulation
were calculated *ex post* by removing the GSA and ITA from the
market and then estimating trends using the resulting price
series. Even under these favorable circumstances, in order to
defend price bands as narrow as ±15 percent around trend
during that period, the ITA would have required a stock that
reached a maximum of at least 100,000 tons [25] for four consecu-
tive years. This figure is far in excess of what has been proposed
for tin and exceeds by a large margin the relative size proposed
for other metals.

It is almost certain that a commodity agreement of this magnitude could never have been negotiated. A rerun of history similar to the 1956-74 period would be very unfavorable indeed to
the ITA in the future. It is also clear from this that the Tin
Agreement cannot be taken as an encouraging example for
supporters of other commodity agreements, since it was never
really called upon to stabilize markets in the way they have in
mind.

Due to their longer-term unpredictability, the full stabilizing
potential of GSA sales has not been achieved. The guidelines
that determine the strategic objective in tin have been changed
several times. Most recently, in 1973 all but 40,500 long tons was
declared surplus and Congress authorized the sale of 50,000
tons. In 1976, the Ford administration reduced the strategic
target to 32,499, but the GSA had practically no remaining
authorization to sell out of the 170,000-ton surplus.[26] The Carter

administration suspended all transactions pending a reevalua-
tion of the guidelines. This study was completed only in October
1977,[27] with a reaffirmation for tin of the 32,499-ton Ford administration strategic target. Congress has yet (March 1979) to
authorize any sales, even though tin prices were well above
$7.00 per pound in New York. Thus, the United States now has
almost 170,000 long tons of surplus tin, markets are very tight,
and no sales are being made.

This erratic behavior, which is by no means restricted to the
examples set forth here, has only increased the uncertainty facing tin producers and stockists. Indeed, recent shortfalls in tin
production may owe a good deal to the natural but mistaken
belief that the GSA would continue to sell surplus stock during
periods of high prices.

IV. THE FIFTH AGREEMENT

In spite of an acrimonious first year,[28] objective conditions on
balance seem to favor significant improvements in the operation
of the ITA and its coordination with the GSA. Greater reliance
on the buffer-stock in place of export control, closer coordination of the GSA with the ITA, and generally more rational
economic decisions seem within reach if the major participants
in the agreement show a reasonable degree of flexibility.

A LARGER BUFFER STOCK?

Twenty thousand tons has again been shown to be woefully
inadequate for the tin buffer stock. That magnitude was neither
sufficient to defend floor prices in 1975-76 without recourse to
export controls nor to defend price ceilings in 1977. How much
larger should the buffer stock be?

The answer to this question cannot be given in a vacuum. It
depends critically upon the *goals* of the buffer stock, the economic structure of tin markets, and upon exogenous shocks—
fluctuations in aggregate economic activity and supply disturbances of various types. In the more technical literature, at least
three general types of goals have been used: (1) Operate the
buffer stock so as to maximize the *expected value* of the dis-

counted sum of consumer and producer surpluses over the life of the buffer stock. This involves the typical Neo-Classical criterion of economic efficiency, which takes individual preferences as the ultimate judge of any policy. It is doubtful that a consensus of Tin Council members would accept Neo-Classical economics as binding. (2) More generally, *any* objective function for the "decision-maker" can be specified, although for computational reasons it is convenient to limit the function to a quadratic. This permits the objective to depend not only upon the *expected value* of some variable(s) but also upon degree of fluctuation of these variables. Thus, in a Neo-Classical formulation the objective could be made a function both of *expected* consumer surplus and of its *variance*. Implementation of either of these general types of goals entails derivation of *optimal* buffer-stock rules for the particular market model and stochastic distribution of shocks. To my knowledge, this has never been done for tin.

The third, more realistic but less elegant approach is to make stabilization itself a target and to posit upper and lower bounds on prices within which prices are to be contained. Buffer stocks with such targets can be simulated using market models, either for particular historical periods or stochastically, that is, repeatedly drawing different values of the disturbance terms for each equation. This approach has thus far been the most common, and is the one drawn upon in this paper. It seems to reflect more closely actual ITA operations and is thus likely to obtain more realistic estimates. But it should be emphasized that they are not *optimal estimates* in the sense that the first two are.[29]

As stated in the previous section, at least 100,000 tons maximum would have been required during 1956-74 to achieve stabilization of ± 15 percent around (known) long-run trends, even admitting extensive export controls. The subperiod 1966-74 was much more stable for tin and hence would have required less buffer-stock activity. Even so, depending on the price bandwidth, stocks on the order of 40,000 (± 15 percent) to 70,000 (± 5 percent) tons would have had to be maintained.[30]

Unfortunately, these figures can serve as only rough guides for future requirements. The stockpile's size is very sensitive to the pattern of the exogenous shocks, which is virtually impossible to model satisfactorily. Thus, sporadic recurrence of massive sales of Chinese tin [31] would inflate the buffer stock considerably, as would a repetition of the business-cycle pattern of the late 1950s and 1960s—prolonged stagnation followed by prolonged expansion. On the other hand, stop-go business cycles of more frequent periodicity would tend to reduce the required buffer stock.[32] It is true that sensitivity analysis can yield upper and lower limits, but in tin these are likely to be far apart. In any case, sensitivity analysis was not performed for this study.

Another serious problem in using commodity model simulations as guides to buffer-stock needs is that none of the models with which I am familiar has satisfactorily specified private stocking behavior and the impact of a buffer stock upon it. Some substitution for private stocks seems inevitable—in the extreme when the private behavior is in fact socially optimal, the substitution would be one for one.[33]

One apparent sign that such substitution has been significant in tin has been the relative ineffectiveness of massive GSA-ITA sales in reducing prices to more reasonable levels in 1964-65 and 1973-74, and the rapidity with which the Tin Council's 20,000-ton buffer stock (about one month's world consumption) was exhausted in 1976. Seemingly, the *expectation* of GSA-ITA sales caused private stockists to reduce their speculative inventories. Later, when sales from public stocks were insufficient, private speculators retained tin in anticipation of higher prices. Further study on this issue is clearly warranted.

In spite of these qualifications to judging stockpile requirements, the current *potential* ITA buffer stock seems large enough if ceiling and floor prices are chosen carefully. The Netherlands, Belgium, the United Kingdom, Canada, France, and Denmark among the consumer nations are definitely committed to contribute to the buffer stock. The United States has announced publicly that it will contribute, and according to State Department officials, a Japanese contribution is also likely. Evaluated at current floor prices, these consumer contributions would add 12,000 to 13,000 to the 20,000 ton buffer-stock capacity. Furthermore, the ITC can borrow up to 75 percent on tin warehouse warrants in London,[34] which, assuming two such rounds of borrowing, could raise maxium buffer-stock capacity to 70,000-75,000 tons. Based on simulations of historical periods, this should be sufficient to achieve ±15 percent stabilization around trends without export controls except in the most exceptional circumstances. GSA support in times of shortage would probably not be required.

One problem, of course, is that 1977 has been a year of shortage and the buffer stock now is empty. Only as excess supply develops can the buffer stock be replenished. In the meantime, voluntary U.S. contributions of tin metal could help ease the situation as well as augment the purchasing power of the buffer stock in the future. Since the tin would only be sold at prices above the lower limit of the upper sector,[35] the United States would earn about the same profit on such contributions as it would selling directly to the market. If necessary, the United States should be prepared to contribute more than the 4,000 to 5,000 tons mentioned so far or, if this is impossible, at least to condition future GSA sales to the ITC ceiling price until the market tightness eases.

GSA SALES

Although the *potential* of the buffer stock is sufficient to maintain reasonable floor and ceilings without outside help, it is not at all clear that it is in the U.S. interest to use that full potential. Ultimately, the question of the size of the ITA buffer stock cannot be isolated from U.S. stockpile disposal policy. Under current administration targets, almost 170,000 tons of tin will be freed for other than strategic uses. Even if 60,000 tons additional were kept as an economic stockpile to guard against cartel-type action in tin, 110,000 tons would still be available for disposal. How should this be done? One way that would yield high sales revenues to the United States would be to dedicate a portion of this stockpile each year to defend ITC ceiling prices. The United States could then support export quotas as the primary mechanism to defend price floors. This would be not unlike the past arrangements except that now the tin stockpile would be more explicitly committed to implementing a stabilization policy. The buffer stock could remain fairly small, large enough so that really extreme quotas could be avoided, but certainly not large enough in and of itself to retain prices within the ceiling. Producing nations probably would oppose such an approach, since compared with the other alternatives it would impose larger adjustment burdens on them in periods of depressed prices, while the United States would rake in the profits from sales at high prices. Narrow economic advantage would probably vitiate the potential benefits anticipated from U.S. membership.

The other extreme would disassociate stockpile disposals entirely from the ITA's stabilization effort. This appears to be the way the U.S. government is leaning. No restrictions would be placed on GSA sales, although it would be understood[36] that the GSA would not "disrupt" the tin market with its activity. The old uncertainties would continue, particularly if congressional authorizations to sell were to be as irregular in the future as they have been in the past. Presumably, U.S. policy in the Tin Council would then advocate a larger buffer stock, thus acceding to the desires of tin producers who want to avoid the necessity of severe export quotas, but not one so large that it could almost certainly defend price ceilings without GSA aid. Thus, consumer contributions would be urged, but probably the United States would not find it in its interest to push for borrowing to expand the size of the buffer stock.

At very little additional cost, U.S. political gains from the agreement could be increased by two changes in the preceding scenario. First, the United States could agree explicitly not to sell below the lower bound of the upper sector of the price range. Second, Congress should vote an authorization to sell all surplus tin, so that the GSA would not be caught without authorization, as it is now, when prices are high.

This combination—somewhat larger buffer stock to satisfy producers and these minor amendments to GSA policy—would probably yield the most satisfactory compromise for the United States.

THE CHOICE OF CEILING AND FLOOR PRICES

The biggest source of conflict within the Tin Council is bound to be over the determination of floor and ceiling prices. Two related issues are involved: the *range* between floor and ceiling prices, the bandwidth, and the price *level* around which the floor and ceiling prices are centered.

The Bandwidth. Assuming the proper level of prices, the band-width is important in at least two ways. First, the narrower the bandwidth, the greater the direct social cost of any buffer-stock scheme. The stock's gross profit depends on selling at a higher average price than that at which it bought. Profits, then, are an offset to storage costs and the social opportunity cost of the capital tied up in the stockpile. If the band is too narrow, costs will exceed gross profits.[37]

Second, the narrower the bandwidth, the greater the inter-ference with the operation with private storage and future mar-kets. Very cursory interviews with copper tradesmen in New York in 1975 indicated that they could survive with ± 10 percent stabilization, but with some pressure. Typically, the ITA price bands have been wider than ± 10 percent.[38] In July 1977, ± 11 percent, on the low side, was chosen by the Tin Council.[39]

A somewhat wider bandwidth, say ± 15 percent seems desir-able. This would insure that the private market would not be seriously impaired in its shorter-term storage function. The costs of physical storage for tin are basically negligible, while an 8 percent real interest rate is almost certainly not too low for such operations. Tin prices under the ± 15 percent band would be free to rise 35 percent from floor to ceiling, a range that would permit profitable storage for perhaps two to three years from low to high prices. Working stocks would not be affected at all. On the other hand, truly effective defense of the ± 15 percent band would almost surely eliminate private storage for longer periods of time. This effect seems inevitable if the buffer stock is to bring substantially greater stability to tin than the private sector would provide.

Longer-term private storage could in principle be preserved were the ITC to rely on subsidies to private storage rather than on its own buffer stock. This could be accomplished by interven-tion in the forward market for tin, buying to stimulate private storage and selling to reduce the private stocks when appropri-ate. As a practical matter, this approach would seem to have little chance of adoption. More generally, it is not at all clear why longer-term private stocks are needed at all as long as the U.S. stockpile contains almost 170,000 tons of tin.

Price Levels. The importance of the level of the target price is obvious, at least for competitive industries. If the price is set too high, net accumulations by the buffer stock will occur, or export quotas will be required. If it is set too low, actual instability will be greater than that allowable by ceiling and floor prices, since the buffer stock will make insufficient purchases in slack markets and will be unable to defend its low ceiling prices when markets are slack.

Until 1974, ITC target prices usually lagged behind true long-run trends, which partly explains the relative ease with which floor prices were defended.[40] In the words of the former secretary of the International Tin Council, "The Council's decisions on changes in its price range were naturally often determined by political reasons, or more simply, by following with a time-lag the actual movement of prices in the market."[41] Since that time producers have pushed rather aggressively for higher support prices, and the issue of the criteria to be used in setting target prices has come to the fore.

At one extreme are the Bolivians. They delayed ratification of the Fifth Agreement for several months in order, among other reasons, to express their discontent with the way prices had been fixed in the past. The Bolivians are on average the highest-cost producers in the Tin Agreement. They argue that floor prices should be set sufficiently high to cover their costs of production, including taxes and royalties. Only in that way, they say, can a steady expansion of investment in tin production for the future be guaranteed.[42]

Application of this criterion in a competitive industry[43] would inevitably lead to oversupply, requiring the net accumulation of stocks and/or export quotas: even marginal producers would be guaranteed against losses in the most depressed markets. Average price over the cycle would be raised above market levels, and the ITA would act as a mild cartel arrangement for the transfer of resources.

In practice, it is not quite that simple, since the cost data supplied by tin producers are *average* costs for whole *industry* segments at the *actual* operating rates of the period in question. Presumably, marginal operations have higher costs than the averages suggest. How much higher is unclear, but presumably more accurate and detailed data could be developed.

The Bolivian criterion probably shoud be, and is being, opposed within the context of general U.S. commodity policy, since it would introduce an explicit element of resource transfer into a stabilization agreement. True, the total costs to the United States are likely to be minuscule from such a concession, but it might set a precedent for other commodity agreements.

Malaysia is the lowest-cost producer in the agreement.[44] While it has certainly pushed for higher floor prices, it is more concerned than Bolivia is about the impact high ceiling prices will have on materials substitution away from tin. Its criterion might be said to keep ceiling prices low enough so that the threshold of substitution in tinplate is avoided.[45]

In July 1977, floor and ceiling prices were approved that have the marks of a compromise between the Bolivian and Malaysian approaches, with the United States, Japan, and West Germany abstaining in disapproval. Five dollars per pound is the "magic substitution" price for tin[46] in that the steel companies will push ahead with blackplate development if they expect prices of that level to persist. Tin priced below $5.00 is not likely to bring substantial further substitution away from the metal. The ceiling price was fixed at $4.55 in Malaysia, which, adding transportation to the United States, is slightly below the $5.00 limit! The floor price, on the other hand, almost covers Bolivia's average costs (including duties) in underground mines during the second half of 1976 ($3.64 versus $3.81).[47] Bolivia did not quite get the price it wanted, but almost. Recognition of the cost-of-production, floor-price principle was not given, however.

In principle, the United States correctly supports the view that floor and ceiling prices should be based upon long-run equilibrium prices and that the goal of the ITA should be to stabilize prices around that equilibrium. One problem is that no one really knows what the equilibrium price is and how it will change. However, projections of the 1961-75 price trend, which was used in the simulations discussed above, suggest a price band centered on approximately $3.20[48] per pound in London instead of the $4.10 per pound in Malaysia fixed in July 1977. Even allowing for some underestimation of real trend price increases in recent years, these figures suggest that producers have probably been successful in using a temporary market shortage to increase the *price band above equilibrium levels.* This happened before, in 1966-68, in the wake of a severe tin shortage.[49] Given the pace of worldwide inflation, no great and lasting economic harm need arise from this high price band. The hard-line[5] countries will have to act more aggressively at future Tin Council meetings in order to prevent further (nominal) price increases. It should be noted, however, that frequent changes in real floor prices introduce one more element of uncertainty into tin markets.

This discussion illustrates the difficulties of negotiating prices in a commodity agreement, even one of relative unimportance such as the ITA. Cost-of-production, long-run equilibrium, and similar concepts are difficult to quantify and apply objectively. In the last analysis, concepts must be backed by the votes, and there is some danger that the United States will be caught in the dilemma either of supporting resource transfer through a stabilization agreement or, by opposing it, dissipating the political capital it had hoped to obtain from membership in the ITA.

V. THE TIN AGREEMENT AND U.S. POLICY

Tin and what happens with the ITA are not of great direct economic importance to the United States. In recent years, the United States has been importing 50,000 to 55,000 metric tons of tin. Each dollar per pound price change translates into about $110 million in the import bill. Thus, if the ITA took the path of higher and higher real prices supported by export controls, the direct impact on the U.S. import bill would be small. But unless the hard-line countries acquiesce, this will never happen within the Tin Agreement. Even if the ITA fell apart in disputes over prices and producers decided to form their own cartel, again highly unlikely, the United States would be only marginally injured. Tin could be eliminated entirely from the production of sanitary containers (40 percent of primary tin use) within a few years, and part of the surplus GSA stock could be used to ease the transition. The effect on employment would be negligible, and the same industry, steel, would be producing blackplate instead of tinplate.

On the other hand, even if the ITA succeeded gloriously in bringing price stability around long-run trends, only Bolivia and Malaysia would be major gainers. In the simulations discussed above, greater price stability is accompanied by more stable producer incomes, unlike the situation with many agricultural products. But for most countries, tin accounts for such a small share of foreign-exchange earnings that the impact on overall balance of payments is bound to be small.[51] For consumers, the benefits from greater stability would be virtually imperceptible, since tin accounts for such a minor portion of the costs of the final products in which it is contained.

The importance of the Tin Agreement to U.S. policy is mainly as a *symbol* of our willingness to cooperate in reasonable agreements run along "economically sound" principles. It remains to be seen what course the United States will in fact follow. It can try to make the ITA an *exemplary* symbol of what a stabilizing agreement can accomplish. The United States can be forthcoming in its contributions and forceful in its opposition to pricing policies it believes to be incorrect. On the other hand, the United States can continue as it has during the first year of its membership—dragging its feet both in contributing to the buffer stock and resolving once again its stockpile disposal policy, while at the same time refusing to alienate certain producing countries to voting against prices it believes to be wrong.

The argument in this paper is that U.S. policy should follow the first course: contribute to the buffer stock, heavily if necessary; coordinate tin disposal policy more directly with ITA goals; and use the veto power of the hard-line countries to establish realistic price bands. In the long run, this orientation should maximize the political benefits and yield some positive economic gains also.

APPENDIX

The governing body of the Tin Agreement is the International Tin Council, which, in turn, is divided into several committees. Major decisions, such as to change the price bands or to declare export controls, require a majority of *both* producer and consumer votes in the council (the distributive majority rule). Under the Fifth Agreement, the price bands are reviewed every six months. The day-to-day operations of the buffer stock are directed by the buffer-stock manager. The manager *must* buy or sell (subject to resource constraints) only when prices are outside the permissible bands. Otherwise he enjoys considerable discretion. The price band is divided into three sectors. In the lowest the manager is authorized to buy in order to prevent steep declines in the price of tin, while in the highest he may sell to prevent steep rises. Operations while prices are in the middle sector require the Tin Council's permission.

All the major producers and consumers of tin are members of the Tin Agreement except the People's Republic of China and Brazil.

NOTES

1. See Ashley C. Hewitt, Chief of the Industrial and Strategic Materials Division, U.S. Department of State, "Report to the Tin Industry," mimeographed, New York City, April 29, 1977, p. 15.

2. Estimates of trend prices can be very sensitive to the *years included,* the *currency used,* and the *functional form* chosen. Furthermore, there is no guarantee that the trend rate of price change will remain constant at the levels of the past.

3. Only Bolivia, among the major producers, exports tin concentrates in any quantity. However, Bolivia plans construction of smelters sufficient to refine all the country's ore by 1979.

4. On the limits of recycling see Keith L. Harris, "Tin" (Washington, D.C.: Bureau of the Mines [Reprint from Bulletin No. 667], 1975), p. 8.

5. According to Department of Commerce estimates, if recycling of 75 percent of municipal waste should be mandated by law, perhaps 8,000 additional tons of recycled tin could be obtained annually, an increase of 40 to 45 percent over the average production of secondary tin in recent years.

6. Source of all data: *Bureau of Mines Mineral Yearbook* (Washington, D.C.: Bureau of the Mines, 1975).

7. One-quarter-pound per base box instead of one-half pound.

8. All information supplied by George Fitch of the U.S. Department of Commerce.

9. See Wharton Econometric Forecasting Associates, Inc. (WEFA), *Forecasts and Analysis of the Tin Market,* report to the General Services Administration, Philadelphia, June, 1976.

10. Almost 30 percent in real U.S. dollars (deflated by the U.S. Wholesale Price Index) over the fifteen years from 1956-60 to 1971-75. Source: K. Takeuchi, "Tin," mimeographed, World Bank Discussion Draft, 1977.

11. For Bolivia, 46.6 percent, and for Malaysia, 43 percent. Source: "Export and Production Taxes on Tin," mimeographed, Washington, D.C., U.S. Department of Commerce, June 1977.

12. Malaysia has the declared goal of 30 percent Malay ownership in the "modern sector" by 1990.

13. Tin-in-concentrates is the standard for measuring production in terms of the tin content of tin concentrates. The latter contain about 70 percent tin in most countries.

14. The number of gravel pump operations has declined from 873 at the end of 1973 to 730 in May 1977. The Malayan Tin Bureau, *Tin News,* 26, no. 9 (August 15, 1977): 6.

15. Source: International Tin Council.

16. Blackplate would be used first in beverage cans, later in food containers. The basic problem is to perfect an economically satisfactory organic coating to take the place of tin. Considerable progress has already been made. See P. J. Van derVeen, D. C. Shah, G. A. Perfetti, and H. Darlington, "Coated Blackplate: Steel's Salvation in Beverage Cans?" *Modern Metals* (January 1977): 60-64.

17. See the appendix to this chapter for a brief description of the structure of the ITA. This section is based upon Gordon W. Smith and George R. Schink, "The International Tin Agreement: A Reassessment," *Economic Journal,* 86 (December 1976): 715-728. The interested reader is referred to that paper for greater detail, particularly as regards the simulations upon which the conclusions are based.

18. For documentation of this assertion, see Comptroller General of the United States, "The Fifth International Tin Agreement—Issues and Possible Implications," ID-76-64, Washington, D.C., August 30, 1976, pp. 9-12. See also William Fox, *Tin: The Working of a Commodity Agreement* (London: Mining Journal Books, 1974), pp. 323-353, for detailed account of U.S. stockpile disposal policy.

19. Smith and Schink, "The International Tin Agreement," p. 719.

20. Ibid., p. 720.

21. Hewitt, "Report to the Tin Industry," p. 7.

22. See Fox, *Tin,* pp. 372-373.

23. See the International Tin Council, *Annual Report for 1969-70,* p. 26, and its *Statistical Bulletin* (November-December 1973): 36-38; and Wharton EFA, *Forecasts and Analysis,* p. 58.

24. See Smith and Schink, "The International Tin Agreement," for details.

25. See ibid., pp. 723-724.

26. *Tin News,* 26, no. 7 (July 15, 1977): 4.

27. Ibid., no. 11 (November 15, 1977).

28. See Hewitt, "Report to the Tin Industry," and *The Wall Street Journal,* July 19, 1977, p. 10.

29. There is some doubt whether optimal rules exist when market participants respond rationally to the actions of the "decision maker." See F. E. Lydland and E. C. Prescott, "Rules Rather Than Discretion: The Inconsistency of Optimal Plans," *Journal of Political Economy* (June 1977): 473-492.

30. Smith and Schink, "The International Tin Agreement," p. 725.

31. As made by the Russians in the late 1950s.

32. The effect of business-cycle patterns on the requirements for a *copper* buffer stock were dramatic for the historical period 1956-74. The price of copper moves fairly closely with the level of industrial production in the Western countries. The years 1957-62 witnessed recession and relative stagnation in much of the West. Thus, the simulated copper buffer stock bought seven years in a row in support of prices. The period 1962-69 was the longest and steadiest upswing in U.S. economic history. The copper industry had not fully anticipated this expansion, and the buffer stock was able to unload much of its copper during periods of tight demand. The 1969-74 period was characterized by stop-go synchronized business cycles in the OECD, and no large stock accumulations were required. See Gordon W. Smith, "An Economic Evaluation of International Buffer Stocks for Copper," consultant's paper for the Department of State, Washington, D.C., October, 1975, pp. 32-33.

33. This requires that private stockists face the true social rate of discount, incorporate rational expectations into their decision, and maximize expected profits. See, for example, R. L. Gustafson, *Carryover Levels for Grains: A Method for Determining Amounts That Are Optimal Under Specified Conditions,* U.S. Department of Agriculture, Technical Bulletin No. 1178, 1958.

34. Bonded warehouses, such as those of the London Metals Exchange, issue warrants representing the quantity of tin-in-stock. These can then serve as collateral against loans, up to 75 percent of the market value of the tin.

35. The buffer-stock manager has *discretion* to sell in the upper sector, the lower limit of which is currently 6.7 percent below the

ceiling price. He must sell if the price is above the ceiling. *Tin News,* 26, no. 11 (August 15, 1977): 2.

36. As indeed it has been mandated by the laws governing such disposals.

37. In the absence of externalities, zero expected profit net of storage and capital costs will be a necessary but not sufficient condition for a socially optimal buffer stock.

38. See Smith and Schink, "The International Tin Agreement," p. 720.

39. Since the ITC could not defend its ceiling, the effective bandwidth was wider.

40. See Smith and Schink, "The International Tin Agreement," p. 720.

41. Fox, *Tin,* p. 391. This is the standard reference on the history of the Tin Agreement.

42. Based upon conversations with State and Treasury Department delegates to the July 1977 Tin Council meeting.

43. There is some question whether state enterprises in minerals can be approximated by the competitive profit-maximizing model. In copper, the model does not seem appropriate at this time for many LDCs that seem to be maximizing foreign-exchange receipts and face stiff borrowing limitations abroad.

44. In the second half of 1976, the costs of its dredging and gravel pump mines (including royalties) were 40 and 18 percent, respectively, below Bolivia's underground mine costs, according to data supplied to the Tin Council.

45. Particularly the move to blackplate.

46. According to Dennis Coursen of the Malayan Tin Bureau. Several government experts on tin expressed some skepticism about this number.

47. Source of cost data: International Tin Council.

48. London Metal Exchange (LME) prices were the target in the simulations. These prices in 1973 pounds were projected to 1977 using the 0.97 percent year growth rate. They were then inflated by the change in the United Kingdom cost of living 1973-77 and converted into dollars at a rate of $1.70 per pound sterling. Exchange changes and relative differences in inflation in different currencies make such calculations fairly rough. Even using a conversion rate of $2.20 per pound sterling, the target would be only $3.80 per pound of tin.

49. See Smith and Schink, "The International Tin Agreement," p. 720.

50. Hard-line countries include the United States, West Germany, and to a lesser extent Japan. They are not sympathetic to the use of commodity agreements to transfer resources to LDCs. They generally insist on hard economic rationales for price changes.

51. In 1970-72, tin accounted for 52 and 18 percent, respectively, of Bolivia's and Malaysia's export earnings. For no other country did the comparable figure reach 10 percent. G. W. Smith, "Commodity Agreements and the New International Economic Order," *Rice University Studies* (Fall 1975): 170.

Chapter 7

CURRENT PRICE AND INVESTMENT TRENDS IN THE WORLD ALUMINUM/BAUXITE MARKET: THEIR EFFECT ON THE U.S. ECONOMY

DOUGLAS W. WOODS

Aluminum Industry Analyst
Charles River Associates

Associate Professor of Economics
Worcester Polytechnic Institute

I. INTRODUCTION

This paper discusses recent investment and price trends in the world bauxite/aluminum industry that may potentially harm the U.S. economy. These trends may result in higher prices for imported raw materials, near-term shortages of aluminum supply, and increasing dependence on foreign sources for our vital supplies, not only of aluminum raw materials, but of the primary metal as well.

209

Fortunately, examination of current economic developments in the bauxite/aluminum industry reveals that major adverse impacts, though possible, are in fact unlikely to occur. For example, in the future the real cost of imported bauxite is more likely to decline than to increase, despite the recent formation of the International Bauxite Association (IBA), an organization of bauxite-exporting countries modeled along the lines of OPEC, and the sharp increase in bauxite prices that accompanied the IBA's formation. With respect to investment trends, analysis indicates that there will be no massive transfer of activity from the United States to other countries, although the U.S. producers' share of the domestic market may decline somewhat over the next few years. The United States remains a more economically desirable location for aluminum smelters and even alumina refineries than many other countries.[1] Three exceptions are Australia (as a location for refineries and possibly smelters), Canada (for aluminum smelters), and Brazil (for both refineries and smelters). We can expect to see continued expansion of the U.S. aluminum industry accompanied by rapid growth of Australian alumina imports. There may also be some increase in imports of primary aluminum from Canada and from developing countries in which smelters may be built as joint ventures of the major aluminum companies and foreign governments in order to take advantage of low-cost hydroelectric power or Middle Eastern petroleum. Despite such growth in other countries, U.S. aluminum capacity should continue to expand. The rate of growth will be slower than in the past, primarily because of a decline in the rate of growth of U.S. aluminum consumption. The final section of this chapter discusses the impact of the expected price and investment trends on the U.S. economy and recommends government policies to deal with them.

II. BAUXITE PRICE TRENDS

In March 1974 the International Bauxite Association was formed with seven members: Australia, Guinea, Guyana, Jamaica, Sierra Leone, Surinam, and Yugoslavia. As of November 1975 four new members had joined: the Dominican Republic,

Haiti, Ghana, and Indonesia. The importance of this development stems from the large proportions of world bauxite production and reserves controlled by the eleven member nations of the IBA. The IBA currently accounts for about 80 percent of world bauxite production outside China and the Soviet Union, and about 68 percent of world reserves. Virtually 100 percent of U.S. bauxite imports, or 90 percent of U.S. bauxite *requirements,* are supplied by the countries belonging to the IBA. Approximately 97 percent of U.S. alumina imports come from IBA members. The goals of the International Bauxite Association, as outlined in Article 3 of the bylaws adopted at the international conference of bauxite-producing countries that created the organization, are "to promote the orderly and rational development of the bauxite industry; and to secure from member countries fair and reasonable returns from the exploitation . . . of bauxite . . . bearing in mind the recognized interests of consumers." Following the creation of the IBA, most of the member countries greatly increased the export taxes they levy on bauxite. Jamaica, a leader in this movement, increased taxes from about $1.80 in 1973 to about $15 to $16 by 1976. The Jamaican tax is tied to the average realized price of aluminum in the United States by a complex formula and increases concomitantly with increases in the price of aluminum. The other IBA countries located in the Caribbean area levied bauxite export tax increases about equal in magnitude to Jamaica's. However, IBA countries in other parts of the world either increased taxes by smaller amounts, as in the case of Guinea, or scarcely at all, as in the case of Australia.

The IBA's goal of furthering the economic interests of its members was apparently almost immediately realized when most of the organization greatly increased taxes on their bauxite exports, and consequently raised the delivered cost of their bauxite to the importing countries. However, even though the IBA appears to have brought about this collective price action, the organization does not constitute a cartel in the sense that it is formation has enabled its members to obtain price increases that would not otherwise have been possible. In fact, each producing country's ability to raise export taxes and maintain them at the new level for a period lasting anywhere from three to eight years does not depend on similar action being taken simultaneously by the other producing countries. The Caribbean area producers such as Haiti, the Dominican Republic, Surinam, and Jamaica have been able to increase their taxes eightfold despite the fact that Australia, the world's largest producer and a country with bauxite reserves equal to sixty-seven years of world supply (at the 1976 rate of consumption) has not increased taxes at all. Guinea, which also has low-cost reserves equal to sixty-seven years of world supply, raised taxes to a level equal to only 40 percent of Jamaica's tax rate; and Brazil, the third largest reserve country, has refused either to join the IBA or to levy bauxite export taxes. Australia, Guinea, and Brazil possess collectively one half of the world's known bauxite reserves.

The ability of the high-tax Caribbean area bauxite-producing nations unilaterally to increase the price of their bauxite by approximately 150 percent over previous levels is caused by three factors. First, these countries have imposed bauxite-production minimums that compel companies to pay taxes on an output equal to the pretax level. As a consequence, companies cannot reduce their tax liabilities by gradually scaling down their rates of output. They cannot transfer production to low-cost sources simply by slowly reducing output in the high-tax countries while slowly expanding output elsewhere; rather, they must undertake quantum expansion of Australia or Brazilian output. In the case of Brazil, this means opening up entirely new mines, a process requiring five years on average. Consequently, it will take a long time before the aluminum companies will be in a position to eliminate their dependence on the Caribbean area producers, even if they strive vigorously to do so.

The variation in bauxite's chemical composition, which requires that alumina plants be designed specifically for each type of bauxite, also gives bauxite-producing countries considerable individual short-term monopoly power. Alumina plants in the United States that are currently geared to handle Jamaican and Surinam bauxite would have to undergo modification in order to accept Australian bauxite as a feed. This is potentially a very serious problem for the companies because even a small increase in operating costs at the alumina stage would be sufficient to eliminate the cost advantage of converting from Caribbean area bauxite to Australian or Brazilian bauxite. However, the specialized nature of the alumina plants may not be as serious a difficulty as is sometimes supposed, because the chemical composition of Australian and Brazilian ores is such that the modifications required by a plant designed to handle Jamaican bauxite will be minor. The increase in operating costs occasioned by switching to Australian or Brazilian ore may be considerably smaller than the savings that would result from the reduction in the after-tax cost of the bauxite.

Third, Jamaica and Surinam enjoy an advantage that may allow them to maintain their very high tax levels indefinitely regardless of the tax actions taken by the other producers. Approximately 14 percent of existing U.S. alumina capacity is actually located in Jamaica and Surinam. Until these plants are depreciated almost fully in a physical sense, it will not become economical to replace them with refineries located in Australia or the United States that would be supplied by Australian or Brazilian bauxite. If the present rapid rate of inflation in capital equipment costs continues, the replacement of these refineries by new ones located outside the high-tax countries may never be economically feasible. It generally makes sense to repair and replace individual components of refineries as they wear out rather than to retire an entire plant. Given a continuation of the present bauxite export tax structure, the companies have an incentive to defer replacement of individual components wherever possible until it becomes economical to replace all components simultaneously by building a new refinery elsewhere. Unfortunately, because of the interdependent nature of an alumina refinery's components, the capacity of the companies to defer replacement of any one component is very limited. Moreover, rapid escalation in replacement costs mitigates against this strategy by imposing a cost penalty on deferred replacement and widening the investment cost differential between a new plant and a newly overhauled old plant.

As presently constituted, the production minimums imposed by the Caribbean area IBA countries will prevent aluminum companies from scaling back bauxite output to the rate required to supply the alumina plants located in these countries. A company with an alumina refinery in a high-tax IBA country will not be able to abandon bauxite mining there without also abandoning its refinery. To determine whether to cease production, a company will compare the total costs of producing alumina in the United States using bauxite from a low-tax country with the variable cost of operating its present refinery in the high-tax country, plus the difference in the cost of bauxite mined there but shipped to the United States for refining and that of the same quantity of bauxite delivered to the United States from a low-tax country. If the refinery in the high-tax country is old, obsolete, and relatively inefficient and absorbs only a small proportion of the bauxite produced to meet the minimums, then the company may be prepared to abandon it in order to obtain bauxite from a low-tax source. On the other hand, if the refinery is efficient and absorbs a large proportion of the bauxite-production minimum, then the company may have no choice but to continue production in the high-tax country, especially if the capital costs of alumina refineries are rising in relation to their variable costs. Depending on what happens over time to the bauxite taxes, the physical condition of the refinery, and its efficiency relative to new plants and to the capital costs of refineries, this situation could last indefinitely.

It is important to recognize that the economic advantage the host country is exploiting derives from the long-run fixed nature of the investment in an alumina refinery located within its borders rather than from the bauxite resource itself. There would appear to be little of an economic nature to prevent any country from appropriating through taxes the quasi-rents of any long-lived plants built by foreign firms—other than the effect the tax would have on foreign investment in the future. Due to the overriding importance of bauxite to the economies of the high-tax Caribbean area bauxite nations, this consideration is outweighed by the export tax benefits. Indeed their tax policies would appear to be rational in terms of their own self-interests even if the high taxes result in a cessation of investment and production growth in their bauxite industries.

Perhaps the best hope the alumina companies have for escaping from this situation is to sell their refineries in the high-tax countries to the governments themselves, provided that a price could be agreed upon that would be fully compensatory, given the cost of replacing these refineries elsewhere. The governments of the producing countries are typically interested in acquiring ownership of both the bauxite deposits and the alumina refineries located within their borders.

The sunk nature of a portion of the investment in the bauxite mines and the rapid inflation in mining capital costs confers a protection on all existing producers similar in nature to the sunk investment of the alumina refineries, but on a much smaller scale, as is noted below.

Without the special factors mentioned above, Jamaica and the other high-tax Caribbean producers would not be able to maintain their present tax rates for very long because of the very substantial discrepancy between the delivered costs of their bauxite and the delivered costs from other sources such as Australia, Brazil, and Guinea.[2] As the relative costs of obtaining bauxite from alternative sources is central to an analysis of the role of the IBA in the bauxite market, these costs will be discussed in some detail.

It is very difficult to make precise estimates of the cost of mining and shipping bauxite from the various producing nations to the United States because information about several of the factors that cause costs to vary among locations is unavailable. For example, data are not easily obtainable on the stripping ratio of the deposits currently being mined, and this factor can cause costs to vary greatly. However, in practice the cost variations among mines due to the differences in the stripping ratio are typically no more than 25 percent. Another major determinant of bauxite-mining costs is the amount of capital required to develop and operate the mine. Capital requirements also tend to vary substantially from location to location, with the more remote sites being more costly than those located in developed areas. Finally, inland transfer costs are extremely difficult to determine with any degree of the precision, and at some locations they can be quite large.

Ore grade is a major factor in determining the relative cost of bauxite from different deposits. A recent Charles River Associates (CRA) study estimated the cost of producing bauxite at various locations throughout the world based on ore grade relative to Jamaican ore grade and published estimates of the cost of producing bauxite in Jamaica.[3] Because these cost estimates did not take into account possible differences due to any of the cost determinants mentioned above, except ore grade, they must be regarded as indicative rather than conclusive. However, the CRA cost figures are reasonably close to those obtained from other sources, principally the Commodity Research Unit (CRU) report to the Overseas Private Investment Corporation and several feasibility studies. All sources indicate that bauxite from Jamaica, Haiti, and the Dominican Republic is now overpriced relative not only to Australian bauxite but to bauxite from Brazil and probably Guinea as well. Bauxite from Surinam is also probably expensive relative to bauxite from the low-cost sources, but it appears to be not as overpriced as that from Jamaica.

The CRA estimates of the 1976 U.S. delivered cost of bauxite, including export taxes from the major producing nations are presented in Table 7.1. The cost estimates in Table 7.1 do not reflect the cost advantage of bauxite from Surinam and Guinea because they are 100 percent trihydrate rather than a mixture of trihydrate and monohydrate, like Australian, Brazilian, and Jamaican bauxite. It may cost as much as $3 to $4 less to refine a metric ton of pure trihydrate bauxite than it does to refine a similar amount of Jamaican bauxite. If $3 is subtracted from the figures given for Surinam and Guinea, then it can be seen that bauxite from Surinam is substantially more competitive than that from Jamaica, and, of course, the cost advantage of bauxite from Guinea over that of the Caribbean area producers is significantly widened.

The additional capital costs involved in opening a new mine or expanding an existing mine are not included in any of the cost figures mentioned above, except those given for Boké, Guinea, the Trombetus River in Brazil, all Australian deposits, and Cameroon. The additional annualized capital costs amount to at least $3.50 to $4.50 per ton at 1976 prices.

The countries with the lowest-cost figures in Table 7.1 are also those with the largest reserves: Australia and Guinea each have 4.5 billion tons and Brazil has 2.5 billion tons, as compared with Jamaica's 1.1 billion tons and Surinam's 600,000 tons. Obviously, the potential supplies of low-cost bauxite are more than ample to meet the growth of consumption and if necessary to supplant output from the high-cost producers.

Given the present bauxite cost and reserve situation, high-tax countries like Jamaica and Surinam can expect to lose substantial market shares over the next few years as companies begin to obtain all of the bauxite needed to meet growing demand from other sources. This factor alone will not be sufficient, however, to induce the high-tax countries to cut their tax rates. These countries are doubtless aware that output from Australia, Brazil, and Guinea would probably have grown more rapidly than output from the Caribbean area even in the absence of the massive tax increases, simply because of the enormous reserves of high-quality bauxite available in the low-tax countries.

At the first meeting of the IBA on November 7, 1974, it was decided in principle to establish a uniform price policy for bauxite among the member countries. A task force was set up to study the problem and to produce a recommendation on pricing policy for the association. IBA staff members are currently collecting information on bauxite-mining costs, reserves, and ore quality around the world to be used as the basis for establishing a uniform price system. Obviously if the IBA succeeds in this endeavor, the bauxite price situation will be radically altered and pressure on the present high-tax countries to lower their taxes will be removed. These countries could then expect to share in the growth of the bauxite market to the same extent that they would have had they not increased taxes at all. It is entirely possible that if the IBA uniform price policy were made a reality, the members of the IBA would increase their taxes still further—possibly to the limit set by the cost of refining the abundant nonbauxitic ores of the United States. Based on the most recently published studies by the Bureau of Mines, which looked into these processes extensively, the delivered cost of bauxite in the United States would have to rise to about $43 per ton before the cheapest nonbauxitic ores would become com-

TABLE 7.1

BAUXITE RESERVES, TAXES, AND DELIVERED COSTS ADJUSTED FOR ORE GRADE OF MAJOR IBA MEMBERS AND POTENTIAL NEW SUPPLIERS OF BAUXITE

Country	Reserves (Years World Supply at 1976 Consumption Rate)	1976 U.S. Delivered Cost/ Metric Ton (Adjusted for Ore Grade) [a]	Taxes/Dry Long Tons (5% Moisture) at a Realized Price of $.44/lb. for Aluminum	Sum of Cost and Taxes
IBA Members				
Jamaica	14.9	12.86	16.9	29.76
Guyana	2.2	15.05	–	–
Surinam	7.4	15.39	14.85	30.24
Dominican Republic and Haiti	1.1	14.96	16.95	31.91
Guinea:				
Bade-Konkouré	67	18.42	8.00	26.42
Boké		18.61 [a]	8.00	26.61
Ghana	4.8	12.99–21.40	N.A.	N.A.
Sierra Leone	1.8	18.60	N.A.	N.A.
Australia:		*Contained in Alumina* [b]		
Western Australia		20.07	0 [b]	23.07
Gove	67	15.67	0	19.17
Weipa		15.23	0.25	18.98

Potential New Sources

Brazil:

Trombetus River	37.2	20.56 [a]	2.00 [c]	22.56
Pocas de Caldos and Serro		15.85	2.00 [c]	17.85
Cameroon	11.2 [e]	22.04 [a,d]	2.00 [c]	24.04

SOURCE: CRA computations based on bauxite deposit characteristics as reported in *Bauxite Reserves and Potential Aluminum Resources of the World*, U.S.G.S. Bulletin 1228 (1967) by Sam H. Patterson, on shipping rates quoted in *Shipping Statistics and Economics* (London: H. P. Drewy). and on reports in the metal trade bulletins.

[a] The delivered cost figures for Cameroon and the Trombetus River, Brazil, and all Australian deposits include an additional $4.00 in annualized capital costs above current Jamaican capital costs to cover the added capital costs that would be encountered in developing mines in these areas. For Boke, Guinea includes an additional $3.00

[b] Australian cost and tax estimates assume shipment to the United States after refining to alumina. Shipping bauxite rather than alumina would add about $6.00 to the costs.

[c] Conjectural.

[d] Plus additional costs for inland transportation, which may be as high as $13.50 per ton.

[e] Bauxite reserve estimates were obtained from the Bureau of Mines. *Mineral Commodities Data Summaries*, 1976 and from Horace Kuntz of the Bureau of Mines. The years of world supply were calculated by dividing the reserves estimates by the 1976 free world bauxite production rate of 67.2 million tons.

petitive, assuming an energy cost of $2 per million Btu's. If the price of energy is only $1 per million Btu's, then the nonbauxitic ores would be competitive at a bauxite price of about $32 per ton.

However, more recent studies have been performed jointly by the Bureau of Mines and the U.S. aluminum industry. These studies indicate that at an energy price of $2 per million Btu's domestic clays are only marginally more expensive sources of alumina than are high-tax foreign bauxites. At an energy price of $1.50 per million Btu's the clays may well be competitive, and at $1.00 per million Btu's they almost certainly will be a less expensive source of alumina than will bauxite from high-tax countries. Further research to refine these cost figures has been undertaken by the Bureau of Mines and the aluminum industry.

Any analysis of future bauxite price trends must consider whether or not the IBA is likely to be successful in instituting its uniform price policy and thereby become a true cartel. To answer this question at least two sets of issues need to be addressed. First, what are the IBA's theoretical prospects for success, given that each of the bauxite-producing countries will determine its bauxite tax and price policies so as to maximize its narrow economic interests in the bauxite market? Second, are there larger economic or political considerations of concern to at least some of the major bauxite-producing countries that will dissuade them from engaging in the monopoly pricing of bauxite?

Space will not permit full exploration of all of the factors that will determine the IBA's ability to become a successful and stable cartel. But, in brief, it appears that if every bauxite-producing country were willing to pursue policies that would maximize their returns from bauxite, the IBA would be successful in emulating OPEC and establishing a uniform price system. To be successful, any cartel must satisfy three basic requirements. First, it must control a sufficiently large proportion of the market so that it faces a demand curve for its output that is not radically more elastic than the market demand. Second, members of the cartel must agree at least implicitly on how their market shares will be determined or the profits obtained by their successful price collusion divided. Lack of agreement inevitably means that competition will occur among the cartel members and that pricing agreements, if established, will ultimately collapse. Third, the cartel must successfully discourage its members from secretly violating established agreements on market share or pricing.

Theoretically, the IBA should be able to satisfy each of these requirements. Its membership comprises most of the major bauxite producers. Brazil is the only very large reserve country outside the IBA that may enter into major production soon, and there is no reason why Brazil or other large reserve countries of future significance such as Cameroon would not eventually find it in their interests to belong to the IBA and to follow its price policies provided that a suitable solution can be found to the second cartel problem—that of agreeing upon mutually acceptable market shares. New producing countries such as Brazil definitely will not accept parity in pricing until their production has increased many times over its present level. A natural solution to the problem of determining mutually acceptable market shares is to bring about at least rough equality among the producing countries in the ratio of production to reserves.[4] That policy would require countries such as Brazil, Australia, and Guinea, whose rates of production are low relative to their reserves, to set their taxes just far enough below the tax rates of the other countries to encourage the aluminum companies to expand mine output more rapidly in these large reserve areas. The tax rates of all producers would be adjusted so as to achieve uniform delivered prices except for these differentials.

Detection of cheating on a market share agreement would not seem to pose a major problem for the IBA. There is a high degree of vertical integration in the industry and companies tend to be active in a number of different countries; the considerable cross-flow of information among countries would make it difficult for one nation to conceal secret tax rebates or secret expansion plans from the others. Moreover, it is difficult to keep mine expansions secret, as they are reported widely in the trade literature and they require a great deal of time to bring to fruition.

It should not be concluded that the IBA would not encounter considerable difficulty in developing and maintaining a uniform price system at a high level of taxes, even if all of the bauxite-producing nations were willing in principle to accept that policy as a long-term goal. However, it does appear that the IBA's prospects for success would be reasonably good.

The IBA's ability to become a successful cartel given that its members are prepared to exploit their collective monopoly position is more of potential than of *actual* current relevance. With each passing year since the IBA's formation, it becomes increasily evident that at least one of the largest bauxite producers, Australia, is unprepared to cooperate in monopoly pricing, not because a suitable agreement that would maximize its income from bauxite could not be reached, but because its bauxite tax policies must be established in the context of a wide range of other economic and political interests. Australia is not a low-income Third World country but rather an industrialized nation with strong cultural and defensive links to the West. Both Australia and Brazil are countries with a wide range of economic interests and development plans in which bauxite plays a relatively small role. Australia's refusal thus far to increase bauxite taxes is not consistent with a desire on her part to maximize bauxite revenues by acting as a Stackelberg output leader (a possibility suggested by Pindyck) [5] or by increasing her market share to a level equal to her share of world reserves without undermining the competitive position of the high-tax countries and forcing a general reduction in prices. Either of these strategies would require Australia to increase bauxite taxes substantially in order to narrow the price differential between her bauxite and that from the Caribbean area.

Despite the IBA's efforts to institute a uniform price policy, there has been little change in taxes since the original round of tax increases in 1974. Both Australia and Brazil have yet to take any tax action—except for the minor increase to $1 per ton in the state of Queensland in 1974. An increase in the tax rate previously scheduled by Jamaica for 1977 has apparently been rescinded, and in fact there may have been a small decrease. It appears likely that the IBA will not be successful, at least in the short to intermediate term, in instituting a uniform price system for bauxite among its member countries or in bringing Brazil into the IBA and into conformity with such a policy. Consequently, the availability of bauxite at much lower prices from alternative sources will continue to exert considerable competitive pressure on the high-tax countries. Their ability to withstand this pressure without being forced to reduce their taxes to narrow the differential between their prices and the prices of alternative sources of supply depends largely on the importance of companies' sunk investments in alumina refineries within their borders. That protection applies only to Jamaica and Surinam. Guyana, another major Caribbean area producer with large alumina refineries, owns 100 percent of these refineries, having nationalized them in 1974 and 1975. It has been reported that since then Guyanan bauxite and alumina have come onto the market at prices well below the delivered cost of Jamaican exports even though Guyana passed a bauxite levy in 1974 that was very similar to Jamaica's. The price at which Guyanan bauxite is currently being sold is so low that the government would appear to be recovering revenues, net of cost, equal to only a small fraction of the bauxite levy passed in 1974. Over the next few years additional supply possibilities will open up as a result of the development of new mines in Brazil and the expansion of existing mines in Guinea and Australia. As that occurs, and the companies are able to contemplate leaving at least some of the high-tax countries, these countries will probably be forced to reduce their taxes. As a result, the average delivered price of bauxite in the United States probably will decline somewhat from its present level in real terms.

III. INVESTMENT TRENDS IN THE BAUXITE/ ALUMINUM INDUSTRY

The discussion of investment trends in the aluminum industry will focus on two issues. The first issue is whether the overall level of investment will be adequate to meet the future demand for aluminum. Costs have been rising rapidly in the aluminum industry due to the increase in bauxite taxes, rising energy prices, and rapid escalation in capital requirements. The lack of a concomitant rapid rise in aluminum prices has resulted in price/cost margins that are near their historic lows. Consequently there is some concern as to whether prices will be adequate in the future to draw forth the large amounts of capital required to expand capacity in line with the growth in demand. The second issue of major importance concerns the geographic distribution of investment in the aluminum industry at the alumina and aluminum stages of production. Will there be significant changes in the location of alumina-refining and aluminum-smelting capacity within the United States or worldwide? Will these changes lead to an increase in U.S. dependence on foreign supplies of alumina and aluminum?

The first issue that will be examined is the adequacy of the overall level of investment in alumina and aluminum facilities. The aluminum industry appears to be characterized by a virtually perfectly horizontal or elastic long-run supply curve. In the long run, capacity and output can expand almost indefinitely to meet demand without incurring increased real costs, given constant input prices. The rate of growth in world aluminum capacity from year to year is determined by the relationship between the transactions price of aluminum and the cost of production, and by the world capacity utilization ratio—primary aluminum consumption divided by primary capacity. Price, in turn, can be explained quite satisfactorily as a function of the cost of production and the capacity utilization ratio. Primary aluminum prices have historically fluctuated in response to changes in capacity utilization around a long-run average level in relation to cost that appears to have stayed quite constant over time.

Price and capacity are interdependent, and both depend on cost. As the consumption of primary aluminum grows relative to capacity, price increases and producers increase capacity. Rising prices and an increased capacity utilization ratio eventually elicit sufficient new investment in the industry to raise capacity to a level adequate to meet the growth in consumption. Unless there is some reason to expect that this process will cease to function in the future, it seems likely that further increases in the real price will occur if they are required to justify additional investment. However, if the U.S. aluminum companies were to anticipate a return to the type of price controls imposed on the industry in 1973, they might be reluctant to expand capacity. They would be concerned that by the time new capacity came onstream their prices might be frozen at a level below that required to return profits on their investments. This concern would have to be balanced against the knowledge that failure to expand while other companies (perhaps foreign) did so would mean loss of market share.

The price/cost capacity relationships described above have been embodied in an econometric model of the world aluminum market developed by Charles River Associates. This model was estimated over a data base ending in 1973; it was used in 1975 to forecast conditions in the aluminum market from 1974 through 1990. The forecast of world aluminum consumption by country, world scrap supply, aluminum prices, and aluminum production generated by this model for the years 1974, 1975, and 1976 compare quite closely with the actual values of those variables.

In August 1977 the forecasts for 1977 to 1990 were updated using the most recent values of the exogenous variables then available. Free world primary-aluminum-production capacity for the years 1977 to 1980 was treated as exogenous in preparing the new forecasts. The estimates of 1977 to 1980 capacity used in the model were those published by the International Primary Aluminum Institute (IPAI). The IPAI forecasts free world primary-aluminum-production capacity to grow from 1977 to 1980 at less than half the normal historical rate of growth. As a result the free world capacity utilization ratio is projected by the CRA model to rise. However, the increase is expected to be small—from 0.85 to 0.87. Capacity will remain adequate to meet demand, worldwide. The increase in capacity utilization is held down by a slower than normal growth in world consumption that stems from the delayed effect of the sharp rise in the real price of aluminum from 1974 to 1977 and the continued increase in the real transactions price from 1977 to 1980. Aluminum consumers respond to price changes with varying degrees of speed, in many cases taking as long as four or five years to adjust fully. Consequently, the impact of a price change on consumption is felt for several years following the change. The ability of U.S. capacity to meet demand from now to 1980 is particularly dependent on this delayed price effect. If the actual price elasticities of U.S. demand and secondary supply are substantially less than the estimates employed in the CRA model, then U.S. demand for primary aluminum will exceed domestic supply, and additional imports will be needed to fill the gap.

Let us now turn our attention to the question of where the additional investment will take place around the world. There are two ways to approach this issue. First, actual trends in investment in aluminum smelters and alumina refineries, and reported capacity expansion plans will be examined to determine whether there is any discernible tendency for actual and planned capacity to grow more rapidly relative to consumption in the less developed countries or Western Europe than in the United States. The economics of smelter and refinery location will then be analyzed to determine whether some areas of the world have become much more attractive sites than others, indicating a potential change in the pattern of capacity expansion that has occurred to date.

Figures on actual and planned capacity are reported regularly by the IPAI, an organization comprising the bulk of the world's aluminum companies. The American Bureau of Metal Statistics also reports capacity figures for virtually all countries of the world, and capacity expansion plans are reviewed annually in *Engineering and Mining Journal (E/MJ)* and other trade journals. Capacity expansion plans reported by *E/MJ* in January 1977 and January 1978 indicate that the amount of new smelter and refinery capacity being planned for the LDCs is about equal to that being planned for construction in the developed countries. As the current level of capacity is much smaller in the LDCs, this obviously implies a much more rapid rate of expansion in smelter and refinery capacity in the underdeveloped countries than in the industrialized nations. Of course, in the past, actual expansions have rarely worked out exactly as predicted in *E/MJ* because many of the reported expansions are in the early planning stages. The estimates of future capacity presented in the IPAI reports are the sum of current capacity plus all capacity additions under construction and scheduled for completion within three years of the date of the report. The IPAI figures indicate a considerably slower rate of capacity expansion than does the *E/MJ* annual capacity review. However, they do confirm that smelter capacity will likely grow somewhat more rapidly in Africa and Latin America than in either North America or Europe. Up to 1976, U.S. capacity growth has kept pace with production and consumption. However, both *E/MJ* and IPAI project a slower rate of growth in U.S. capacity through 1980 than is expected to occur in consumption. Industry sources confirm that U.S. aluminum capacity will increase by no more than 3 percent during the next three years, an annual rate of 1 percent. According to announced expansion plans reported by *E/MJ*, Canadian capacity will also grow substantially more rapidly than U.S. capacity.

In summary, the investment plans reported to date indicate that U.S. producers may lose a portion of their market share to Canadian producers and possibly to new smelters located in the LDCs. However, this information is far from conclusive.

Let us now turn to an examination of the economics of smelter and refinery location. Locational economics must be considered from the point of view of the potential investors. With respect to the aluminum industry, the investors can be divided into two basic categories: the aluminum companies, especially the major producers; and national governments, principally the governments of LDCs. The economic advantages and disadvantages of various locations around the world as sites for aluminum smelters and refineries will be considered first from the standpoint of the aluminum companies.

There are three major inputs into production of primary aluminum: alumina, electric power, and capital. In 1976 these inputs cost, respectively, $360, 380, and $203 per ton of aluminum for an efficient new smelter located in the Tennessee Valley area of the southeastern United States and supplied by Australian alumina. The remaining inputs cost about $312, for a total production cost of $1,255 per ton. Labor appears to account for slightly more than one third of the miscellaneous expenses; and various materials and supplies, local taxes, and insurance account for the rest. These figures were presented in a recent CRA report and are based on published cost estimates available from a variety of sources.[6] They assume that electric power is priced at 25 mills per kilowatt-hour and that alumina costs $187 per metric ton. The capital cost figure assumes that the investment required per metric ton of aluminum in the United States is about $1,730. This figure is consistent both with the capital requirements reported in the *E/MJ* survey of expansion plans and with the other sources of cost information alluded to above, principally reports by Arthur D. Little (ADL) and Stewart Spector of Oppenheimer. To calculate the annualized capital costs, capital requirements per ton were multiplied by a capital recovery factor of 12 percent, which was computed using a *real* before-tax required rate of return (weighted average cost of debt and equity capital) of 10 percent and an investment life of twenty years.[7] The alumina cost is equal to the current operating cost of existing refineries plus the annualized capital cost of a new alumina plant costing $450 per ton of capacity.

The cost items that are most sensitive to plant location are the major ones: alumina, power, and capital. Obviously, labor costs per hour vary considerably around the world. However, the best information available indicates that variations in wages tend to be largely offset by variations in manning rates, that is, labor productivity. Consequently, it is reasonable to assume that labor costs in the aluminum industry are pretty much the same everywhere. Two major exceptions to this rule are the new smelter in Bahrain, which has been plagued with labor problems, and Brazil, where skilled labor is available at low wage rates.

It is possible to determine at least approximately how the major cost items will vary from one location to another in different parts of the world. The important issue is whether foreign sites will have production-cost advantages to offset the additional costs of transporting aluminum to the Midwest where the bulk of this country's aluminum fabrication plants are located. Only in that event is there any possibility of a movement abroad of the U.S. aluminum smelting industry. The Southeast

appears to be the most favorable domestic site for new aluminum smelters.[8]

The five areas outside the United States that appear to be the
best potential sites for aluminum smelters are the Middle East,
using bauxite from Australia or West Africa and Middle Eastern
petroleum to generate electricity; West Africa, using local hydroelectric power and alumina from Guinea; Brazil or the Caribbean, using local hydroelectric power and Brazilian alumina;
Australia, using Australian alumina and thermoelectric power
generated by burning coal; and Canada, using Australian or
Brazilian alumina and Canadian hydroelectric power. The costs
of producing aluminum at each of these locations and shipping
it to the United States is presented in Table 7.2. The notes at the
bottom of the table explain how the cost estimates were
computed.

Aluminum costs at these foreign locations (except Australia)
range from about $50 to $125 less than the previous estimate of
the production cost of the Tennessee Valley plus $12 in trans-
portation—$1,267. The sum of higher capital costs and addi-
tional transportation costs abroad cancels out about half of the
savings in energy, resulting in a delivered cost of primary aluminum from foreign locations that is about 10 percent less than
that produced in the southeastern United States.

Up to this point there has been no consideration of the appropriate rate of return to use in determining the annual capital
costs of aluminum smelters at various locations. It has been
implicitly assumed that the 10 percent before-tax U.S. cost of
capital is an appropriate interest rate for investments in foreign
smelters. However, it is obvious that the companies, at least, will
assign a substantial risk factor to any investment in a developing
Third World nation. This would have been true even prior to the
formation of the IBA and the round of massive tax increases by
Jamaica. Today, given those developments, the degree of risk
perceived by the companies will be quite large. As noted previously, it is primarily the companies' sunk investments in alumina refineries in Jamaica and Surinam that confer on those
countries the economic leverage that may enable them to main-

TABLE 7.2

ANNUAL COSTS PER METRIC TON OF PRIMARY ALUMINUM ASSUMING NO ALLOWANCE FOR DIFFERENCES IN RISK

	United States (SE)	Middle East	West Africa	Brazil	Australia	Canada
			Country/Area			
Electricity [a]	$380	$170	$170	$170	$380	$170
Capital (at a 10% rate of return before tax) [b]	203	264	264	264	250	250
Alumina [c]	360	360	374	349	336	380 (360 in BC)
Transportation [d]	12	60	60	60	80	20 (60 from BC)
Tariff		22	22	22	22	22
Miscellaneous [e]	312	312	312	262	312	312
Total	1,267	1,188	1,202	1,127	1,380	1,154 (1,174 in BC)

[a] The electricity cost figures assume that a smelter will pay 10 mills per Kwh for hydroelectric power or electricity generated in the Middle East using local petroleum and 25 mills per kwh for thermoelectric power from plants burning inexpensive U.S. midwestern or Australian coal.

[b] Annualized capital costs per ton are based on investment requirements per ton in 1976 dollars of $1,730 in the United States, $2,150 in Canada and Australia, and $2,230 in the rest of the world. These are averages of the costs of planned expansions reported in the metals journals. They agree closely with estimates obtained from other sources. No allowance was made for variations among the alternative locations in the required rate of return due to risk.

c In computing alumina costs it was assumed that the only inputs into alumina production that vary in cost with location are bauxite and transportation. This is a conservative assumption. In reality the other inputs are likely to be generally more expensive abroad than in the United States. The cost of alumina in Australia is approximately $174 per metric ton (1976 dollars). The cost of transporting Australian alumina to the United States, western Canada, or the Middle East is about $12 per ton. Alumina costs $7 to $20 more per ton in Brazil and Guinea than in Australia due to higher bauxite prices. About 1.93 tons of alumina are required to produce a ton of aluminum.

d Transport costs from foreign locations are inclusive of the cost of shipping aluminum from the ports of entry to the Midwest—about $13 to $14—and are based on charges reported on ocean shipments of aluminum from Surinam and Norway to the United States in 1975 and 1976.

e Miscellaneous expenses are assumed to be the same at all locations, except for a 50 percent saving in the cost of labor in Brazil.

tain their taxes at current levels for many years. In the long run, these taxes amount to the expropriation of a portion of the quasi-rents the companies earn on their investments in the alumina refineries. Jamaica took her tax action unilaterally, in violation of existing contracts with the companies. Although the companies protested the Jamaican action to the International Center for the Settlement of Investment Disputes (ICSID), that organization has to date been unable to help them obtain tax relief. These developments are likely to make the aluminum companies very wary of future investments in either alumina refineries or aluminum smelters in bauxite-producing countries that may emulate the Jamaican action. Investments in smelters and refineries are very long-lived, almost indefinite, and this increases the companies' need for safety and security. The absolute risk involved with a smelter investment, of course, is much greater than that involved with a refinery because of the much larger amounts of capital required. A host government could levy an export tax as high as $200 per ton before it would become worthwhile for an aluminum company to abandon a smelter located in that country. If the ICSID treaty cannot provide protection against that type of action, the companies will obviously be reluctant to invest in aluminum smelters in developing nations.

It is very difficult to estimate the kind of interest-rate premium that companies might require to induce them to make investments in LDCs. They may very well want a rate of return of 50 percent or more above the rate obtained in the United States. That would be high enough to eliminate the cost advantage of the foreign locations, increasing the annualized costs by $125 or more. In analyzing risky investments, business firms frequently give great weight to the payback or discounted payback period. The latter is the time required to recover the initial capital outlay plus the cost of capital. If the aluminum companies required a discounted payback period of five years to provide them with adequate protection, that implies an internal rate of return of 26 percent, assuming a twenty-year life for their smelter or refinery, and a cost of capital of 10 percent. A discounted payback of ten years is equivalent to an internal rate of return of 15 percent.

The companies are not likely to insist upon a substantial risk premium on investments in either Australia or Canada—although there is some investment risk in Quebec, given the present political situation there. Though certainly unlikely, it is possible that Quebec will secede from the rest of Canada. Even if this does *not* occur, the efforts of the Quebec government to make French the business language of the province, if enforced against the aluminum companies, will unquestionably create significant managerial problems for them.

Available evidence indicates that smelter locations in Brazil or elsewhere in Latin America, West Africa, or the Middle East are at least marginally uneconomical vis-à-vissoutheastern United States for delivery to the U.S. market, largely because of the risk factor. An Australian location would also be uneconomical if energy costs were equal to those in the U.S. However, the cost of coal generated in some areas of Australila is substantially less than in the U.S. due to less stringent pollution abatement standards. Given power costs in the 10 mill range these locations would be competitive with U.S. domestic sites. Moreover, either eastern or western Canada would appear to be quite competitive, assuming satisfactory hydroelectric sites can be found and that their remoteness does not make capital costs prohibitive.

It should be noted that two new developments in smelter technology—the Aluminum Company of America (Alcoa) chloride process and titanium diboride cathodes—will significantly reduce electricity consumption in smelting, thus improving the cost position of domestic via-à-vis foreign sites. These new processes may become available commercially in about five to ten years.

The focus to this point has been on aluminum smelters. The situation with respect to the alumina refineries is both simpler to analyze and more difficult to resolve. Because alumina is a bulk commodity containing twice as much aluminum per unit of weight as does bauxite, there is a substantial transportation cost advantage to locating alumina refineries close to bauxite mines.

On the average, about 2.3 long dry tons of bauxite are required per long ton of alumina, and the transportation costs per ton of bauxite and alumina are approximately the same. Thus, the transport cost savings that arise from locating alumina refineries close to mines are equal to 1.3 times the cost of shipping bauxite. The latter is $10.00 to $12.00 per ton from Australia, $8.00 from Brazil, and $6.50 from Guinea. With the exception of Australia, where costs are about the same as in the United States, most of the potential alumina refinery locations abroad are likely to have somewhat higher fuel and labor costs than U.S. refineries. However, these differences will probably be relatively minor; thus, the desirability of locating alumina refineries in bauxite-producing countries depends on the difference between the transport cost savings realizable by doing so and whatever additional capital costs may be incurred. The capital requirements per ton for an alumina refinery constructed in the United States are currently (1976) about $450. Multiplying this investment by a capital recovery factor of 12 percent gives an annualized capital cost for alumina refining of about $54. Obviously, only a small percentage increase in capital costs would be sufficient to eliminate the transportation cost savings from foreign locations. Many of the potential alumina refinery sites abroad are in fairly remote areas and have substantially greater infrastructure requirements than plants located in the United States and in many areas of Australia. Consequently, the greater capital requirements per ton would be sufficient by themselves without any increase in the required rate of return to eliminate the transport cost advantage. But in fact, as has been pointed out above, the aluminum companies are certain to require a very substantial risk premium on any investment in an alumina refinery in a developing bauxite-producing country, making alumina refineries in all of the bauxite countries except Australia unattractive propositions. However, it is not clear that the aluminum companies will refuse to make such investments, despite their economic undesirability. Most bauxite-producing nations wish to achieve some degree of downstream integration in the aluminum industry by building up their domestic alumina refinery capacity. Aluminum companies are likely to come under pressure to build alumina plants in bauxite-producing countries as a condition of obtaining the bauxite. It is virtually impossible to predict what the outcome will be. It seems very probable that Australian alumina capacity will expand rapidly in the future because it is there that the transportation cost savings from locating the alumina plants close to the mines are at a maximum and the capital cost disadvantage is at a minimum. Beyond that it is very difficult to predict what will occur. It is conceivable that there will be a compromise in which some alumina refineries are constructed in bauxite-exporting countries in exchange for their permission to export bauxite to alumina refineries in the United States.

Until now the economics of aluminum smelter and alumina refinery location have been analyzed from the point of view of the aluminum companies. However, it is quite likely that future investments in either refineries or smelters in developing countries will be undertaken by the governments themselves, either in joint ventures with the aluminum companies or, in some cases, entirely on their own.

It is generally agreed that by contracting with a major aluminum producer, the government of a developing country can obtain the technology required to construct and operate a smelter or refinery. It is less clear whether a government-owned aluminum smelter could get sufficient help through a contract arrangement with an established producer to enable it to be run at top efficiency. This would require assistance from the aluminum company in training not only management but skilled workers. The enormous labor problems that have been experienced in the new aluminum smelter in Bahrain illustrate clearly that obtaining an adequate supply of skilled labor will often be one of the major problems confronting a new aluminum smelter operation in an underdeveloped country.

A second major problem a government-owned and -operated aluminum smelter will face is that of marketing its output. Most aluminum producers are integrated forward into aluminum fabrication. Consequently, the market available to an independent smelter consists largely of independent semifabricators, which, in the United States and Europe, account for only a relatively small portion of the total market.

The advantage the government of a bauxite-producing nation would possess over a private aluminum company in investing in aluminum smelters in that country is presumably a lower cost of capital due to the absence of any risk of nationalization or unfavorable tax action. The cost of capital a government would use in evaluating an aluminum smelter investment would probably be close to the international lending rate as established by such organizations as the World Bank. However, this rate is not a true cost of capital in the sense that if the borrower is prepared to pay that rate of interest, funds are guaranteed to be available. In fact, international lending organizations do not have sufficient capital to make all investments in developing countries that are profitable or earn a return greater than the rate of interest charged on the loan. If the government were to use a shadow price of capital, one that reflected capital's true scarcity, the return the government would require on an aluminum smelter would be much larger than the international lending rate, especially if the return included a risk premium large enough to compensate for the risks inherent in an aluminum smelter investment due to potential operating difficulties and problems in marketing the output.

The above discussion indicates why joint ventures involving both governments and companies are frequently proposed. Equity participation by a firm reduces the marketing and labor problems that would pose substantial risks for the government if it invested alone. Heavy financing from the government reduces the firm's exposure to expropriation. Both factors work to reduce the cost of capital. It should not necessarily be concluded, however, that the aluminum companies will aggressively seek participation in joint ventures. The arrangements have significant disadvantages from their standpoint. They lose full control over a vital stage in the highly integrated and interdependent flow of production from mining to semifabrication. By accepting partial ownership, they fail to secure all of the pure profits their dominant positions in the industry might in the long run enable them to earn. The key question is whether the determination of countries with large supplies of low-cost electric power to enter aluminum smelting and the competitive pressure exerted by the aluminum companies to participate in joint ventures. Are, for example, the Middle Eastern petroleum-exporting countries likely to move into aluminum smelting on a large scale, and if so will they be successful in persuading the aluminum companies to participate? After all, depending on what these states regard as the opportunity cost of their oil, they may view themselves as possessing virtually unlimited supplies of low-cost power. Many smelter projects have in fact been proposed for the Middle East over the last five years. However, many of these have apparently been abandoned or postponed. In appraising this trend, it is important to realize that the cost figures presented in Table 7.2 very probably understate Middle Eastern smelter costs. These figures do not include an allowance for higher labor costs such as those experienced by the plant in Bahrain, and in all likelihood they understate the capital costs as well. Inflation is rampant in the Middle Eastern petroleum-exporting countries and the costs of most capital investment projects have turned out to be both much higher than forecast and much higher than the costs of similar projects in other parts of the world.

My expectations with respect to future investment trends in the aluminum industry can be summarized briefly as follows. Investment will continue to be made in alumina refineries in Australia, and Australian refinery capacity will grow rapidly. Alumina refineries will also be constructed in Brazil and Guinea. There will be a substantial expansion of Brazilian smelter capacity and isolated examples of investment in aluminum smelters in other developing countries in various parts of the world. The latter will occur when cheap power and low-cost government financing are available and when the major aluminum companies can be induced to participate. But the aluminum companies will be reluctant to surrender a substantial portion of the U.S. market to foreign joint ventures. Therefore, I do not expect this to take place on a scale sufficient to alter radically the present balance in the United States between domestic aluminum production and imports from the LDCs.

However, it is quite possible that Canadian aluminum capacity will expand more rapidly than that of the United States and that Canadian exports to the United States will increase. The conclusion that domestic smelter capacity will continue to grow rests on the assumption that the siting difficulties currently facing electric power companies attempting to expand will not result in power shortages in the southeastern or midwestern United States that could compel the aluminum companies to build their new smelters abroad.

IV. BAUXITE/ALUMINUM PRICES AND INVESTMENT IN THE U.S. ECONOMY

By the early 1980s the average price of bauxite imported by the U.S. either directly or contained in alumina will have stabilized at a level approximately $6 to $7 greater (in constant 1976 dollars) than the level it would have reached without the 1974-75 round of tax increases. The price of bauxite should remain at this level in real terms for the next several years. In 1976 the United States imported about 20 million long tons of bauxite either as bauxite or in the form of alumina from the member countries of the IBA. These imports are expected to grow at the same rate as U.S. aluminum production and consumption, approximately 4.5 percent per annum. Through the 1980s and 1990s the average additional tax that will be paid on these imports will be about $6 in constant 1976 dollars; consequently, the present value of the total additional tax payments that will be made by U.S. aluminum companies to the bauxite-producing nations from 1976 to 2000 over and above the taxes that would have been paid at the 1973 rate of taxation, equals

$$\$120,000,000 \sum_{t=0}^{24} \left(\frac{1.045}{1.1} \right)^{t} = \$1,614,282,800.$$

The additional tax of $6 per ton is an average of zero for Australia (whose share of U.S. imports will have increased substantially by 1980; and $8 to $9 or more for most of the other

IBA countries. This estimate assumes that by the early 1980s some of the additional high-tax bauxite-exporting countries will have reduced their taxes by several dollars per ton in order to make their delivered prices more competitive with those of bauxite from Australia and Brazil.

The 1974 increase in export taxes on bauxite, of course, increased the cost of primary aluminum. Since approximately 4.4 long dry tons of bauxite are required to produce a long ton of aluminum, the total increase in the cost of aluminum was $26 per ton or $.012 per pound in 1976 dollars. This increase is small in percentage terms, equaling about 2 percent. As this cost increase ultimately will be passed on to consumers in the form of higher prices, the price of aluminum will also rise by about 3 percent. The long-run elasticity of U.S. aluminum consumption with respect to the price of aluminum is a little under one. Consequently, the reduction in U.S. aluminum consumption resulting from the higher bauxite taxes will be in the neighborhood of 2 percent. This reduction will take several years to materialize, since there is a lagged response on the part of aluminum consumption to price increases.

The increase in the price of aluminum and the concomitant reduction of U.S. consumption due to the bauxite export tax increases will result in a deadweight loss of U.S. consumer surplus. However, because the elasticity of demand is low and the percentage changes in price and output are small, the magnitude of this deadweight loss will be negligible compared with the direct cost of the bauxite taxes—the income transfer from U.S. consumers to the bauxite-producing nations.

If the IBA becomes a successful cartel by securing the full cooperation of Australia and Brazil and bauxite prices proceed to climb toward the ceiling level set by the cost of refining nonbauxitic ores in the United States, both the transfer cost and the deadweight loss resulting from higher bauxite taxes are likely to be substantially greater than presently forecast. For example, if the bauxite price at which nonbauxitic ores may become competitive is as high as $43 per ton, the percentage increase in price and decrease in output will be about four times the changes resulting from an average increase in bauxite taxes over 1973 levels of only $6 per ton. The income transfer and the deadweight loss will also be three times as large, although the latter will still be relatively small.

Because of higher bauxite prices and rapidly increasing capital requirements and energy prices, the price of primary aluminum is likely to rise by the early 1980s to a level approximately 10 to 15 percent in real terms above its level in the mid-1970s. The real price of copper, on the other hand, is forecast to be lower by a similar magnitude over the next five to ten years than it was in the mid-1970s. The price of copper is an important determinant of U.S. aluminum consumption, having a cross-elasticity with the latter of approximately 0.2. As a result, U.S. aluminum consumption will not grow as rapidly in the future as it has in the past: from 1977 to 1987 the annual rate of growth will be in the neighborhood of 4 percent versus 6.5 percent in the past. Nevertheless, this rate of growth is high enough to permit employment in primary aluminum to increase, provided U.S. producers continue to maintain their share of domestic and foreign markets. In the past, labor productivity in the aluminum industry has increased at an annual rate of about 3 percent per annum. If this rate of productivity improvement continues into the future, total employment will have to increase at an annual rate of 1 percent in order to meet th. expected rate of growth in consumption and output of 4 percent. The rate of change in the ratio of total U.S. primary aluminum consumption over domestic output must be subtracted from this 1 percent growth rate to obtain the rate of change in employment in the event that U.S. import dependence grows. The effects on U.S. employment in primary aluminum production of increases in the import share of the market from its present level of 10 percent to various higher levels by 1987 is shown in Table 7.3. Current 1977 employment is approximately 34,000. An import share of 40 percent that will reduce employment to three quarters of its present level as shown in Table 7.3 represents essentially a worst possible case, implying no growth in U.S. aluminum output from 1977 to 1985.

A large proportion of the bauxite needed to meet future growth in U.S. bauxite consumption will come from Australia

TABLE 7.3

THE IMPACT OF ALUMINUM IMPORT GROWTH ON U.S. EMPLOYMENT IN PRIMARY ALUMINUM

Aluminum Imports as a Percent of U.S. Consumption in 1987	Rate of Growth in U.S. Primary Aluminum Employment	U.S. Primary Aluminum Employment in 1987 as a Percent of 1977 Employment	U.S. Primary Aluminum Employment in 1987
10.0	+ 1.0	110	37,400
20.0	0	100	34,000
30.0	−1.5	86	29,240
40.0	−3.0	74	25,160

after being refined into alumina. Consequently, the growth in U.S. alumina capacity will be much slower than in the past, and given the continued growth in output per man, it is possible that total employment in the alumina stage of the industry may actually decline somewhat.

V. U.S. GOVERNMENT POLICIES

Aside from the 1974 increase in bauxite taxes and the continued income transfer from the United States to the bauxite-exporting countries to which the tax increases have given rise, developments in the bauxite/aluminum markets that will create major economic problems for the United States are not foreseen. It is unlikely that bauxite taxes will be further increased in real terms. And the U.S. aluminum industry is not expected to transfer a substantial portion of its operations abroad during the next couple of decades. Consequently, there would appear to be little need for the U.S. government to develop new policies to deal with economic trends in this industry.

The role of the government can probably be limited to such obvious measures as the pursuit of diplomatic policies designed to encourage and support Australia and Brazil in their refusal to go along with the rest of the IBA in raising taxes and, of course, the continued sponsorship of research into alternative methods of refining our plentiful nonbauxitic ores. Ongoing government participation in this research is essential because the economic stake which the country has in lowering the cost of bauxite alternatives exceeds the economic return to the aluminum companies from doing so. A socially adequate level of investment in research in this area will not be forthcoming unless the government is directly involved. It now appears likely that the cost of obtaining alumina from domestic nonbauxitic ores can be brought down to equality with the cost of refining Jamaican bauxite by continued improvement in the energy efficiency of the processes for refining nonbauxitic ore. If so, it may be desirable for the government to encourage the aluminum firms to build a full-scale test plant by supplying loans and offering, if necessary, to indemnify the companies against future declines in the price of bauxite.

Two government policy options that occasionally are brought up in discussion of bauxite prices are the application of economic and diplomatic pressure on the high-tax Caribbean area countries to induce them to cut their export taxes, and the stockpiling of bauxite in the United States. While space does not permit a thorough evaluation of either of these policies, it is important to indicate why neither option is particularly desirable.

The stakes of the Caribbean area producers in the bauxite industry are much larger than their stake in any industry (such as tourism) that might be vulnerable to U.S. pressure. Consequently, efforts on the part of the United States to compel the Caribbean area countries to reduce bauxite taxes are apt to fail. Such a policy involves many negative aspects that may be more than sufficient to discourage the U.S. government from adopting it.

The option of stockpiling bauxite has been analyzed extensively by CRA.[9] It was concluded that while there is no justification for a massive increase in the government stockpile of bauxite, it would probably be desirable to retain a large portion, if not all, of the present stockpile. The latter is equal to approximately one year's domestic bauxite consumption. Collectively, and in the case of Jamaica individually, the Caribbean bauxite-producing nations possess enormous short-run monopoly power because of the difficulty the United States would have in replacing their bauxite in a period of less than two to three years. Consequently, there is concern that these countries might utilize their monopoly advantage to increase bauxite taxes greatly in the short run. There is also concern about the possibility that an embargo against the United States might be initiated by these countries. The probability that either event will occur, especially the latter, is extremely low. However, aluminum is inelastic in demand even in the long run and has only a limited number of substitutes that could be utilized in the short run. Moreover, a loss of aluminum raw materials would result in the idling of large amounts of U.S. resurces presently engaged in the aluminum industry. The economic harm to the United States from either short-run monopoly pricing or an embargo would be very large, and even a small probability of such an occurrence justifies holding a moderate-sized stockpile of anywhere from six months' to one year's supply. This stockpiling cannot be left to the aluminum companies themselves because the amount that would be optimal for them to stockpile is only a small fraction of what would be socially optimal; the loss the aluminum companies themselves would suffer from the embargo is only a small fraction of the total loss of economic resources that would be suffered by the economy as a whole. Consequently, policies designed to encourage private stockpiling such as the development of a forward market for bauxite, if that were possible, would not make much of a contribution to meeting the nation's stockpiling requirements. Even if a forward market for bauxite were organized, it would be too inactive to have much impact on stockpiling, since very little bauxite is currently traded on the open market.

Such movement abroad as may occur in the primary aluminum industry will be in response to cost advantages possessed by foreign locations having plentiful supplies of low-cost power. Utilization of these sites will be in the economic interests of both the United States and the countries involved, as long as the savings in power cost are not offset by greater capital costs due to higher risk. The aluminum companies would seem to be well qualified to make that judgment. Any increase in U.S. dependence on foreign aluminum supplies will be too limited to raise significant defense considerations, especially since a major portion of the increase in imports may well be from Canada.

In the event that the import share of the U.S. aluminum market grows more rapidly than expected, the government may wish to consider more active intervention. Growth of the domestic industry could be stimulated by increases in tariffs or special investment tax credits, although these stops might create problems with GATT. Such policies would probably have to be justified on the basis of defense considerations rather than on those of economic efficiency. The usual economic arguments for tariffs (e.g., infant industry and improving the terms of trade) would hardly seem to apply here. Exports to the U.S. market are likely to be too widely distrubuted among different countries to raise much of a threat of cartelization. Investment incentives might take the form of tax credits given to offset the cost of pollution abatement, possibly including that embodied in the cost of power.

A governmental action that would both promote economically efficient international specialization in aluminum production and foster employment in the U.S. aluminum industry would be the reduction of the legal and institutional impediments to the construction of coal-fired power plants in the southeastern and midwestern United States. Conceivably, these impediments may prevent the aluminum industry from taking advantage of the relatively favorable domestic energy cost situation and force it to shift abroad. The chief necessity is for a streamlined site selection and approval procedure that would greatly lessen the lead time required to bring new power plants on-line—currently six to eight years—and ease the problem of finding sites. Clarification and reduction of the cost of meeting sulfur dioxide emission standards through government research assistance would also be helpful, as would elimination of the requirement to install scrubbers on plants that can meet the emission standards more economically by burning low-sulfur coal.

NOTES

1. There are two stages in the production of aluminum beyond the mining of the aluminum ore, bauxite. In the first stage, bauxite is refined to isolate alumina, a compound containing aluminum and oxygen. Then, in the smelting stage, the oxygen and aluminum metal are separated by electrolysis. Table 7.2 presents the costs of producing aluminum at various locations around the world. Given no differences in the required rates of return on capital, production costs at most foreign sites range from $75 to $150 less than in the United States. This differential is likely to be fully offset by higher capital costs due to greater risk.

2. The substitution of low- for high-cost bauxite would not be limited by any clear tendency for the cost of the former to rise as its output was expanded. The propensity for unit costs to increase as the rate of output from a deposit increases, because the producers are forced to exploit lower-quality deposits, is offset by two factors. Producers do not have detailed knowledge of the quality of every portion of a deposit when

they begin mining. (It is not cost effective to conduct the intensive explorations and analyses necessary to obtain that detailed knowledge given that much of the deposit will not be mined for decades.) Moreover, according to bauxite mining engineers, unit capital costs fall sharply as the rate of output from a mine is expanded. Much of the cost of opening up a mine, of setting up the inland transportation system and the necessary infrastructure, is fixed in the long run. It was suggested that the response of unit capital costs to changes in the rate of production could typically be approximated by the relationship $C = kx^{\frac{2}{3}}$ where C is capital cost per ton and x is the rate of output.

3. Charles River Associates, Inc., *Policy Implications of Producer Country Supply Restrictions: The World Aluminum/Bauxite Market* (Cambridge, Mass.: CRA, March 1977). Prepared for the Experimental Technology Incentives Program, National Bureau of Standards, U.S. Department of Commerce.

4. There might possibly be differences due to variations in relative bargaining strength as defined by the Zeuthen-Nash theories of bargaining. Those countries with lower costs (excluding taxes) might be able to insist on higher ratios of output to reserves. See Charles River Associates, *Policy Implications,* chap. 4.

5. Robert S. Pindyck, "Cartel Pricing and the Structures of the World Bauxite Market," paper prepared for the Ford Foundation World Commodities Conference, Airlie, Virginia, March 18, 1977.

6. Charles River Associates, Inc., *Aluminum Industry Production Costs and Smelter Location Decisions* (Cambridge, Mass.: CRA, June 1977). Prepared for the General Accounting Office.

7. A real *before-tax* rate of return of 10 percent will yield a real *after-tax* return of 6 percent, given an effective corporate tax rate of 40 percent. If the rate of inflation is 6 percent, a 6 percent real rate of return is equivalent to a nominal after-tax rate of return of 12 percent.

The capital recovery factor is equal to the required rate of return plus the sinking-fund factor. The Patten is the constant by which an initial investment is multiplied to obtain the sum that must be invested annually in a sinking fund if the amount of the fund, including accumulated interest, is to be equal to the initial investment outlay at the end of the investment's life.

8. Substantial fabrication capacity is also located in the northwestern United States. However, the smelting capacity in that area is already much more than sufficient to supply the local western fabrication plants and currently substantial amounts of aluminum ingot are shipped from the Northwest to the Midwest for fabrication. There is no question that in the past the northwestern United States has been an economically suitable location for aluminum smelters largely because of the availability of cheap hydroelectric power. Since this cheap power seems to have been fully utilized, it is unlikely that there will be a further

expansion of the aluminum-smelting industry in the Northwest. Due to the lack of cheap fossil fuel, the marginal cost of supplying additional thermoelectric power to aluminumplants in the Northwest is about 50 percent greater than the cost of supplying power to the aluminum plants in the Midwest, where inexpensive coal is available.

9. Charles River Associates, *Policy Implications*, chap. 4.

Part IV

CAPITAL FLOWS

Chapter 8

EXTERNAL FINANCE AND THE BALANCE OF PAYMENTS OF THE NONOIL LESS DEVELOPED COUNTRIES: AN OVERVIEW *

MILLARD LONG

Professor of Economics
Boston University

FRANK VENEROSO

International Financial Consultant

* The research on which this report is based was financed by the Ford Foundation as part of their study on World Economic Order. Additional funding for the preparation of this paper was provided by the United Nations Association. We should like to thank Deepak Bhattasali for much helpful discussion, and Stephen Bennett for invaluable assistance as discussant, editor, and interpreter of statistical information.

251

I. INTRODUCTION

The years since 1972 have been a period of financial turmoil for the nonoil less developed countries (NOLDCs). Especially during the years 1974-76 they suffered a significant deterioration in their balance of payments and borrowed extensively abroad—increasingly from commercial banks—to finance extremely large current account deficits. At the end of 1972, outstanding loans from commercial banks to the NOLDCs amounted to $20 billion; by the end of 1976 this total had quadrupled to $80 billion. This rapid increase in loans has caused considerable alarm and discussion. Some are concerned that the NOLDCs may prove unable to service these debts, thereby creating problems for the banks, the reverberations of which could affect the entire world financial system. Others are concerned lest the banks stop lending on the same scale, necessitating drastic retrenchment in the economies of the NOLDCs. Some observers feel that the increase in indebtedness merely postponed the date of difficult but necessary adjustments in the NOLDC balance of payments, while others hold that due to world inflation the real burden of the increased nominal debt is not much greater than before 1972, so that overmuch concern about the issue is largely irrelevant. We shall not pretend that we can provide definitive answers to all of the important analytical and policy questions raised by our research, but we do feel that a survey of the issues involved is useful to help outline the dimensions of the problem and to provide a background for future research.

The present paper is an overview and summary of a larger research program the authors have undertaken on the debt-related problems of the nonoil LDCs.[1] In the course of this investigation we have learned that many of the issues are difficult to unravel because: (1) much of what has been written on the subject has suffered from oversimplified conceptual analysis; for example, it examines the external liabilities but not the external assets of the NOLDCs; (2) much of the data collected by other investigators have been based on such oversimplification; and (3) frequently used concepts, like the resource transfer,

the real rate of interest, and the real value of NOLDC debt—
concepts that are crucial to informed judgments about the central issues—are, in a world of inflation, changing relative prices,
and disequilibrium exchange rates, far from clear-cut and are
susceptible of measurement in alternative ways suggesting differing answers to our questions.

Section II of the present paper is a factual-historical review of
basic information on the debt of the nonoil LDCs and is organized around specific problem areas where both the available
data and their interpretation are subject to dispute. Section III
builds on the (sometimes tentative) conclusions of our factual
review and tries to place the more controversial aspects of
NOLDC debt-related issues within the context of a continuing
policy discussion among analysts of the financial aspects of
economic development. The general summary of the chapter is
presented in Section III, to which the reader who is mainly
interested in our results is invited to turn.

II. FACTUAL HISTORICAL REVIEW

THE STOCK OF DEBT OF THE NONOIL LDCS

The period since 1972 has been one of unprecedented current
account deficits for the nonoil less developed countries
(NOLDCs). Taken together, their current account deficit increased from $9.8 billion in 1972 to $29.6 billion in 1974, and to
$37.7 billion in 1975, though it has been falling since that time.
Preliminary indications are that the deficit was reduced to $26.8
billion in 1977, still a substantial figure. The main source of
external finance for these increased deficits was the international
commercial banks (see Table 8.1). In nominal terms the combined debt of the NOLDCs increased by 154 percent between
1972 and the end of 1976. Of the $96 billion in added debt, $60.5
billion, or 63 percent, was provided by commercial banks. Between 1972 and 1976 the stock of outstanding loans from multilateral and bilateral lenders doubled, while that from
commercial banks increased almost fourfold.

The debt figures reported in Table 8.1 are considerably in

TABLE 8.1

THE DEBT OF THE NONOIL LDCs, 1972–76 [a]

(billions of U.S. $)

	1972	1973	1974	1975	1976
External Capital Obligations	99.5	117.1	146.5	179.1	212.0
Direct Investment	36.9	40.2	43.9	48.6	53.0
Debt:	62.6	76.9	102.6	130.5	159.0
Official Lenders	34.4	39.4	47.5	57.1	67.8
Commercial Banks	20.2	29.2	45.8	63.7	80.7
Suppliers' credits, bonds, & others	8.0	8.3	9.3	9.7	10.5

[a] Figures are for the stock of debt outstanding at year end. See pages 000–00 for information on how these figures were calculated.

excess of the usually cited numbers provided by the World Bank.[2] The major difference is in coverage. The World Bank reports include only debts that are public or publicly guaranteed and are of more than one year in duration. We have attempted to provide more comprehensive data by including nonguaranteed long-term loans, short-term loans,[3] and borrowings from the International Monetary Fund (IMF).

Despite its attempt at broader coverage, the approach used in this chapter still probably underestimates the debt of most countries studied, since it excludes some commercial bank lending not captured by data of the Bank for International Settlements (BIS),[4] some suppliers' credits, and debts related to the purchase of military equipment, which in many countries are not reported. Overall, the underestimate is probably between $10 and $15 billion, but it could exceed these levels.

Debt is not the only source of capital financing for the NOLDCs. In addition, there is a substantial amount of foreign direct investment. Whether direct investment should be included in a discussion of debt is debatable, but it must be so included if we wish to have a complete picture of capital inflows. The Organization for Economic Cooperation and Development (OECD) collects information on direct investments in the less developed countries,[5] and the IMF provides some data on dividends paid. As reported in Table 8.1, the OECD estimates that the book value of foreign direct investment in the nonoil LDCs was $53 billion at the end of 1976, and that the annual flow of new investment is about $4.5 billion. However, this information is subject to greater potential error than the debt statistics.[6]

Since the period under discussion has been one of worldwide inflation, nominal figures on debt may not be very informative unless they are either deflated, using an appropriate price index, or expressed in relation to another nominal figure, such as the GNP. In this paper we make use of both approaches; they are alternative means of expressing what we are really interested in, which is the size of the debt calculated at constant prices, that is, in constant purchasing-power terms. However, since our investigation reveals that the choice of a deflator for NOLDC debt is a controversial and complex issue, we shall postpone a fuller discussion of it until the next subsection.

THE RESOURCE TRANSFER

Many people equate the funds borrowed by the nonoil less developed countries with a corresponding flow of real resources; that is, they assume that the borrowed funds are used to finance the trade deficit exclusively. In fact, such financing is only one, and in some years not the major, use of the funds obtained abroad. The NOLDCs also used borrowings to meet interest payments, to roll over maturing debt, and to acquire foreign financial assets. If we ignore refinancing to concentrate on net borrowings alone, in 1976 and 1977 borrowed funds spent on interest payments and external financial asset accumulation were approximately 60 percent of expenditures on the trade deficit. It is important to bear this qualification in mind when we consider the question: What transfer of real resources to the nonoil LDCs has corresponded to the financial transfer the borrowings represent? For the purpose of investigating this topic, we define the *resource transfer* as the net flow of resources to a country as a result of its international transactions in goods and services.[7]

The resource transfer to the NOLDCs, expressed in nominal terms, increased significantly during the period 1972-77. This nominal increase reflects both growth in the NOLDC economies and general world inflation. To explore changes in the resource transfer over time, independently of growth and changes in the world price level, we can compare its dollar value to the dollar value of the NOLDCs aggregate gross national product. We have done this in line IV (ii) of Table 8.2, which indicates that the resource transfer/GNP ratio increased markedly in 1974-75, after the oil price increase and the world economic recession. Financing the increased trade deficits of these years required a more rapid flow of external borrowing relative to national income. However, substantial progress was made in reducing the deficit in 1976-77, and it appears that the resource transfer to the NOLDCs as a group was narrowed to 2.4 percent of GNP by 1977, a level that is slightly higher than the general experience of these countries in the period 1970-72.

The resource transfer/GNP ratio is not the only method of measuring the flow of resources to a country. During the period since 1972 there have been substantial changes in the relative prices of NOLDC imports and exports, and these have contributed to changes in the values of the resource deficit as well. There are two aspects to such relative price changes. First, in general terms, there was an increase in the prices of NOLDC traded goods relative to other world prices. Such an increase tends to increase the size of the nominal deficit relative to GNP, since the definition of GNP includes nontraded goods as well. Second, though there were fluctuations in import prices relative to export prices within the period 1972-77, if one considers the entire period (end point to end point), then NOLDC import prices rose somewhat faster than export prices, and this movement contributed to a further increase in the dollar value of the resource transfer.

One can attempt to screen out the effects of price changes on the resource transfer. If one deflates exports by an NOLDC export price index,[8] and imports by a comparable import price index and then takes the differences between the resulting double series, these differences are a measure of the resource transfer that would have occurred had there been no price changes in NOLDC traded goods, but simply changes in physical quantities of imports and exports, measured from the base year (in this case, 1972). Line IV(i) of Table 8.2 shows the results of this calculation.[9] It is an index in which the effects of both relative and absolute price changes have been eliminated, that is, it is a measure of the resource transfer corrected for changes in the terms of trade and for changes in the level of world prices. Line IV (iii) shows the ratio of this series to aggregate NOLDC national income expressed in 1972 prices. Measured in this way (i.e., assuming we still live in a world of 1972 prices), the resource transfer has fallen recently from its peak of 2.7 percent in 1974 but has remained at levels that are considerably higher than those recorded in the period before 1973.

The implication of this exercise is that the nonoil LDCs apparently suffered a significant deterioration in their terms of trade in 1974-75, the years of the largest deficits. Relative price changes over the entire period 1972-77 were on balance adverse, and to bring the resource transfer down to its current (1977) level has required a contraction of the value of the flow of goods and services to the nonoil LDCs from the levels of 1974-75. Had these adverse price changes not occurred, the ratio of the resource transfer to GNP would be higher than it was before 1973, but not nearly as high as it was in the years of the greatest deficits. In effect, the adjustment in physical terms that has been accomplished by these countries in the past two years has been more significant than most observers realized.

INTEREST PAYMENTS AND NOLDC DEFICITS

Payments of interest and profit remittances constitute a significant portion of the current obligations of the nonoil LDCs and contribute importantly to their current account deficits, and hence to increases in the stock of their indebtedness. Largely because of this increase in debt, nominal interest payments and profit remittances more than doubled over the period 1972-77, as indicated in Table 8.2. During the years 1974-76, when the resource transfer to the NOLDCs increased sharply, the increase in net factor payments abroad was large, but not nearly as large as the increase in the resource transfer. However, during the most recent period when the resource transfer has been falling (1976-77), the volume of NOLDC external debt still increased.

TABLE 8.2

BALANCE OF PAYMENTS OF THE NONOIL LDC's, 1972–77
(billions of U.S. $)

	1972	1973	1974	1975	1976	1977 [a]
I. Goods & Services	−9.8	−11.5	−29.6	−37.7	−32.7	−26.8
A. Resource Transfer (goods & services *less* interest & dividends)	−5.5	−5.8	−22.9	−29.6	−23.8	−17.0
B. Interest & Dividends	−4.3	−5.7	−6.7	−8.1	−8.9	−9.8
(i) interest paid	−5.3	−7.4	−10.1	−11.0	−11.4	−12.6
(ii) interest received	1.0	1.7	3.4	2.9	2.5	2.8
II. Financial Transfers	15.8	23.6	38.2	44.0	46.8	42.5
A. Capital Movements	*12.2*	*17.6*	*29.4*	*32.6*	*32.9*	
B. Unrequited Transfers	*3.6*	*6.0*	*8.8*	*11.4*	*13.9*	
(i) public	1.9	3.4	6.2	8.4	10.4	
(ii) private	1.7	2.6	2.6	3.0	3.5	
III. Reserves & Other Assets	*−6.0*	*−12.1*	*−8.6*	*−6.3*	*−14.1*	*−15.7*
A. Official Reserves	−5.6	−7.6	−1.7	−0.5	−8.6	
B. Assets Unrelated to Reserves	−1.8	−4.7	−6.0	−2.7	−5.1	
C. Net Errors & Omissions	1.4	0.2	−0.9	−3.1	−3.8	
D. Balancing Item [b]					3.4	

IV. Calculated Values

(i) real exports less real imports [c]	−5.5	−8.8	−11.2	−10.0	−10.8	n.a.
(ii) resource transfer/ GNP (nominal)	1.5%	1.4%	4.5%	5.5%	4.0%	2.4%
(iii) (real X − real M)/ GNP (1972 prices)	1.5%	2.2%	2.7%	2.4%	2.4%	n.a.

[a] Figures for 1977 are preliminary.

[b] In order to make the balance of payments data consistent with the recorded increase in debt, it is necessary to include a balancing item for the year 1976.

[c] See p. 000 for information on the calculation of this figure.

259

The large resource deficits of 1974-76 have contributed to an increased volume of debt that has left these countries with a higher debt-service burden. One of the difficulties faced by an analyst of the NOLDC debt situation is to evaluate what these increased nominal debt payments imply in real terms; our own evaluation is given in section III, pp 000ff. Another major problem is to determine exactly the factors that contributed to changes in the nominal interest burden in the past, and to consider what the implications of these may be for the future.

Credits to the NOLDCs from official lending institutions, such as governments and the World Bank, are ordinarily long-term credits and carry a fixed-interest coupon; the rates charged are either subsidized or are roughly equivalent to the U.S. market rate on long-term instruments. By contrast, interest rates on commercial bank loans (except very short-term loans), both to governments and to private borrowers in the NOLDCs, typically are floating rate and often carry a fixed spread of between 1 and 2 percent above LIBOR, the London interbank offer rate, which is the overnight, or "call money" rate, of the Euromarkets. These commercial bank loans are usually either short-term or medium-term loans; typical maturities through 1977 rarely exceeded seven years. In addition to these two categories of loans, there is a variable proportion of fixed-interest-rate private lending to borrowers in the NOLDCs, largely in the form of suppliers' credits for long-range investment projects.

During the period 1972-76, the debt component of total NOLDC external obligations (as opposed to the direct investment component) increased by 154 percent; over the same period, nominal interest payments increased 135 percent. Since interest payments increased less rapidly than debt, it would appear that the average interest rate on NOLDC debt declined during the period. However, as noted above, our estimates of NOLDC debt for the years before 1975 are likely to be understated. Adjusting the base year (1972) debt figures slightly upward makes the percentage increase in debt approximately equal to that of interest payments, indicating that the average rate of interest on NOLDC debt did not change appreciably from 1972 to 1976.

As the 1970s are generally considered to be a period of rising inflation and rising nominal interest rates, this constancy of the interest rate requires some explanation. Breaking gross debt into its components, it can be seen that some components—namely, the long-term fixed-interest component, and some of the short-term components—exhibited a modest increase in rates, while the remainder—principally floating-rate Eurodollar short-term and medium-term debt—experienced a very slight decline in rates. Between 1972 and 1976, long-term interest rates in the Eurocurrency and U.S. markets increased somewhat, which tended to raise the rates on new fixed-interest-rate borrowings from sources tied to these markets, principally suppliers and multilateral institutions. For example, World Bank loan rates, which are tied to the dollar bond markets, rose during this period from 7.25 to 8.75 percent. However, the *average* rate on all official (including sources other than the World Bank) loans outstanding increased only from 2.9 percent in 1972 to 3.2 percent in 1975, the last year for which country data (as opposed to aggregate data) on interest rates are available.

Rates on short-term fixed-rate loans from national (as against Euromarket) banks in the developed countries, which are tied to bank prime rates, also increased slightly as prime rates tended to rise over the period. However, the floating-rate credits tied to LIBOR appear to have declined slightly between 1972 and 1976. As the increase in long-term rates affected average rates only through their impact on incremental borrowings, while the decrease in Eurodollar rates affected the average rate on the entire stock of floating-rate Eurocredits, it is understandable that the average rate of interest on NOLDC debt remained virtually unchanged over the period.

In addition to calculating average rates at the end points of our period, it is informative to examine the course of rates during the intervening years. The year 1974 was characterized by a cyclical peak in interest rates, both in the national money markets of the developed countries and in the Euromarkets. This cyclical increase primarily affected the floating-rate component of NOLDC debt, and as a consequence, the average interest rate paid on all debt rose to a cyclical peak level 1.6

percentage points above the level of 1972. In fact, rates on all maturities of floating-rate debt were extremely volatile over the period; LIBOR rose to a quarterly average peak of 11.44 percent in 1974 and then declined by 1976 to a cyclical nadir of 4.83 percent. As a growing proportion of NOLDC debt is commercial debt of this sort—whose *average*, as opposed to marginal, interest-rate changes with LIBOR—the average interest rate on NOLDC external debt has become quite volatile. Since the end of 1976, Euromarket rates have been rising steadily. By mid-1978, LIBOR reached the 8 percent level; presumably, the average interest rate on NOLDC debt has risen markedly as a result. In addition, the 1974 experience in the Euromarkets indicates that a further significant rise in average rates may lie ahead as the world economy and world credit markets approach another cyclical peak.

Parenthetically, we should note that the nominal interest rate on outstanding debt is still very low for the poorest countries (in real terms it is negative), who receive most of their loans from official sources at subsidized rates. For example, the average rate on India's outstanding debt was only 2.1 percent in 1975. But countries at more advanced stages of development, who now borrow mainly on commercial terms, pay considerably higher average rates—Mexico's, for example, was 7.5 percent in 1975.

What happened to *real* rates of interest over our period? If we calculate them by taking as our measure of inflation the U.S. implicit GNP deflator, a comparison of the end points (1972 and 1976) indicates that some interest rates were more or less constant in real terms over the period, while others declined somewhat. Nominal rates on new fixed-rate borrowings rose roughly with the U.S. rate of inflation. As noted above, World Bank loan rates, which are tied to U.S. bond market rates, though with a lag, rose from 7.25 percent in 1972 to 8.75 percent in 1976, while the U.S. implicit GNP deflator increased from 3.4 to 5.5 percent, resulting in a more or less constant real rate. By contrast, some short-term rates and particularly LIBOR, actually declined over the period from 5.4 to 4.83 percent, implying a significant decline in real terms for the rate on that portion of NOLDC debt that depends on LIBOR.

It is usual to regard the inflation premium in interest rates as the difference between the nominal and the real rate of interest, though actually the real rate is calculated as a residual after comparing the nominal rate and the rate of inflation. Looked at another way, we say that the inflation premium is that addition to the real rate that is intended to compensate the lender for the reduction in the real value of his principal that is due to inflation. In the national accounts, interest payments normally appear in the current account category, but an inflation-adjusted (constant value) system of national accounts would, more logically, show only a portion of interest payments in the current account deficit, while the remainder would be treated as a capital account transfer—that is, as an amortization of principal. In fact, at the present time some of the most important nonoil LDC borrowers, such as Brazil, would show significantly smaller deficits on current account if such as inflation adjustment were made.

In summary, nominal interest payments on NOLDC external debt have risen in recent years, but this is due entirely to the increase in debt. Nominal interest rates over the period 1972-76 fluctuated widely but were quite similar when compared end point to end point. The average real interest rate on NOLDC borrowings, in the aggregate, was marginally positive in 1972 but had become practically zero by 1976, if the U.S. rate of inflation is used to compute real interest rates. However, though much of the borrowing of recent years appears to have been costless in real terms, this will not necessarily be so in the future—a point we consider more closely below.

THE SHORTENING OF MATURITIES

Some observers have recently expressed concern over the apparent shortening of maturities on the aggregate debt of the NOLDCs. Some of this concern, in our opinion, has been misplaced, since our research indicates that though maturities have shortened for the NOLDCs taken as a group, they have *not* shortened significantly for individual countries. We shall attempt to explain this statistical anomaly in what follows. On the other hand, not enough attention has been focused on the fact that persistent inflation has had the effect of shortening "real" maturities, though nominal maturities remain unchanged.

Our research indicates that the average maturity of NOLDC debt has shortened in recent years, simply because a greater percentage of such debt is now commercial bank debt, which continues to carry shorter maturities than loans from official sources. Bilateral and multilateral loans typically carry maturities of between twenty and thirty years; by contrast, half of the credits from private banks are short-term credits with maturities of less than one year, whereas for most private medium-term credits maturities range up to seven years. Overall, the average maturity on commercial bank loans outstanding is approximately one and one-half years.[10] As noted above, 63 percent of the additional debt contracted by the nonoil LDCs in the period 1973-77 was from commercial banks. Thus, the shifting mix of debt from official to private lenders turns out to be the prime cause of the recent shortening of maturity structures.

But despite the greater preponderance of private borrowing, leading to an *overall* shortening of maturities (for the NOLDCs taken as a group), a recent World Bank study showed that maturities for individual countries were little affected. The reason for this is that the poorer countries, which in the past received most of their credits at longer maturities from official lenders, still continue to borrow primarily from those sources, whereas while the wealthier NOLDCs, such as Brazil and Mexico, who continue to rely primarily on private sources, have increased their borrowings both absolutely and as a percentage of total NOLDC debt.

The second factor affecting maturities is inflation. In normal national accounts statistics, the inflation premium in interest rates is treated as a current account item. But since this premium really represents a repayment to the lender for the declining value of his assets, it should more logically be treated, like amortization, as a capital account item.[11] Thus, the NOLDCs are currently paying inflation premiums in interest rates that cause them (actually, though not nominally) to have to amortize a considerable portion of debt each year, thus reducing "real," though not nominal, maturities.

Shortened maturities are likely to be a problem for countries that depend heavily on commercial bank financing, little of which credit has an original maturity longer than seven years. Such countries typically have to refinance between 40 and 50 percent of their debt annually; under normal conditions, however, this refinancing creates few problems, as debt is simply rolled over. But what of the possibility of abnormal conditions arising when lenders become reluctant to roll over debt? Such a situation could arise either if the banks became suspicious of the long-run solvency of a particular country or if world financial markets became generally tight, even though the solvency of particular countries were not in doubt. Up to now, individual country problems have been worked out in bilateral negotiations though with varying degrees of success, depending on whether one takes the creditor's or the debtor's point of view on the negotiations. Still, though individual countries have been technically in default on their commercial bank obligations for varying periods of time, there has been no example of a massive and absolute individual country default in recent years. The second situation—that of general financial market tightness making the commercial banks as a group reluctant to lend—is potentially more serious, since it would have repercussions for many NOLDCs, not just on particular countries. Speculation about the possibility of such an event requires a broader analysis, which we attempt below in our review of alternative debt policies

FINANCIAL ASSET ACCUMULATION

Our discussion to this point has considered only the external liabilities of the nonoil LDCs. But we must not ignore the fact that the capital accounts of these countries would, if more complete information were available, show considerable foreign financial asset holdings. The extent of the foreign asset acquisition that has led to these holdings is hard to gauge, since statistics on such asset holdings, other than official reserves, are only fragmentary. In what follows, therefore, we shall be painting only a rough impression of some rather murky waters.

What is indubitable is that, in addition to financing the transfer of real resources, and interest and dividend payments on foreign obligations, the external borrowing of the nonoil LDCs has been used to purchase foreign financial assets. Though official borrowings from commercial banks have received a great deal of attention, there has been a roughly comparable reverse flow of funds from the NOLDCs into deposits with the international commercial banks, which has gone largely unnoticed in the literature.

The BIS issues quarterly statistics showing the aggregate loan and deposit positions of the Group of Ten commercial banks with individual countries. In this usage a "country" means the government, government agencies, state enterprises, private businesses, and individual residents; and it is the total of the positions of all these different groups that makes up a particular country's loan-and-deposit position with the banks. These statistics indicate that the NOLDCs are net borrowers from the Group of Ten banks, but their net borrowed position (gross bank borrowings *minus* deposits held in the same banks) is only a fraction of their gross indebtedness. At the end of December 1977, their gross indebtedness to the banks was $90.5 billion, their gross deposit position was $62.4 billion, and their net indebtedness amounted to only $28.1 billion, or 31 percent of their gross indebtedness.[12]

If private as well as official holdings of foreign financial assets are considered, it is likely that the net debt position of the NOLDCs with respect to the international commercial banks is even lower. Countries that are important banking centers, such as Switzerland, are very large sources of deposit funds flowing into the Group of Ten banks. It is known that these funds do not originate in these countries but are, rather, funds of nonresidents held in trust by banks and other institutions. To a great extent, these trust funds are funds from oil-exporting countries. However, it is known that individuals, corporations, and institutions in the NOLDCs also hold foreign financial asset balances, including bank deposits, with these trust companies, and inclusion of the deposits attributable to asset holders in the nonoil LDCs would further reduce the net borrowed position of the NOLDCs vis-à-vis the banks.

Because of the absence of adequate time series data, it is difficult to determine with accuracy the pattern of annual flows of funds from the nonoil LDCs to the Group of Ten banks. However, we estimate that these flows may have averaged approximately $4 billion per year over the last half decade. We also estimate that more than half of these deposit stocks and flows are not official reserves but are deposits held by corporations, individuals, and state enterprises.[13]

This estimate applies only to the acquisition of deposits in the Group of Ten banks. Owing to data deficiencies, it is difficult to determine the precise magnitude of holders of other foreign financial assets by asset holders in the NOLDCs, which correspond to other sources of external borrowing: suppliers' credits, official credits, direct investment, and so on. However, we do know that asset holders in nonoil LDCs, especially in regions such as Latin America, hold substantial volumes of foreign securities and that firms in these countries have trade claims on the rest of the world as well. Overall, it is possible that, when the entire financial accounts of the NOLDC's are considered, it might appear that net borrowings were even less than our analysis of commercial bank loan-and-deposit figures suggests.

Even if better information about NOLDC foreign asset holdings were available, a significant interpretive problem would remain. A country's overall balance sheet cannot be analyzed like that of a firm's. Foreign assets held by one individual or corporation may not necessarily be available to meet the liabilities of others. It is not at all clear whether, and to what degree, private holdings of foreign financial assets would be made available to service national obligations. Such assets have been accumulated for various reasons, so that availability will depend heavily upon the motive for their accumulation and upon prevailing country conditions, both economic and political. But the analyst cannot overlook the existence of these assets, since NOLDC borrowing may have contributed directly or indirectly to their acquisition, and since the question of their ultimate availability affects a country's ability to repay external borrowings.

III. DEBT POLICY FOR NONOIL LDCS'

Prior to 1970, commercial bank lending to the NOLDCs was of only limited significance. Credits to NOLDCs were not an important part of the international commercial banks' loan portfolios, nor were the banks significant sources of external funds for the nonoil LDCS. Neither of these statements is true any longer. Since 1972, commercial banks have provided approximately 63 percent of the external finance of the NOLDCs as a group, and for particular countries the share is much higher. Further, such loans are now a substantial part of the portfolios and profits of the international commercial banks, and in particular the major U.S. money center banks.

These developments, viewed in the context of the substantial increase in NOLDC indebtedness in recent years, pose important policy issues for several groups—official lenders, nonoil LDC borrowers, and the commercial banks themselves. The issues posed are complex and not easily analyzed. Rather than pretending to provide answers, our intention in this section is simply to identify problem areas and to indicate alternative lines of approach to them, based on the material presented in section II. In the following section we attempt to: (1) provide a review of the major developments in the NOLDC balance of payments during 1972-77; (2) examine alternative approaches to evaluating NOLDC indebtedness; (3) identify what developments might cause the NOLDCs to experience debt-related problems in the future; (4) examine the problems raised for the commercial banks in future lending to the NOLDCs; and (5) discuss the implications of the changed position of official lenders vis-à-vis the nonoil LDCs.

INSTABILITY AND PAYMENT ADJUSTMENTS IN THE NOLDCS'

The period since 1972 has been one of extreme instability in the balance of payments of the nonoil LDCs. The causes of the instability have been many, and the impact on individual countries has varied. Rapidly rising prices for exports and imports, which on average doubled between 1972 and 1976, were one major source of instability. Of course, not all prices moved together. Depending upon a country's mix of imports and exports, these price movements have brought both favorable and adverse movements in the terms of trade. For most of the nonoil LDCs, the movement in the terms of trade was favorable in 1973, adverse in 1974 and 1975, and again favorable in 1976 and 1977. Overall, of all factors influencing the trade account, adverse movements in the terms of trade in 1974 and 1975 contributed most to the increased deficits of the NOLDCs as a group. Another factor contributing to balance-of-payments instability for the NOLDCs was a decline in the rate of growth of real exports. The developed countries constitute the major market for NOLDC exports; when the boom of 1972 and 1973 became the recession of 1974 and 1975, nonoil LDC export growth slowed, and for some countries the physical volume of exports actually declined. Again, export volume recovered in 1976 and 1977. For some NOLDCs, severe domestic price inflation coupled with inadequate exchange-rate policy was an important additional source of balance-of-payments instability. Many of the nonoil LDCs experienced severe domestic inflation during the period 1973-77, and this often led to an overvalued exchange rate with concomitant deterioration in the trade account, and in some cases to associated capital flight.

In general, it is believed that the rapid growth in commercial bank financing of the NOLDCs during the difficult years 1974-76 made it easier for the nonoil LDCs to adjust to the disturbances in their balance of payments. Of course, even in the absence of direct commercial bank lending, the international financial system would have responded in some degree to the disturbances by making credits available through an alternative channel, most probably through increased financing from multilateral lenders, who themselves would have financed their position by borrowing from the oil surplus countries. But, to the extent that substitute credits would not have been available, more of the balance-of-payments adjustment of the nonoil LDCs would have had to be made in other ways. Because the reserve to import ratio of the nonoil LDCs had declined so significantly in 1974 and 1975, from 30 percent to under 20 percent, a substantial further drawdown of reserves to meet the balance-of-payments deficit was probably unfeasible. To the extent that external funding had not been available, therefore, the adjustment would have had to be made in the trade accounts of the NOLDCs. This would have required either more rapid and more drastic exchange-rate adjustment, more restrictive domestic demand management, direct intervention in the markets for imports and exports, or some combination of the three. It can be argued that this type of adjustment would have reduced the short-run rate of growth (but not necessarily the long-run rate) of the NOLDCs and would have compounded the severity of the world recession and the concomitant contraction in world trade. On the other hand, for a few countries the availability of compensatory financing from the commercial banks may simply have deferred necessary adjustments and allowed them to follow for a longer period the policies that were in part responsible for their balance-of-payments difficulties.

The above generalized account of disturbances and adjustment does not apply to all nonoil LDCs. Our research has demonstrated that there has been an extraordinary degree of heterogeneity in the balance-of-payments difficulties experienced by these countries, in the adjustment paths they have followed, and in the role commercial bank financing played in such adjustments. Countries that were not reliant on oil imports, such as Peru or Mexico, experienced some of the most severe balance-of-payments difficulties during this period, and they have had some of the most difficult problems in their relations with commercial banks in recent years. Other countries, such as India, whose terms of trade were gravely affected by relative price changes during this period and which had limited access to compensatory balance-of-payments financing from commercial banks, had a minimum of balance-of-payments difficulties. Overall, owing to the heterogeneity of these countries and their adjustment paths, a careful country-by-country analysis is called for; and an understanding of the role that commercial bank financing and balance-of-payments adjustment ought to play for nonoil-developing countries should be a product of such more detailed, country-specific analysis.

Despite the problems mentioned above in determining the exact level of nonoil LDC debt, there is little doubt that such debt has expanded significantly since 1972. Unfortunately, as this period has been one of substantial world inflation, we cannot say precisely what has happened to the debt in real or constant purchasing-power terms. On one hand, some economists, responding to the concern voiced in the press over the rapid growth of NOLDC debt, have argued that its real value has been greatly reduced by inflation and that in real terms its expansion is no great cause for alarm. On the other hand, we believe there is considerable evidence that the debt of the oil-deficit countries has in fact grown rapidly, even in real terms, and that it expanded significantly faster than one very important real variable—NOLDC output. Corresponding to these differing positions are different appraisals of the seriousness of the problem, and varying concomitant policy implications.

To a large extent, this controversy comes out of special problems encountered when attempting to choose a price index for deflating international debts. Deflating a nominal series of values with a price index is straightforward when one is dealing with a determinate basket of goods whose composition does not change. Then the deflation exercise eliminates changes in value due to price changes and provides a measure of changes in physical quantities of goods alone. However, financial asset aggregates correspond to no unique basket of physical goods; they are money values that can be exchanged for equivalent money values of *any* basket of real goods. To deflate financial assets, we must in effect single out, from all possible baskets of goods, a particular basket that is most likely to correspond to the purchasing power represented by the asset. If we believe that the appropriate basket of goods for our deflator is the combined output of debtor *and* creditor countries, then we should construct our deflator using a very broad world price index. If we focus on the economic activity of the creditor countries alone, then an index of developed country output, such as the United States or OECD gross national product deflator would be appropriate. But if we regard the economic activity of the *borrowing* countries as most relevant to the real size of their debt, then an NOLDC gross national product deflator or export or import price index would be most appropriate. This technical problem in the construction of a deflator would not be important if, as is normally the case, differently constructed price indices had moved comparably in the period 1972-76; but since the period was one of frequent and substantial relative price changes, deflators constructed using different indices do not move together, introducing wide discrepancies into estimates of the real size of NOLDC debt, which are apparent from Table 8.3.

TABLE 8.3

ESTIMATES OF THE GROWTH OF NOLDC DEBT
IN CONSTANT PRICES
(billions of U.S. $)

	1972	1973	1974	1975	1976
Nominal Debt	99.5	117.1	146.5	179.1	212.0
Debt Deflated by Price Index (1972 = 100):					
U.S. GNP	99.5	110.4	126.3	141.0	158.2
OECD GNP	99.5	102.7	116.2	126.1	145.2
NOLDC Exports	99.5	86.1	78.3	98.4	109.3
NOLDC Imports	99.5	92.9	77.1	89.6	107.0
Nominal Debt/					
Nominal GNP	.26	.28	.29	.33	.35

Almost all writers [14] on the subject have taken the last position noted above—that is, that the borrowing country's economic activity should establish the appropriate basket—and have used an index of NOLDC gross exports to deflate the nominal debt figures. Because of large increases in the relative prices of NOLDC tradables in recent years, this results in the striking conclusion that the real value of NOLDC debt has not grown significantly in spite of its large nominal growth. Now the choice of this basket—NOLDC exports—requires a rationale or justification, especially given the surprising character of the results it generates. Though it has not been explicitly discussed in the literature, it appears that NOLDC exports have been chosen as the basket for constructing a deflator because exports constitute the goods and services that generate the foreign exchange that pays external debt service. If indeed this is the rationale for the choice, we believe it suffers from important drawbacks.

First, foreign exchange from export sales must be utilized to purchase imports, some of which are used directly in the manufacture of exports, as well as to meet prior fixed obligations. Only the *value added* in exports generates foreign exchange that is available for debt payments. To be consistent, the rationale given implies that the basket for deflating debt statistics should be the value added in exports rather than gross exports. Second, we are most likely dealing with fairly long-term debt contracts. The composition of a country's imports and exports can change rapidly even though current domestic factor prices remain constant (in which case the price of domewtic value added remains constant) if profit-seeking entrepreneurs undertake reorganization of the structure of local production in response to newly perceived export or domestic demand for particular commodities. Consequently, national income or output, which is the ultimate source of both present and future possible exports, may be a more appropriate basis for constructing our deflator. There is good precedent for such a choice: an entire analytical approach—the so-called growth-cum-debt literature—which explicitly considers this problem, has rested its results on this very assumption.[15] Then it is the international price of the GNPs of the nonoil LDCs rather than the price of their gross exports that constitutes the appropriate index for constructing our deflator.

Whatever the basket of domestic goods and services chosen, we have found that calculating an index of prices of domestic value added, so that it is expressed in the same international currency terms as is external debt, is a difficult problem that admits of no straightforward analytical solution. Thus, what appears at first to be an arcane technical problem—finding an index with which to deflate international debt statistics—has turned out to be an essential step in evaluating the real burden of NOLDC debt. We have undertaken this evaluation more thoroughly in another paper,[16] which argues that though there is probably no single "correct" deflator for NOLDC debt, there are many reasons for thinking that a price index for total world output (such as the U.S. or OECD gross national product deflators) is the closest available approximation to it. As we saw above, the use of such an index indicates that real debt has grown significantly faster than calculations based on an NOLDC gross export price index. This conclusion is further supported by the fact that nominal NOLDC debt has grown more rapidly than nominal income or exports, and since both of these have grown appreciably in real terms over the last five years, it appears that the growth of real NOLDC debt has been even greater.

CRITICAL FUTURE DECISIONS FOR THE NONOIL LDCS

Above we gave a brief general account of the adjustment path followed by the nonoil LDCs in response to the generalized balance-of-payments crisis of the years 1974-76. By the end of 1977 a significant recovery from the problems of that period was apparent to most analysts. In most of the NOLDcs, export growth was strong in 1976 and at least adequate in 1977. Measures were taken to reduce the level of imports, so that the physical quantity of imports declined in 1975 and 1976. The deficit on current account was still large, but the ratio of the resource transfer to GNP had been reduced, though not to the levels of 1970-72. Two legacies remain from the years of balance-of-payments difficulties: an increased debt, which had been accumulated to finance the extraordinary increase in the current account deficit; and smaller but still uncomfortably large resource deficits, in which interest payments on inherited debt are a significant component.

How might this legacy of debt affect the future development of the nonoil LDCs? Our research indicates that the course of future events for these countries depends importantly on what happens to three critical variables, all of which are determined by world events and thus are largely outside the direct control of the NOLDCs:

(1) changes in the terms of trade;
(2) changes in the real interest burden; and
(3) factors affecting future availability of external finance.

We now turn to a brief consideration of these critical factors.

1. Small changes in the relative prices of NOLDC imports and exports can have a substantial impact on the current account deficit. Over the period 1972-76, NOLDC export prices increased by 94 percent, and import prices by 98 percent, so that the resulting 4 percent differential was quite small compared with the overall change in both export and import prices. Had 1972 prices ruled in the year 1976, the resource deficit in the latter year would have been 2.4 percent of aggregate NOLDC gross national product; but the actual figure for 1976 was 4 percent—an uncomfortably high, and probably unsustainable, number.[17]

As an illustration of the potential effects of changes in terms of trade, we have calculated that a 10 percent increase in NOLDC import prices with no change in export prices would double the resource deficit; while a 10 percent decrease in import prices with no change in export prices would eliminate it entirely. In three out of the last four years the nonoil LDCs have experienced changes in the terms of trade of 9 percent or more, though this experience was unusual in the context of a longer run of years going back to the mid-1950s. Still, changes on the order of those recently experienced—and thus not wildly improbably in the future—could become crucial for the size of the current account deficit.

Our conclusion is that any unusual shift in relative prices—even a shift that did not appear very great in percentage terms—could alter both the resource deficit and the current account deficit significantly. If the shift were adverse, it would greatly increase demand for external financing on the part of the NOLDCs, while at the same time it might affect their creditworthiness (since prices would have moved against them) and hence their ease of access to external finance.

2. The real value of NOLDC debt has undoubtedly increased appreciably in recent years, regardless of the particular measure

chosen. Interest payments associated with the higher debt have increased both absolutely and as a percentage of GNP. Do these higher nominal interest payments impose a higher real interest burden on the NOLDCs? Our answer to this question is that up to now they have not, since world inflation has insured that most real interest rates have been zero or only marginally positive. However, this happy state of affairs may not continue to obtain in the future.

Though it has received little attention, we suspect that the gravity of the NOLDC debt problem depends very much on the real interest rate paid on external obligations. At present, with world market interest rates on new loans at negative or marginally positive levels, and with negative rates on long-term NOLDC loans written earlier at fixed-interest rates, the real interest burden appears to be low. However, a decline in the rate of inflation—a turn of events welcomed by most, including those concerned about the NOLDC debt problem—would, it appears to us, seriously increase the real burden of interest obligations. Loans written at fixed-interest rates that now seem relatively low given the current rate of inflation could prove to be burdensome in coming years if the rate of inflation declined substantially.[18] Also, on short-term and floating-rate commercial loans, the real interest burden would rise if the higher real interest rates that prevailed in the past, when the rate of inflation was much lower than today, were to materialize once again.

Of course, the prevalence of negative real interest rates in the industrial world in recent years remains something of an enigma. It is quite possible that it reflects no more than money illusion and lagging expectations; if so, the real level of interest rates on the outstanding short-term and floating-rate component of NOLDC external debt could rise significantly in the future, even if no change occurs in the rate of inflation. Such a rise, coupled with expirations of old long-term, low-interest-rate loans and their necessary refinancing at higher nominal interest rates, would act to raise the real level of the NOLDC interest burden. By contrast, if the rate of inflation were to increase still further, the real interest burden on the nonoil LDCs would probably decline, at least in the short run.

Of course, these conclusions focus mainly on the interest burden associated with *gross* indebtedness; to the degree that the *net* indebtedness of the NOLDCs is smaller, the effect of interest-rate changes on the real interest burden will be correspondingly less.

On balance, we believe that market and institutional factors, such as those described above, will have a major bearing on the real interest burden paid by the NOLDCs, and should be a major concern of both lending institutions and policy analysts. Unfortunately, the determinants of real interest rates in international financial markets are obscure; and the degree of flexibility open to important lending institutions, such as the World Bank, to adjust nominal interest rates on their long-term contracts is an issue that is clouded by institutional and political uncertainties. Last, the severely impoverished state of information about the financial asset portfolios of the NOLDCs and the degree to which those financial resources and their interest earnings are available to finance national obligations leaves us in a poor position even to measure changes in the real interest burden of *net* NOLDC debt, let alone analyze such changes in depth and make policy recommendations on the basis of such analysis.

3. In addition to the potential problems associated with a high real interest burden, the larger debt of the NOLDCs carries with it the need for a higher level of refinancing. In addition, shortening of maturities has added to the cash-flow burden on these countries. As a result, conditions in world financial markets, or in the economic condition of a country or countries, which might affect debt rollovers and renewals, pose more serious problems to the NOLDCs today than in the past. In effect, the NOLDCs are now more dependent on external financial market conditions than they were before the balance-of-payments disequilibriums of 1974-76. Furthermore, the increase in relative NOLDC indebtedness has tended to erode their general creditworthiness, thereby straining relations with external financial markets. These and other problems associated with the potential unavailability of finance are discussed below.

CREDIT RATIONING, MATURITIES, AND EXTERNAL FINANCE

To this point our discussion has largely been restricted to the factors influencing *demand* for external credit on the part of the

NOLDCs; but it is necessary to turn our attention now to factors affecting the *supply* of external finance, since one of the principal problems connected with the high level of debt is that, under certain conditions, lenders may be unwilling to extend additional credit.

Credit, it is often asserted, is rationed among borrowers, that is, loans do not necessarily go to those willing to pay the highest rate, but are allocated according to creditworthiness criteria determined by the lender. Clearly this is true of credit to the NOLDCs from official sources. Most bilateral credits are granted on generous terms, and the demand for such credits exceeds supply, which is determined by national aid policies. To a lesser extent, the same has also been true in the past of multilateral credits; that is, they were available on better terms than most NOLDCs could borrow in world credit markets. Demand exceeded supply, and so multilateral agencies rationed their loans. In recent years, these credits have become relatively more expensive, and the extent of such credit rationing has probably been reduced, at least in regard to the subclass of NOLDCs that have access to the commercial banks.

Whether commercial banks also ration credit to the NOLDCs is more difficult to determine. Certainly, descriptive accounts of the market from the trade literature suggest that credit rationing exists. Bank behavior is described as "setting country credit limits," with each bank setting separate limits for medium-term and short-term loans. Poorer risks are granted only short-term loans for trade financing. While better risks can borrow at medium-term rates, they do not necessarily obtain the amounts desired. Rather than being able to obtain additional loans by offering to pay higher rates, countries that have reached bank-imposed limits are apparently unable to get more credit.

Furthermore, there is some evidence of what has been called *dynamic* credit rationing; that is, banks increase their degree of credit rationing during periods of tight money and relax their constraints on borrowing during periods of ease. Data on publicized Eurocredits to the NOLDCs show a narrowing in the distribution of commercial bank lending to the larger traditional NOLDC loan clients in 1974 and 1975, during and immediately following severe strains on the international banking system at the time, and a broadening in the distribution in 1976 as loan demand slackened, and after the banks had rebuilt their overall liquidity. In general, as indebtedness increases, country credit-worthiness is impaired to some degree. Since this strains the willingness of commercial banks to continue to finance large current account deficits while refinancing outstanding obligations, it is an open question whether the NOLDCs will find commercial bank credit as available in a future period of balance-of-payments and international financial market crisis as they did in 1974 and 1975.

The problem of shortened maturities, noted above,[19] is significant mainly in the context of the vastly increased debt of the nonoil LDCs. In general, the existing burden of debt could lead to three classes of potential problems: (1) A country could have short-run difficulties rolling over maturing debt; this is the problem of *short-run illiquidity.* (2) A country might have difficulties meeting interest payments when due. In such a case we would speak of *long-run insolvency.* (3) Though liquid and solvent, a country might have to curtail borrowing if it had already exhausted officially or informally imposed credit limits, and as a result would be constrained to grow more slowly.

The circumstances under which these various potential problems might arise differ considerably. Insolvency can be either a generalized or a particular country phenomenon: a world recession could threaten the solvency of several developing countries at the same time, while a particular country, say a single-commodity exporter, could become insolvent if the price of its only foreign-exchange-generating export fell drastically. By contrast, illiquidity is more likely to be a generalized phenomenon, since it implies tight money in world financial markets, which could affect several countries at once. Under equilibrium conditions, where credit markets are under no strain, maturing debts are, in general, rolled over, while the inflation premium in interest rates is financed out of the new loans that are forthcoming as a result of the increment to nominal deposit balances demanded by asset holders in an inflationary world. Under such conditions, the maturity structure of country indebtedness is relatively unimportant. However, under disequilibrium conditions, if credit rationing prevails, such refinancing of principal-and-interest payments is not automatic.

Of course, liquidity difficulties will affect most severely those borrowers who have proportionally more debt due—that is, those with high levels of debt, short average maturities on their debt, or a bunching of maturities at the time, *and* those borrowers who are considered marginal by the commercial banks—marginal because, when credit tightens, they will not be considered qualified to receive further credits. Nevertheless, since almost all NOLDCs have considerable recurrent repayment obligations outstanding at any one time, and since so many of them are likely to be considered marginal borrowers under conditions of cyclical disequilibrium and tight credit in financial markets, such liquidity difficulties are likely to affect many countries at the same time.

Certainly tight money prevailed in 1974, the most recent period of cyclical economic difficulties, and it resulted in liquidity difficulties for some nonoil LDC borrowers; but fortunately, most of the large borrowers were able not only to refinance maturing obligations but to borrow large additional amounts to compensate for the imbalances in their trade accounts. Money may again become tight in the next world business-cycle disturbance, but with their larger legacy of indebtedness, liquidity difficulties are likely to prove more severe for the NOLDCs, and less additional compensatory financing may be forthcoming. In such a situation, adverse conditions in credit markets and in the world economy may tend to reinforce one another. If the world's "real" economies are depressed, it is likely that several of the other conditions that can deteriorate the balance of payments would also be experienced. By impairing creditworthiness, these other adverse changes in the balance of payments could have a "feedback" effect and act to further limit the availability of finance. Analysis of the risks associated with NOLDC debt should therefore focus on the entire complex of debt repayment problems that could occur at such a time. Not only should it concentrate on maturity analysis, but it should also investigate commercial bank rationing behavior toward the NOLDC's as well, since both are likely to be significant in future critical periods.

LDC LENDING, BANK REGULATION, AND OFFICIAL LENDERS

The expansion in lending by the international commercial banks to the nonoil LDCs has created new problems for the commercial banks as well as for the authorities responsible for supervising them. When such loans were only a small part of their portfolios, the commercial banks incurred only limited exposure and limited risks in this area and could evaluate such loans by applying traditional measures of assessing customer risk. Today, their NOLDC risk exposure is substantial, and banks are now forced to assess country as well as customer risk— that is, they are now forced to assess the risk that, even though their particular loan client did well, for one or another reason the borrower might be unable to obtain the foreign exchange to service the loan.

A major question now facing both banks and regulatory authorities is: What is a tolerable level of country exposure, and how does one evaluate country risks in general and NOLDC risks in particular? The problem of country risk exposure has been discussed extensively in conjunction with the nonoil LDCs in recent years. The trade literature contains various checklists of factors to be used in appraising country risk. The foundation for most country risk analysis is the approach to this problem developed by the World Bank.[20] This approach has two basic components: first, it attempts to identify criteria of country credit risk; second, using a small-growth-model framework, it attempts to define the critical macroeconomic relationships that make a given country's debt structure immune or subject to debt default. In recent years, several studies have been done that build on the World Bank's original work in this area and that try to identify more precisely the indicators of country debt default and the acceptable limits of country indebtedness.[21] However, much of this work suffers from neglect of some or all of the critical variables identified above: changes in the terms of trade, in real interest rates, and in conditions in international financial markets.

The problem of estimating debt magnitudes and of relating them to other economic magnitudes to obtain a measure of their significance is complicated. Obtaining a satisfactory solution to it, while screening out the distorting effects of inflation on changes in country debt, income, and exports, is a necessary first step in evaluating debt burdens and debt default risk. Also, while most country debt description and analysis focuses on gross indebtedness, a more adequate debt evaluation would view the entire financial structure of a country, including its financial asset holdings and their characteristics. Again, country credit analysis has been concerned with interest rates, but in almost all cases with nominal as opposed to real rates. We have suggested that real rates are the critical variable in assessing country interest burdens, and we have pointed out some of the complications that arise when one attempts to determine the real level of country interest burdens. Lastly, though maturities have been another focus of country credit analysis, we have argued that overall country cash-flow analysis is incomplete unless it considers such cash flow obligations in the light of the peculiarities of bank behavior, especially rationing behavior, and the impact of world financial market conditions on flows of credit for financing loan principal-and-interest payments when they come due.

Obviously, the problems involved in assessing country risk are imposing. Still, if we are to attempt such analysis, it is better to start with concepts that capture the relevant variables—for example, *net* indebtedness, the real rate of interest—rather than with concepts that ignore the complexities of the real world.

These novel problems regarding country credit assessment carry over into the area of bank regulation and risk management in the financial system by regulatory bodies in the developed countries. What is of interest here is not only the level of country risk assumed by individual banks but the level of risk assumed by the international commercial banks as a group as well. In general, bank regulation limits a bank's exposure to a single borrower and requires diversification of bank portfolios. In dealing with international credits, especially those involving the developing countries, data deficiencies and the lack of information about foreign borrowers pose special problems for bank regulators responsible for supervising bank loan activities and maintaining the quality of bank loan portfolios. Further problems arise in applying these limits on bank portfolio composition to international loans. Regulatory authorities are now considering how to assess and control a bank's total exposure in a foreign country and are investigating methods of limiting country as well as customer risk.[22] But without a more thorough understanding of what is involved in country risk, and how to measure it, the appropriateness of any regulatory procedure must remain open to question.

When establishing principles for bank regulation, regulatory bodies must concern themselves with the health of the entire banking system as well as with that of individual banks, since at the broadest policy levels the two are no longer separable. However, lending to the nonoil LDCs is done in large part by the foreign Euro-subsidiaries and branches of the international commercial banks, and loans are usually syndicated among banks with home offices in different developed countries. The multinational character both of the banks and of their syndicated NOLDC loans may require that regulation and supervision of these loan activities be performed on an international, rather than a national, basis.

The emergence of commercial banks as a significant source of external financing for the nonoil LDCs raises other policy issues as well. One corollary of this development has been a lessening of the influence of the major official lenders, since they are no longer exclusive sources of compensatory financing for the NOLDCs. Thus, relationships between official lenders and commercial banks have become an emerging area of policy concern.

The official lenders have been a source of policy advice for developing countries, and their special role as concessional lenders under conditions of economic and balance-of-payments duress has given them considerable policy leverage with particular countries. This has been especially true of the IMF, which prior to the emergence of the commercial banks as important compensatory balance-of-payments lenders was the principal source of emergency financing for developing countries in balance-of-payments difficulties. The availability of commercial bank financing for balance-of-payments support provides many developing countries with a new policy option during periods of payments duress, and it poses questions regarding the appropriate relations between commercial banks and official lenders when supporting countries during balance-of-payments adjustment periods.

To some extent, it has appeared that the presence of commercial bank financing, by offering an alternative external channel of finance, has reduced the effectiveness of intervention by the official lenders, as countries with access to commercial financing may now bypass official strictures by obtaining external finance from other sources. On the other hand, the banks have come to realize that the ultimate solvency of their balance-of-payments loans depends in large part on the adoption of adequate adjustment policies by recipient countries. To a limited degree, they themselves have attempted to use their leverage as lenders to influence developing country policies; but they have not been conspicuously successful in their role as advisers on macroeconomic policy. On occasion, the commercial banks have refused to lend unless the borrowing country followed the policy advice of official lenders, but on other occasions the banks have not observed such restraints.

Future developments in the relations between the commercial banks, official agencies, and the nonoil LDCs are as yet uncertain. As the issues involved are complex, and as their ramifications extend to many areas of the world financial structure, a more detailed investigation of them is likely to be an appropriate task for concerned analysts and policymakers.

IV. SUMMARY AND CONCLUSION

The research program of which this paper forms a part began with a fairly straightforward objective—evaluating the significance of the increased debt of the nonoil less developed countries. Since debt is incompletely reported in official publications, we first had to assemble our own statistics. The estimates we arrived at proved to be substantially larger than those reported by the World Bank, primarily because we included certain classes of loans not reported by the World Bank. Our figures show a gross debt (excluding direct investment) of $159 billion at year-end 1976, against $108.8 billion using the World Bank's numbers, for a comparable group of countries.

That the nominal debt of the NOLDCs was growing throughout the period 1972-76 there can be no doubt, since it has more than doubled over those years regardless of whose figures are chosen. But since we are dealing with a period of significant world inflation, we had to separate that part of the increase in debt which simply represented a rise in world prices from the increase in real value. It is not clear what deflator is appropriate for this calculation, since international debt is not used to buy, and is not repaid with, any clearly defined basket of goods whose prices could be used to construct a deflator. Employing different price indices as deflators for nominal debt gives us divergent results: using one measure (the NOLDC export price index) the real value of debt grew by only 9 percent, while another measure (the U.S. GNP deflator) indicates a rise of 58 percent from 1972 to 1976. Another approach, that of comparing nominal debt to nominal GNP, indicates that for the NOLDCs taken as a group, the ratio of debt to GNP has grown from 26 percent in 1972 to 35 percent in 1976—a substantial increase in *relative* indebtedness over a period in which it is estimated that real NOLDC output grew by 28 percent, which implies that the increase in the real value of debt must be considerably greater than the latter figure.

However, *net* NOLDC indebtedness does not necessarily have to move proportionally to gross indebtedness. Investigating the question of how borrowed funds have been utilized by the NOLDCs, we discovered that these countries hold foreign financial assets equal to more than half of their external liabilities, though the precise figure is indeterminate, given the poor quality and coverage of the information available. Our first result indicates that the debt (in real terms) is increasing more rapidly than is usually reported, but this second finding appears to mitigate the seriousness of the situation, since net debt is apparently much smaller than gross.

We then investigated the real interest burden, both currently and in the recent past, imposed on the NOLDCs by the stock of their outstanding debt. Our conclusion here is that the increasing nominal interest payments of 1973-76 were not very significant, since throughout that period the average real interest rate on NOLDC debt was around zero, or only marginally positive, as interest rates generally failed to keep pace with world inflation. However, our analysis suggests that the existence of a large overhang of debt could prove to be a substantial burden *if* real interest rates become significantly positive at some point in the future.

In the course of our research we reviewed the financial history of the nonoil LDC's during the most disturbed period since the end of World War II. The major factor behind the increase in debt was a three-year episode of massive balance-of-payments deficits. Investigating these deficits, we found that here also it is important to distinguish price from real effects. Doing so, we found that had no price changes occurred from the base year 1972 on, the ratio of aggregate resource transfer to aggregate GNP (for the NOLDCs) would have increased in 1974 and 1975 but would have fallen by 1977 to levels closer to, though not as low as, those typical of the period 1970-72. That the oil-deficit countries had taken significant measures to close the resource gap was obvious; equally obvious also was the fact that relative prices have moved against them; and, as a consequence, despite policies designed to control physical quantities of imports and exports, the resource deficit of the NOLDCs remains uncomfortably large.

Much of the recent literature on our topic falls into one of two categories: optimistic or pessimistic, alarmist or "comforting." Alarmist analysis holds that the debt of the NOLDCs is a grave cause for alarm, while the "comforting" school of thought implies that the problem, if there is one, has been exaggerated by sensationalist writers. We have tried to avoid taking a position on this point, since our research has shown us how difficult it is to state even simple declarative propositions about any part of this complex problem without significant qualification. We observe that to date the existence of the debt has not caused major problems (except in special cases, which are fortunately not generalized), but that there are certain conditions—not wildly improbably ones, either—under which it could become one, both for the NOLDCs themselves and for international financial markets and their participants.

We have no means of evaluating the relative probabilities of optimistic or pessimistic predictions being proved correct. But we can attempt an assessment of the situation by painting a number of different scenarios and let the reader choose between them. The optimistic scenario presents a world of relatively tranquil but fairly rapid growth accompanied by mild inflation, in which price changes for NOLDC imports and exports lead to favorable, or at least neutral, movements in the terms of trade for the nonoil countries. In this world, the relationship between inflation and interest rates is such that the NOLDCs continue to pay low, or even zero, real interest rates, while the growth of international liquidity and the absence of serious disturbances in international financial markets assures that credit rationing never becomes a significant problem.

Against this, the pessimistic or alarmist scenario can be divided into two subtypes: the first displays a picture of generally conservative macroeconomic policies in the developed world, largely motivated by the experience and fear of recurrent inflation. This is a world of slow growth and deflationary policies, though given the experience of the last several years it is unlikely that prices would actually decline. Still, tight financial markets in the developed countries could mean that, in this picture, real interest rates would be high, so that the real interest burden on the NOLDCs could become oppressive, while this oppression would not be mitigated by a rapid increase in the growth of NOLDC exports to a demand-constrained developed world.

Finally, the second version of the alarmist scenario shows us a world quite similar in many respects to the one of the recent past. Here we observe a continuation of inflationary boom-and-bust cycles like those of 1973-75, leading, perhaps, to further deterioration in the terms of trade of the nonoil LDCs as short-lived commodity booms are succeeded by busts brought about by installation of new capacity and falling developed world demand. Though the high inflation of such a world is likely to be favorable to real interest rates, keeping them low or negative, at the same time the persistence of inflation is likely to lead to episodes of extremely tight credit in the industrial countries, which could lead to periods of credit rationing by the banks toward the NOLDCs. Of course, whether this last scenario is really optimistic or pessimistic depends in large part on the relative length and strength of boom and bust: a prolonged inflationary expansion could increase demand for NOLDC exports while inflation was wiping out new debt as fast as it could be borrowed. If such a situation were to continue long enough and were followed by a *short* world recession, the NOLDCs might be much better off than if the boom had never happened. However, the experience of the recent past indicates that the depth of any future world recession is likely to be proportional to the height reached by the preceding boom.

In the long run, we suspect that the seriousness of the NOLDC debt situation depends in large part on the ability of these countries to bring their trade accounts with the rest of the world closer into balance. The most likely way of accomplishing this is either by expanding labor-intensive exports to the developed world (here the lower real wage rates that prevail in the NOLDCs will be a factor in their favor), or by exploiting currently underutilized national resource endowments that become relatively cheaper due to the exhaustion of easily obtainable supplies in the "older" developed economies.

However, in the short run *and* for a future extending beyond that, debt is definitely a problem for these countries. We are in no position to judge which, if any, of the scenarios we had painted is most likely to occur. It is obvious, at least, that the potential problems posed by the existence of NOLDC debt are serious enough to merit concern and are deserving of more detailed investigation on the part of analysts, both of the prospects of the developing countries and of world financial markets.

NOTES

1. We have attempted to make this paper a relatively broad and nontechnical survey. The reader will judge whether we have succeeded in our intention. For a fuller discussion of theoretical issues and technical and statistical arguments, see our forthcoming papers: (1) "The Debt-Related Problems of the Non-Oil Less-Developed Countries;" (2)"The Real Value of International Financial Assets: The Case of the Non-Oil LDC Debt"; and (3) "Disturbances in the Balance of Payments of the Non-Oil LDC's' Retrospect and Prospect." All are available from the authors upon request.

2. World Bank, *World Debt Tables*, vols. 1 and 2, September 1977. Though we have expanded our definition of the debt of the NOLDCs, we have adopted the IMF's narrower definition of non-oil-developing countries, which excludes southern European countries. For a comparable group of NOLDCs, World Bank estimates of debt are $49.5 billion in 1972 and $108.8 billion in 1976.

3. Some analysts prefer to exclude short-term debt, as much of it is trade-related and self-liquidating. While any particular loans may be easily liquidated, this is not true of the stock of such debts. Furthermore, if short-term debt is neglected, refinancing short-term debt with long-term debt will indicate a deterioration rather than an improvement in country liquidity. With available statistics, one cannot separate accurately the short-term from the long-term debt for most countries. For the NOLDCs as a group, recent estimates are that the short-term debt amounts to about $50 billion.

4. BIS, *Annual Report* no. 47, Basle, 1977.

5. OECD, Development Assistance Committee, Chairman's Report, Paris, various issues.

6. As a final caveat, we should point out that all available data on the size of the debt are far from perfect. The World Bank gathers statistics only on government and government-guaranteed debt of more than one year. Those desiring more comprehensive statistics must assemble them themselves by piecing together figures from various sources. The resulting figures given in Table 8.1 undoubtedly contain errors of unknown sign and magnitude.

7. Our measure of the resource transfer is equivalent to the current account deficit as usually stated in the balance of payments, *less* net interest payments and profit remittances. We hesitated before settling on this definition, as it would be equally logical to subsettling on this definition, as it would be equally logical to subtract unrequited private transfers as well from the current account deficit. These private transfers consist primarily, at least for those countries for which data are available, of remittances of nationals working abroad, and hence are

equivalent to a service export. If this latter definition of the resource transfer had been adopted, it would appear to be 20 to 35 percent smaller each year, and the ratio of the resource transfer to GNP would be correspondingly less. If the reader prefers to take this alternative definition, he will have sound grounds for doing so: balance-of-payments categories are largely conventional, and good arguments can be made for altering them to suit the purpose at hand.

8. *International Financial Statistics,* 30, no. 5 (May 1977); 31, no. 6 (June 1978).

9. Real exports = volume of exports/export price index; similarly for real imports. Since imports exceeded exports, the resulting values are negative.

10. BIS News Release, June 1977.

11. Consider a case in which the nominal value of debt does not change, while the real value falls 5 percent per annum due to inflation. If the borrower pays a 5 percent inflation premium (the lender adds 5 percent to the real rate), the result is equivalent to amortizing 5 percent of the total debt each year. See also our discussion of the inflation premium in section II on interest payments.

12. BIS, *Quarterly Report* (Spring 1978), Table 7: "External Positions in Domestic and Foreign Currency of Banks in Group of Ten Countries and Switzerland and of the Foreign Branches of U.S. Banks in the Caribbean Area and the Far East."

13. For a complete discussion of the mechanics of these estimates, see our paper, "The Debt-Related Problems of the Non-Oil Less-Developed Countries." Mimeo available from the authors.

14. See, e.g., Helen Hughes, "The External Debt of Developing Countries," *Finance and Development,* 14, no. 4 (December 1977): 22-25; Gordon W. Smith, *The External Debt Prospects of the Non-Oil-Exporting Developing Countries* (Washington, D.C., Overseas Development Council, 1977); and Robert S. Solomon, "A Perspective on the Debt of Developing Countries," *Brookings Papers on Economic Activity,* no. 2 (1977): 479-501.

15. Dragoslav Avramovic et al., *Economic Growth and External Debt* (Baltimore: Johns Hopkins University Press [for the World Bank], 1964); Benjamin B. King, *Notes on the Mechanics of Growth and Debt,* World Bank Staff Occasional Paper No. 6 (Baltimore: Johns Hopkins University Press, 1968); and Gershon Feder, *Economic Growth, Foreign Loans and Debt Servicing Capacity of Developing Countries,* World Bank Staff Working Paper No. 274, Washington, D.C., February 1978, are some (though not all) of the important works in this area.

16. See our paper, "The Real Value of International Financial Assets: The Case of the Non-Oil LDC Debt." Mimeo available from the authors.

17. See pp. 255ff., on the Resource Transfer for the source of these figures, and Table 8.2.

18. The degree to which high fixed nominal rate debt becomes costly as rates of inflation decline will depend in part upon the willingness and ability of fixed-interest-rate lenders, such as the World Bank, to call their own outstanding high-cost bonds and to refinance at lower prevailing interest rates and pass on the interest savings to their LDC loan clients.

19. See pp. 253 for a discussion of the Stock of LDC Debt.

20. Avramovic et al., *Economic Growth and External Debt.*

21. King, *Notes on the Mechanics of Growth and Debt;* Feder, *Economic Growth, Foreign Loans and Debt Servicing Capacity;* Solomon, "A Perspective on the Debt of Developing Countries."

22. See Federal Reserve Bank of New York, "A New Supervisory Approach to Foreign Lending," *Quarterly Review,* 3 no. 1 (Spring 1978): 1-6.

Chapter 9

INSTITUTIONAL ASPECTS OF DEVELOPING COUNTRIES' DEBT PROBLEMS *

CONSTANTINE MICHALOPOULOS

Agency for International Development

I. INTRODUCTION

The rapid rise in developing countries' international indebtedness, especially in the aftermath of the 1973 oil price crisis, has given rise to serious concerns about their future ability to service

* I wish to express my gratitude to Neal Riden of for his valuable assistance and advice in the preparation of this paper. Over the years, he has been the source of a huge amount of information and wise counsel on the issue of international indebtedness and the functioning of the U.S. and foreign private capital markets. In addition, I would like to express my thanks to David Denoon of the EXIM Bank and Keith Jay of AID for useful comments on previous drafts. Gerry Benedick and Deborah Miller of AID contributed greatly to the collection of statistical material for this paper. All remaining errors are my responsibility. The author is Deputy Assistant Administrator for Economic Affairs of AID. This paper expresses solely the personal views of the author and does not necessarily reflect the policy of AID.

their foreign debt without compromising development objectives. The bulk of the additional credits to developing countries during the last few years has been extended by private institutions, mostly commercial banks. If the developing countries were to have general difficulties in servicing this debt, some feel that the viability of the international monetary system would be undermined.

On the other hand, the bulk of the increases in debt to private institutions has been concentrated in a few of the more advanced developing countries. An important question is whether the existing international institutions and policy instruments are adequate to deal with future debt-servicing problems that might arise in these countries.

Foreign debts of the low-income developing countries have also increased in the last few years. But in the case of these countries, the key question for the future is whether the net inflow of resources is adequate to meet their development objectives and, in this connection, whether debt relief should be used as an instrument to augment net resource flows.

The future ability of the developing countries to service their foreign debts depends on various factors affecting their balance payments, the international private capital markets, and aid flows from the developed countries. The first part of the paper examines the balance of payments, resource flows, debt structure, and development prospects of developing countries as well as the international economic environment in which they will be operating in the short term and up to 1985. For this purpose, projections by the World Bank in its *World Development Report* are used, modified in some instances by projections from other sources. In the following section, this general economic framework is used to place in perspective the different types of debt problems likely to be faced by developing countries. Subsequent sections examine the evolving international institutional structure and policy instruments that deal with developing countries' debt problems and evaluate proposals for their modification. First, the question of using debt relief as an instrument to increase net resource flows to low-income developing countries is discussed. Then debt issues arising from increased commercial borrowing by the more advanced developing countries are addressed. Finally, various proposals designed to strengthen the capacity of the international community to prevent, as well as deal with, debt crisis situations are assessed.

II. FUTURE ECONOMIC PROSPECTS
OF DEVELOPING COUNTRIES

For the purposes of debt analysis, developing countries can be divided into three major groups: (1) the low-income countries (LICs) with per capita income less than $300 per annum in 1977 prices; (2) the middle-income countries (MICs) with per capita income over $300 to roughly $3,000 per annum; and (3) the oil-exporting, capital-surplus developing countries. Debt issues arise in the context of the first two groups. However, the uses to which the capital surplus of the oil exporters is put and the international financial instruments they employ have an important bearing on the prospects of the other two groups and their ability to cope with mounting foreign indebtedness.

World Bank and other projections point to the following conclusions about the future prospects of developing countries: [1]

1. Economic growth in the low-income countries primarily in South Asia and Sub-Sahara Africa will continue to be slower over the next few years than rates of growth for the middle-income group and the developed countries. The IBRD estimates low-income country growth to be 4.7 percent per annum compared with 5.3 percent for the middle-income countries, between 1975 and 1985. This compares with a 3.9 and 6 percent annual growth rate, respectively, achieved by these countries in the period 1960 to 1970.

2. Export growth is critical to the future development prospects and debt-servicing ability of developing countries. In the simplest sense, the higher the export growth, *ceteris paribus,* the more external debt can be serviced. Moreover, the higher the export growth, the lower the requirements for net borrowing and debt accumulation. Finally, the stronger the export growth prospects, the greater the willingness of private creditors to extend additional credits, because the country is considered more

creditworthy. The World Bank projects that developing country exports will grow at a rate of 6.1 percent per year between now and 1985, compared with 5.9 percent in the period 1960 to 1975.

Export growth depends critically on the rate of expansion in the economies of the industrialized countries of the OECD, their degree of protectionism toward developing countries' exports and the developing countries' own policies in providing the proper incentives for an outward-looking, export-oriented development strategy.

The World Bank forecasts noted above assume a rate of economic expansion in the OECD of approximately 4.2 percent per annum for the 1980s. However, the near-term forecasts in the OECD are for significantly lower rates of growth. Unless growth in the OECD picks up significantly in the latter part of the period, developing countries' export and GNP growth prospects may have to revised downward.

Protectionist tendencies in many OECD countries have led to the erection of nontariff barriers on items of importance to the developing countries' trade. These tendencies have been manifested even in the GATT Multilateral Trade Negotiations (MTN) which aim at reducing overall barriers to trade. OECD offers for tariff or other NTB reductions on items of interest to developing countries have tended to be less generous than on items of interest to other OECD countries. On the other hand, a number of developing countries with more diversified manufacturing export structures are likely to benefit from the general liberalization of trade barriers in the OECD countries resulting from the MTN. Similarly, the developing countries, especially in the MIC group, would continue to enjoy some, although small, benefits from the Generalized System of Preferences. On balance and despite the MTN, there is considerable uncertainty at the moment about the future trade policy of developed countries and its impact on developing countries' export growth.

In terms of their own policies, many developing countries have learned the lessons of unbridled import substitution of the 1960s and have moved toward more outward-looking, export-oriented policies. However, the incentives they offer in the form of export subsidies are running into increasing opposition in the

OECD in the form of countervailing duty or selective safeguard actions.

3. To maintain the rate of economic expansion projected, developing countries will need a multifold increase in Official Development Assistance (ODA) flows from the multilateral development banks and especially from the private sector. The World Bank estimates that ODA would need to grow in real terms by 2.3 percent per annum from $19.6 billion in 1975 to $52.5 billion by 1985, while private flows, especially Eurocurrency and other banking loans, would need to rise 3.9 percent per annum, from $26.0 billion in 1975 to $55.1 billion in 1985. If developing countries' export growth is lower, there may be need for additional borrowing, particularly by middle-income countries, to finance imports associated with the pace of economic activity projected.

4. There is a significant difference between low-income and middle-income countries in terms of the source of external financing. Low-income countries depend heavily on ODA and other official flows [2] for the bulk of their external financing. Middle-income countries, while continuing to be significant recipients of ODA in absolute terms, rely on such assistance only for a relatively small proportion (22 percent) of their total financing needs. The World Bank projects needs for ODA flows to low-income countries at $23.6 billion or 45 percent of total ODA. This estimate may well be too low, as it seems to have been derived—as most such estimates are—by reference to projected current account deficits.[3] However, resource needs in low-income countries may well be higher if measured by reference to domestic savings gaps, which may tend to be more limiting of development prospects in such countries. This is especially true for countries that embark upon programs aimed at addressing basic needs of their population and that tend to have large components of local fixed and recurrent costs.

5. Total outstanding public and publicly guaranteed debt of the developing countries reported by the World Bank was $197.7 billion as of the end of 1977.[4] To this must be added approximately $45.4 billion of private nonguaranteed debt.[5]

Public and publicly guaranteed debt for the LICs amounted to $48.3 billion, compared with $149.4 billion for the MICs. The bulk of the private nonguaranteed credits ($43.2 billion, or 95.2 percent) was accumulated by middle-income countries. If one excludes the major oil-exporting countries, public and publicly guaranteed debt for the remaining developing countries rose from $73.4 billion in 1973 to $166.5 billion in 1977.

The implications of the future aid and capital flow projections are clearly that the growth of developing countries' indebtedness to private creditors will continue. The IBRD estimates imply that total developing countries' outstanding long-term debt [6] by 1985 will be $740 billion, of which $302 billion will be to official creditors and $438 billion to the private sector. Most of the increases in debt, especially of debt owed to private creditors, will occur in the MIC group. LIC debt will also grow substantially, but most will be in the form of soft ODA credits.

The absolute size of this debt is quite large. While the increase in debt is a widespread phenomenon, most of the debt is concentrated in a few countries. The top three debtor countries constitute 41 percent and the top ten 70 percent of total commercial bank debt outstanding.

The scenario of growth in product, exports, and debt sketched out above is one which, while perhaps not close to achieving developing countries' aspirations, will enable them to promote their economic development at a pace somewhat better than in recent years. The feasibility of the overall scenario clearly hinges on the willingness of official and private lenders to extend additional credits and hence, in a sense, to contribute to the accumulation of further debt. But more foreign debt is not necessarily a bad thing. The other side of increased foreign indebtedness is increased availability of foreign resources for domestic development. While availability of foreign credits should not result in decreased efforts to raise developing countries' internal savings, it is doubtful that these countries' development objectives can be achieved solely through increased internal savings or improved resource allocation. The key issue, then, is how to develop institutions and policies that will promote the productive use of foreign credits as well as permit the developing countries to manage a rising level of foreign indebtedness without disrupting their development process.

III. DEBT ISSUES

Within the overall economic setting outlined above for the 1980s, the capacity of individual countries to cope with rising levels of indebtedness and the likelihood that they might encounter debt-servicing problems will vary significantly. For several, debt management will continue to be a vexing problem defying easy solutions. The problem, moreover, may be more widespread and severe if a slightly more pessimistic general economic scenario develops for a variety of reasons; for example, slower growth or greater protectionism by the developed countries. In either case, however, the types of problems developing countries are likely to encounter will tend to vary according to their level of development and the degree of reliance on official or private credits.

THE NET RESOURCE TRANSFER PROBLEM

For some low-income countries whose outstanding debt and current financing of capital inflows is heavily dependent on official development assistance, the key problem is that debt-service payments in some instances can be expected to remain for some time at a high level relative to gross capital inflows. Gross disbursement of total official aid and private credits to these countries in 1976 amounted to $13.4 billion. However, debt service absorbed slightly more than a quarter of this amount, so that net transfers were only $9.9 billion.

Debt service on outstanding ODA debt is usually fairly small because of the relatively soft terms on which ODA credits are extended. However, for some countries debt service on harder commercial credits adds significant amounts to their annual debt-servicing burden. In general, though, and with some notable exceptions such as Sudan and Bangladesh, low-income countries do not have high debt service to exports or debt to

GNP ratios. Debt service ratios of LICs averaged 7.6 percent in 1977 compared with 9.2 percent for MICs.

On the other hand, the economies of the low-income countries are more frail and less flexible that those of MICs and thus more prone to internal disruption or debt crises when subjected to external shocks. The problem of low-income countries is that they have been experiencing low growth rates of output and that their net inflow of resources is inadequate to raise their overall rate of economic growth to levels consistent with their long-term development objectives. This pattern will continue in the 1980s, with the result that income disparities betweeen low- and middle-income developing countries will widen.

This is not, strictly speaking, a general debt problem. Rather, the problem faced by the international community in the low-income countries is how to raise the net resource flows to these countries on terms consistent with their debt-servicing ability in order to raise their lagging rate of economic growth. The debt issue is whether efforts to increase net resource flows should include provision of debt relief in the absence of an imminent default situation, that is whether debt relief measures for these countries should be used as alternatives to development assistance for the purpose of increasing net resource flows.

MATURITY STRUCTURE

For some developing countries, especially but not solely in the middle-income group, the total size of their outstanding debt relative to such aggregates as GNP may not be excessive. However, this debt might consist of a heavy proportion of short- and medium-term credits, primarily in the form of Eurocurrency bank lending. This debt might give rise to servicing problems for a variety of reasons. The credits obtained may not result in increases in production and domestic savings in time to permit repayment in accordance with the predetermined schedule. An extreme case of this problem might arise when a developing country is borrowing heavily to sustain consumption import levels and the credits do not directly or indirectly result in increments of domestic capital formation. Under such circumstances, the country may be forced to curtail its future rate of growth and imports in order to service debt. Alternatively, problems might arise if a developing country is unable, because of domestic structural difficulties or because of conditions in international markets, to expand its exports in a timely fashion so as to permit servicing of the debt.

In such cases, the willingness of private creditors to roll over debt and thus *de facto* lengthen maturities is critical. The willingness to roll over debt as well as increase the volume of gross lending, which is projected to be necessary if these countries are to continue to grow in the 1980s, is a function of many factors: confidence in the long-term management and economic performance of the debtor is obviously critical. However, some more technical factors are also important. For example, individual international banks may be approaching exposure limits in individual countries, thus requiring that the number of private banking institutions engaged in lending to developing countries increase in order to assure increases in total gross private bank lending.

A problem related to the maturity structure issue is that of bunching. In some instances, the overall term structure and long-term profile of the developing country debt portfolio may well be appropriate, but, due to unusual circumstances, there are sharp deviations leading to a heavier than optimal debt-servicing burden for a short period. This could well be a problem in the late 1970s and early 1980s for developing countries that borrowed very heavily from private banks in 1974-76 to finance large current account deficits during that period.

The potential magnitude of such problems is higher for the middle-income countries that have accumulated and are projected to accumulate the bulk of short- and medium-term private credits. While these countries are usually better able to use credits productively and their export structure is more diversified and dynamic, the vast and unprecedented amounts of private medium-term debt already accumulated and the amounts projected for the future have raised general concerns about their overall ability to service such debt. The rapid expansion of private debt and the ability of the developing countries to service it without compromising their growth objectives or undermining the viability of the international monetary system poses the single largest overall challenge to be faced by the international community on the matter of developing countries' debt in the next few years.

While the attention here and elsewhere has focused on the middle-income countries, maturity structure problems arise also in the lower-income countries, some of which have accumulated significant amounts of short to medium-term debt from a variety of sources. Improved development performance in these countries hinges on overcoming serious deficiencies in physical and human infrastructure, raising productivity in the agricultural sector, and general transformation of subsistence economies. Such changes can occur only over a period of years. Payoffs for social and infrastructure projects are typically quite long. In addition, emphasis on domestic investment in public service sectors or other sectors aimed at increasing production of goods and services critical to meeting the basic needs of the poor may well not permit adequate expansion in production of exportables. Saddling these countries with debt of short maturity and hard terms, especially in the context of addressing short-term balance-of-payments problems, is a sure way of courting debt crises in the future.

DEBT CRISES

By debt crises we mean situations where for a variety of reasons a developing country finds it impossible to service its debts *and seeks relief from its creditors* (official and/or private). If a rate of economic expansion that is viewed as desirable proves unsustainable, developing countries usually take steps to prevent facing default on their external debt. The cost is simply borne in terms of lower rates of economic growth than could be sustained for any given level of gross capital inflows. However, developing countries often do face debt-service crisis situations, either because of circumstances beyond their control or because of bad management or inadequate planning. These arise essentially when further domestic and import retrenchment is so costly in terms of suppressing domestic consumption or political survival of a particular government that it proves necessary to seek recourse in debt relief or default on foreign obligations. Since default penalizes the debtor in terms of his ability to obtain new private or official credits as well as the creditor who is not getting paid, few defaults actually occur. Rather, countries facing imminent default situations seek debt relief. Questions arise as to what are the best institutional mechanisms and policy instruments available to the international community for handling debt relief in crises situations.

The actual incidence of formal debt relief operations has not been large over the years. Since 1956, there have been thirty-eight multilateral debt renegotiations involving only eleven developing countries.[7] Four countries (India, Indonesia, Ghana, and Chile) have accounted for half of the reschedulings. Of these negotiations, seventeen occurred in the context of the so-called creditor club mechanism. Another fourteen occurred in the context of IBRD or OECD-led aid consortia, and the remaining involved special ad hoc arrangements. Since 1973, there have been two to three reschedulings a year, a number not significantly different from the average in previous years.[8]

To the extent that developing countries and the international community can take action through existing or new institutions and policy instruments to address the problems outlined above, the likelihood that debt crises will arise in individual countries will diminish. But they may occur, nevertheless. Thus there are two types of institutional issues that need to be addressed for the future. These concern what actions are needed, if any, to improve: (1) existing international institutions and policies that are aimed at addressing developing countries' problems and preventing the incidence of individual debt crises; and (2) the international community's ability to deal with individual debt crises as they arise and prevent them from recurring or being generalized.

IV. DEBT RELIEF AS AN INSTRUMENT OF INCREASING RESOURCE FLOWS

Net resource flows to the low-income countries through Official Development Assistance have increased only slightly in real terms over the last decade. Given the problems most developed countries are facing in increasing assistance, can and should debt relief be extended as a regular means of increasing net resource flows to developing countries? If so, what institutional arrangements are appropriate for this purpose? Without doubt, this has been one of the main issues of contention in the debt area between developing and developed countries in the past three to four years—ever since the oil crisis and recession in the West contributed to a serious deterioration of the balance-of-payments positions for oil-importing developing countries.

GENERALIZED DEBT RELIEF

The developing countries proposed in the Manila Declaration, at UNCTAD IV, and at the Conference on International Economic Cooperation (CIEC), generalized debt relief to take the form of cancellation of ODA debts for the Relatively Least Developed Countries (RLDCs) and Most Seriously Affected countries (MSAs), as well as moratoriums on debt repayments for other low-income developing countries.[9]

These proposals encountered strong opposition from the major donors, who argued that generalized relief is an inequitable form of resource transfer since the benefits from such relief do not necessarily correspond to current aid needs; that the burden of relief would fall disproportionately on donors that have extended assistance over long periods of time; that this form of assistance is not likely to be additional to other forms of assistance—and that in any case, several countries (including the United States) were prohibited by law to cancel debts or provide generalized reschedulings. As the debate progressed, especially in UNCTAD, the more drastic of these developing countries' demands for general relief were abandoned. At the same time, various donors took action to provide relief on past ODA debt for groups of developing countries (see below). Donors that did so were careful to stress that their action was aimed at increasing net resource flows to beneficiaries and not because the beneficiaries of such actions were suffering from a debt problem per se.

THE UNCTAD TDB MINISTERIAL MEETING
AND RETROACTIVE TERMS ADJUSTMENT

This process of rapprochement between developed and developing countries culminated at the UNCTAD Trade and Development Board (TDB) Ministerial Meeting in March 1978.

The substance of the agreement reached at this meeting can be summarized as follows: (1) The developed countries agreed "to seek and adopt measures to adjust terms of past ODA or other equivalent measures as a means of improving the net ODA flows." This concept of so-called retroactive terms adjustment (RTA) typically involves converting past ODA loans into grants, and as such is equivalent to debt relief. (2) The definition of the beneficiaries of such action was left rather vague through the use of such terms as "poorer developing countries and particularly the least developed." Several of the donors, however, explicitly stated their intention to limit their actions to the least-developed group. (3) It was agreed that each donor country would "determine the distribution and the net flows involved within the context of its own aid policy." This implies that the beneficiaries would be chosen by each developed country. It represented a *de facto* abandonment of developing countries' requests for generalized relief for whole categories—except to the extent that the beneficiaries were to be chosen among the group of the "poorer" and particularly the least developed.

The Ministerial agreement essentially involved a further commitment by developed countries to increase resource flows to the poorer countries but to do so through a variety of instruments, including RTA. It was possible, for them to agree to this because the commitment was made in the context of increasing resource flows and not through the explicit provision of generalized, debt relief, about which most continue to have serious reservations. Developed country agreement was facilitated by the fact that RTA or equivalent measures were limited to the poorer countries and especially the least developed, whose level of outstanding ODA debt is relatively small. This meant that the cost to the developed countries in the form of additional resource flows would also be modest. The developing countries, on the other hand, were able to agree because they saw that they were obtaining a fairly concrete commitment for additional resource flows linked in some manner to their overall debt situation.

It should be stressed that the concept of RTA has inherent logic and is not important merely because it provided a basis for a diplomatic bargain. In recent years, many developed countries have been extending aid to the least-developed countries solely or predominantly through grants in recognition of the long-term difficulties faced by these countries in achieving their development objectives. It was thus logical that terms of previous ODA to these countries should be adjusted to reflect the more recent recognition of their problems.

The total developing country benefits from the agreement are likely to be modest in comparison with their total debt-servicing obligations. On the basis of imcomplete information, it appears that the total debt that may be effectively cancelled might be of the order of $4.5 billion, involving perhaps $150 to 200 million in annual servicing. However, the amounts will not be inconsequential for individual low-income countries.

The United States has obtained congressional authority to provide retroactive terms adjustment for the least-developed countries. The total outstanding ODA debt to the United States by these countries is approximately $1 billion. The extent to which the United States actually provides RTA in any given year and in total, however, will depend on the amounts appropriated by the Congress for this purpose. This cannot be predicted with any accuracy at this time.[10]

DEBT RELIEF AS AID ON A CASE-BY-CASE BASIS

While the TDB agreement would involve only modest benefits to developing countries, it represented a nice diplomatic bargain that put to rest the contentious issue of *generalized* debt relief as a form of development assistance. However, the UNCTAD agreement did not resolve the issue of whether to use debt relief on a *case-by-case* basis as an instrument of increased resource transfers. At the UNCTAD Ministerial Meeting, this issue was put aside. It is being considered in the current UNCTAD discussions of the definition of "features" for future debt renegotiations.

The issue is whether debt relief would be provided, in the absence of an *imminent default* situation, in the context of providing economic assistance and in light of a developing country's development plans and prospects. For example, developing Countries' representatives at the December 1977 UNCTAD experts meeting stressed that "future debt reorganizations shall be established in the context of international cooperation and development," meaning in the context of aid; also, that "international actions (including debt relief) should be taken early, before the occurrence of a debt crisis"; and finally that "analysis of the economic situations of the developing debtor country should be carried out within the framework of internationally agreed "development targets." [11] The latter reference would presumably permit a developing country to seek and obtain assistance, including rescheduling of debt payments due, if its GNP fell short of such general targets as the 6 percent per annum agreed upon as desirable for the United Nations Second Development Decade. While debt rescheduling has been extended in nonimminent default situations in the past, and although it is envisaged that debt reorganization could be undertaken in nonimminent default situations under the US/EC proposal (see section VII pp. 321), some donors, and especially the United States, have been reluctant to use debt rescheduling as a regular mechanism to provide assistance to low-income developing countries.

It is necessary to dwell briefly on this attitude about debt rescheduling because it might appear at first glance quite peculiar. After all, the impact of debt rescheduling on a recipient's economy is not unlike that of new aid. Indeed, it can be high-quality aid insofar as it is untied, quick disbursing, and its terms could be highly concessional. And yet there are problems. First, if the debtor country knows that the likelihood of obtaining reschedulings on a regular basis is high, there is less pressure to manage its economy effectively and in a manner that is consistent with its international obligations. Another type of problem arises from the developing countries' demands that development objectives as well as international targets be taken into account when judging the need for debt rescheduling or other remedial action. While promoting economic development of developing countries is in general a shared objective between aid donors and recipients, it is quite clear that a debt crisis and/or a need for additional external financing can result from the recipient's setting unrealistic goals; similarly, if a developing country falls short of attaining international development targets, this could be caused as much by its own ineffective policies as from the lack of adequate international finance.

In addition to these fundamental difficulties, the United States has had a number of other concerns. In the United States unlike many other developed countries, provision of debt rescheduling under current procedures essentially bypasses the budgetary appropriation process and tends to be additional to other aid funding. This poses a number of problems. First, the United States may bear a disproportionate share of the burden in terms of overall assistance given to a particular country, since it might be providing both regular aid *and* debt relief—whereas other donors could *substitute* debt relief for aid. Second, and most important, there is a distinct possibility that use of debt relief in such fashion would not be tolerated for long by Congress, which would demand that funding for debt rescheduling be subject to the regular appropriation process.[12]

If indeed debt rescheduling is to be viewed as a substitute to aid, it is altogether reasonable that it be subjected to the same congressional scrutiny as other aid programs. The problem is that under current procedures this process is quite lengthy. While this is not necessarily a handicap, if debt relief is provided in an anticipatory mode, there are many cases where quick action is necessary to remedy a rapidly deteriorating imminent default situation. Under these circumstances, subjecting *all* debt relief to the vagaries of the congressional appropriation process might indeed be counterproductive.

It is possible, of course, to amend current procedures and

legislation to require appropriations of amounts extended for debt rescheduling but also to provide the executive with flexibility; for example by imposing a ceiling on how much debt rescheduling could be undertaken each year but not specifying the countries to which it would be extended. Such flexibility is indeed quite desirable. However, it is questionable whether Congress would be willing to provide it in light of its strongly expressed desire to decide which countries the United States assists in any form. Even if it were possible to obtain such flexibility, debt relief would have to be weighed against other uses of development assistance funding. It is doubtful that flexibility by itself would result in significant additional resource flows to low-income developing countries. Indeed, support for assistance to low-income countries among the U.S. Congress and public is far stronger if such assistance is extended for explicit, targeted activities helping the poor than on general balance-of-payments or debt relief grounds, although the net financial effect of each type of assistance may well be quite similar. On balance, it would appear that use of debt relief on ODA debt in order to increase the net flows to low-income countries over the years ahead will have to be used with care and on a limited basis when alternative sources for additional aid are not readily available or appropriate. As a result, it cannot be considered as a useful instrument for either significantly decreasing their overall debt outstanding or significantly increasing their net resource flows.

V. THE MIDDLE-INCOME COUNTRIES AND COMMERCIAL BORROWING

Since the oil price increase and recession in the West forced oil-importing developing countries to borrow increasing amounts in the international private capital markets in 1973-74, grave concerns have been expressed about their ability to sustain this pace of borrowing in the future and, more broadly, about the possibility that failure to meet their obligations will trigger an international crisis that will endanger the viability of the international financial system.

But, while there have been many prophecies of doom, the international private capital markets have exhibited a remarkable ability to function smoothly and to absorb and channel funds; and the international community has come to the rescue of the few countries that have encountered significant debt-servicing difficulties related to their private borrowing. As a result, no general crisis has occurred, although one has been repeatedly predicted in the last five years.

Those who argue that the middle-income developing countries face a general problem in relation to their ability to service private debt point to the following considerations:

- That the size of debt and debt servicing has risen relative to key economic variables that have a bearing on developing countries' ability to service this debt.
- That the debt has been incurred by some developing countries to maintain consumption as opposed to investment. As a result, developing countries would face general difficulties in repayment, since they would be unable to generate the rate of savings necessary to repay the borrowing.
- That the terms on which borrowing has been extended are too hard and especially that the maturities are too short in comparison with the time frame over which investment projects in developing countries will start paying off.
- That if lending in the Eurocurrency market that has provided the bulk of the developing countries' credits is significantly curtailed—even for reasons unrelated to the developing countries' performance—developing countries will suffer disproportionately on the "last-in, first-out" principle.
- That defaults or serious financial crisis in one or a few important developing country debtors will undermine confidence in all of them, reduce the willingness of the private banks and other investors to lend to all of them, and thus lead to a general crisis.
- That since middle-income developing countries are de-

pendent on the private market for *additional* borrowing, reductions in new lending will cause them to default on outstanding loans, thus causing a general financial crisis because several important banking institutions have already lent to them heavily.

These are serious considerations that need to be addressed in reaching a judgment as to the future of the middle-income developing countries. First, with respect to debt-servicing capacity as reflected in various indicators, such as the debt-servicing ratio, debt relative to GNP, and so on, the evidence is mixed; but in general it does not show a significant general deterioration for the middle-income developing countries as a group. The weighted average debt-servicing ratio (relative to exports of goods and services) moved from 10.2 percent in 1970 to 11.8 percent in 1977. Similary, the weighted average ratio of debt servicing relative to GNP went from 2.0 percent in 1970 to 3.3 percent in 1977.

On the other hand, there is perhaps a legitimate concern that the overall maturity structure is too short, that the developing countries have borrowed to meet consumption needs, and that, in many instances, the structural changes necessary to produce increased earnings may take longer to achieve than the present terms or repayment. This may result in some *individual* countries are facing debt-servicing difficulties in the years ahead.[13]

There is little evidence that the developing countries are being squeezed out of the Eurocurrency market. In 1977, as many as forty-eight developing countries obtained $20.3 billion in Eurocurrency bank credits, or 59 percent of the total. This is about the same percentage but a higher absolute amount than that obtained in the previous two years. In 1978, sixty two developing countries obtained about $37.9 billion of the $71.6 billion raised during the period, with the non-oil-exporting countries alone raising over $36.6 billion. This was almost double the amount raised during a comparable period in 1977. In addition, developing countries have been having success in increasing both the absolute amount and their share of borrowings in the Eurobond market, thus improving the overall maturity structure of their debt. In 1978, twenty six developing countries raised $3.2 billion or 20 percent of the total Eurobond offerings.

But the past period may not be a good test, since the market had been growing. The international system has had ample liquidity, in part because of OPEC members' initial inability to use the bulk of their oil earnings for directly productive investment, in part because developed countries' demand for borrowing was restrained by relatively slow growth in these countries. On the other hand, some of the OPEC deposits in the immediate post-1973 period were very short. This has changed in recent periods, with beneficial effects on the maturities and interest-rate spreads of private sector lending to developing countries.

The question of reduced lending from Eurocurrency and other banking sources should be broken down in two parts: First is the possibility of reducing lending because of "reduced confidence" in developing countries, which is linked to their own performance; second is reduced lending because *total* lending is going down, and the developing countries are cut off because they do not appear to be good credit risks relative to developed countries.

With respect to developing country performance, while there are considerable concerns as noted above, the prospects do not appear to be so bad as to warrant the conclusion that a general confidence problem will arise. Debt is concentrated in a few countries, and with a few exceptions they have been able to cope with the servicing burden. Their future prospects often depend critically on developed country performance, as, for example with respect to their export earnings.

How the private banking community reacts to individual country difficulties is a crucial question. It has been argued that the private sector takes too narrow a perspective on individual country performance, focusing only on short-term prospects of repayment to particular credits. Others have argued that as the private banks accumulate an increasingly large share of total debt, they will become more "responsible" and take a broader and more long-term perspective on particular county difficulties, restricting credits where necessary or rolling over debt when appropriate.

In the past few yars, making Eurocurrency loans to developing countries has been an extremely profitable business for the major banks. Indeed some have argued that the banks are actually eager to overload developing countries with credits; thus, the problem may not be limited supply of funds but too much credit. Presumably, the danger, then, is that at some point banks will realize that the credit extended cannot be repaid, and the whole pyramid of debt will come crashing down. The possibility that this will happen depends critically on how well the commercial banking system evaluates creditworthiness and how responsibly developing countries manage their international borrowing. Proper evaluation of creditworthiness is a function, in large part, of information about policies and prospects of particular debtors. It appears that the major credit institutions are developing improved information systems. Their confidence in particular debtor policy is also enhanced if the IMF is actively involved in providing policy advice as well as support. Thus, the private banking community, whose long-term interests lie in the strong economic performance of their developing country clients and may best be served by rolling over previous credits, may well act in tandem with the IMF in support of particular countries facing difficulties. The challenge for the international banking community will be to avoid generalizing the confidence problem from the few problem cases that will undoubtedly continue to occur to apply to all developing countries. If it did, there would indeed be a crisis, given the continued need or middle-income countries to expand private borrowing. So far, it appears that the banking community has risen to that challenge, and individual crisis situations have not been generalized.

With respect to reductions in Eurocurrency lending for reasons unrelated to developing country performance, here the issues have to do, in large part, with the supply of funds for such lending. There are several developments to watch in this respect.

First, a supply problem may arise because Eurocurrency lending has been concentrated in a relatively small number of primarily North American insitutions, and some of these have been approaching the limits of their lending exposure to individual developing countries. However, there is evidence that new banking institutions, especially in West Germany and Japan, are becoming more actively involved in lending to developing countries—a trend that will have to be strengthened in the years ahead.

Second, to the extent that growth in the developed countries will be higher in the next few years than it was in the 1973-76 period, it is possible that developed countries' demand for credits from the international banks will rise and that, as a result, developing countries will encounter greater difficulties in rolling over debt as well as in obtaining new credits. There is a possibility that this will occur, but the extent to which it will occur is hard to determine, especially since it is critically dependent on domestic developed country monetary expansion and policy. In any case, a slowdown would still permit increased net borrowing for developing countries in the decade ahead.

Third, policies by the national banking systems of the OECD countries of OPEC members may have the result of inducing international banks to reduce Eurocurrency lending. If the supply of funds from these sources were sharply limited, given the continued dependence of developing countries on increased private borrowing, the result could well be the type of large-scale default everybody wishes to avoid. While there can never be complete certainty about future policies, it is not clear what circumstances might prevail in the near future that would induce either the developed countries or OPEC to take actions that would limit Eurocurrency bank lending. The adverse implications for the overall system may well be sufficient to avert such action, were it actually considered. Indeed, it is hard to see how massive default, which would undermine the whole financial system, would occur without massive ineptitude in developed country management of the banking system. The developing countries themselves are not likely to cause a massive crisis due to their own economic performance; the international banking community has not so far showed tendencies of trying to generalize a crisis of confidence from one developing country to others; and the developed countries have an array of instruments to bail out individual commercial banks hard hit by exposure in developing countries facing financing difficulties.

In circumstances where balance-of-payments problems arise in which debt servicing is an important element, the IMF is the key institution. It is important that the IMF have adequate liquidity to deal with individual balance-of-payments problems as they arise and to prevent them from lingering on or spreading. In recent years, the IMF has been strengthened in various ways that make it more able to assist developing countries. First and most important, its overall quotas have been increased; second, two facilities have been created that are important in giving the IMF needed flexibility in addressing the problems discussed here. The Compensatory Financing Facility (CFF) permits the IMF to deal with sudden shortfalls in export earnings that could make it difficult for a country with a high debt-servicing ratio to meet its international obligations while maintaining an acceptable rate of economic expansion.[14] Over the period 1976-1978, the CFF provided developing countries with $2.5 billion in financing to offset downswings in export earnings. The Extended Fund Facility (EFF) permits borrowing and re-payments over a longer period, which should be helpful in addressing medium-term structural balance-of-payments difficulties.[15] In addition to these, the proposed Supplementary Financing Facility (SFF) is placing approximately $10 billion in additional resources at the command of the IMF for general lending purposes.[16]

Developed countries can play an important role in averting balance-of-payments difficulties related to the maturity structure problem in MICs by increasing lending to MICs directly or indirectly by expanding the capitalization of the IBRD and other Multilateral Development Banks (MDB), thus permitting increased lending from these institutions to the MICs. At present, consideration is being given to an increased capitalization of the IBRD that would permit it to expand its flow of credits to the developing countries at the rate of 5 percent per annum in real terms in the next few years. Increasing MDB lending to the MICs is important, not only because it can, to some extent, substitute for harder terms credits from the private sector, but also because MDB involvement in individual countries tends to increase the private banking community's confidence in the overall policies pursued by these countries and thus facilitates additional lending where desirable. Bilateral ODA from the major donors is not a significant source of finance for MICs. But in some instances, its soft terms help to ease the overall debt-servicing burden of the recipients.

The availability of these facilities, while not a complete assurance, enhances the prospects that the emergence of a general crisis involving massive default can be prevented. Further, should such a crisis appear imminent despite the application of the full scope of these measures, it is likely that the international community will take sufficient steps to prevent its actual occurrence, given the capabilities and resilience shown in the face of severe international developments over the past several years. This does not mean that middle-income countries' debt problems are insignificant and that the international community need not be concerned. It does mean that international action should focus on institutional changes that could help assure that individual crises are prevented rather than on further efforts to create new facilities with a view to dealing with a generalized crisis. Also, it means that the international community should be concerned about how to handle individual country problems as they arise. For example, even if only a few individual country crises occur at any point in time, their problems might be generalized if they are not dealt with quickly and effectively.

VI. THE INSTITUTIONAL SETTING FOR DEBT RELIEF

CREDITOR CLUB OPERATIONS

Debt reorganizations in recent years have commonly occurred within an institutional setting provided by the creditor club mechanism. The mechanism works as follows: countries experiencing acute difficulties in servicing their debt approach their major creditors in order to seek a debt reorganization, while in the past the chairmanship of the club and its locus used to vary, most recent negotiations have taken place under French chairmanship in the Paris Club.[17] (See Table 9.1 for an inclusive list of multilateral debt relief opeations).

The negotiations usually have three stages. First, there is a

TABLE 9.1

MULTILATERAL DEBT RELIEF OPERATIONS

Year of Agreement	Country	Amount of Debt Rescheduled (millions of U.S. $)
1956	Argentina	500
1959	Turkey	440
1961	Brazil	300
1962	Argentina	270
1964	Brazil	270
1965	Chile	90
1965	Turkey	220
1965	Argentina	274
1966	Ghana	170
1966	Indonesia	310
1967	Indonesia	110
1968	India	300
1968	Peru	120
1968	Indonesia	180
1968	Ghana	100
1969	Peru	(100)[a]
1970	Indonesia	2.090
1970	Ghana	(18)
1971	India	100
1972	Cambodia	4
1972	Chile	258
1972	Pakistan	236
1972	India	153
1973	Pakistan	107
1973	India	187
1974	Ghana	190
1974	Chile	460
1974	Pakistan	650
1974	India	194
1975	Chile	230
1975	India	167
1976	India	(160)
1976	Zaire	(280)
1977	India	(120)
1977	Zaire	(210)
1977	Sierre Leone	(52)
1978	Turkey	(1.100)
	TOTAL	10.720

NOTE: Table does not include debt renegotiated outside a multilateral framework.

[a] ( ) = estimates.

detailed request of information about the recipient's debt, balance of payments, and general economic situation; second, there is the stage of multilateral negotiations aimed at reaching an overall "umbrella" agreement between the creditors as a group and the debtor. The agreement covers such things as the amount of debt due that will be rescheduled (usually not the total amount total debt becoming due in the next twelve months); the types of credit rescheduled, (usually short-term credits are excluded); the overall concessionality of the rescheduling, that is, the average interest rate, grace periods, and rollover period, as well as the distribution of debt to be rescheduled by various creditors. The agreements involve solely public of publicly guaranteed debt from official sources. However, arrangements are usually made for negotiations with private lenders to precede or follow the renegotiation of official debts.

The IMF plays an important part in the negotiations. The creditors usually request that the debtor obtain standby credit from the IMF, commonly involving second or higher credit *tranches.* Of the eighteeen debt renegotiations in creditor clubs, twelve were related to IMF standby arrangements, one involved a first credit tranche, and eleven involved higher credit tranches. In five cases not involving standbys the IMF was requested to monitor the debtors' implementation of their commitments with respect to their financial and economic policy and to keep the creditors informed of their performance.[18] The IMF, in turn, tends to provide standby arrangements only on condition that the debtor undertake considerable retrenchment in terms of its domestic and international financial, credit, and budgetary management, aimed at reducing domestic and international expenditures and thus regain its ability to service its international debt obligations at the soonest time possible. The creditors thus use the IMF conditionality as a means of assuring the restoration of debt-servicing capacity for the debtor.

The last stage of the negotiations involves the signing of bilateral agreements between the individual creditors and the debtor that formally reschedule specific credits. This stage is usually aimed at meeting the individual legal requirements of respective creditors.

Past experience with the functioning of creditor clubs has led to a variety of criticisms. Some of the criticisms have to do with the effect of debt reschedulings under the creditor club format on the debtors; others have to do with the atmosphere and workings of the creditor club operation. The most fundamental criticism is that the creditor club functions as a rescue operation when the deterioration of a country's financial situation has progressed to the point where remedial measures by necessity would tend to retard long-term development prospects. Critics argue that relief operations should occur earlier on so as to permit a more smooth adjustment to balance-of-payments and debt-servicing difficulties. The problem, of course, with such "anticipatory" debt relief is that it becomes difficult to distinguish it from normal aid, a distinction that has been important for some donors such as the United States. On the other hand, it is probably true that the operation of the club has tended to exaggerate the "stop-go" type of policy in developing countries, which analysts have pointed to as being a serious impediment to long-term development [19]

A related problem is that the creditor club focuses on short-term relief measures. There is little concern with long-term development problems and plans. The debtor is kept on a "short-leash" within the period for which debt is rescheduled, generally not exceeding a year—with some exceptions, in earlier periods, such as Indonesia. This may well be appropriate in circumstances when the debt crisis was triggered by bad developing country monetary and fiscal management or overambitious plans and goals. It may not be appropriate in circumstances where the developing country is experiencing debt-servicing difficulties because of circumstances beyond its control: for example, sudden declines in earnings from a key export or increased prices of imports, as well as in cases where the problem is more of a long-term nature and involves the maturity structure of its debt or structural problems in increasing productivity or exports. Under such circumstances, austerity measures and the short-leash appraoch may assure repayments in the short run, but at the expense of long-term development goals as well as long-term capacity to service debt. In extreme cases, short-term conditioning that does not take into account long-term development problems may simply result in repetitive debt crises and successive reschedulings over a period of years.

The operation of the Paris Club, in particular, has come under criticism in recent years for other reasons as well. In several instances, the chairmanship of the club provided France with influence considerably in excess of its stake as a creditor. The willingness to reschedule debt often involves a political commitment by the creditors to the future development of the debtor. Since French foreign policy interests in particular debtor nations may not necessarily coincide with those of other creditor nations, French handling of particular debt renegotiations has come under criticism by both creditors and debtors. Second, the atmosphere of the proceedings is one where the debtor is put in a position of a supplicant for relief to be granted by creditors. Creditors typically caucus and reach agreement among themselves and then confront the debtor with their offer. The atmosphere is not helped by the fact that until recently the debtor could not even have the negotiation documents drafted in its own language—a distinct disadvantage to non-French-speaking representatives of debtor nations.

A final problem with the operation of the French Club is that there is no guarantee that developing countries seeking relief from the club would obtain similar treatment if their circumstances were similar. This is a thorny problem. Obviously, equitable treatment is something difficult to oppose in principle. How to achieve it in practice is a different matter. One alternative would be to set a priori quantitative guidelines that would create a presumption that a recipient is entitled to more assistance or debt relief and the terms for such relief. This has been a persistent developing country demand. Aside from the practical difficulty of setting up such guidelines, the "automaticity" aspect of this approach hits at the heart of the creditor's prerogative and the nature of the debt renegotiations. Ultimately, the creditor wishes to feel that it is up to him to decide whether to extend relief and how much and that he must be persuaded to do so by the debtors' commitment to take remedial measures to assure repayment. Under such circumstances, no guidelines for comparable treatment seem feasible.

If it is assumed that the size and terms of debt relief extended are going to continue to be determined essentially by a bargaining process, it is difficult to see how equitable treatment in similar economic circumstanes could be achieved. The reason is simple. Political considerations involving the overall foreign policy relationship between creditors and debtors are always present and influential in aid as well as in debt relief matters. It is basically impossible to exclude them, and it is equally impossible to assure that they do not result in biasing the results of particular debt negotiations either favorably or unfavorably.

AID CONSORTIA

Critics of the creditor club operations have pointed to aid consortia as a preferable alternative institutional setting for extending debt relief, especially for ODA. Debt reorganization has occurred in consortia for the express purpose of increasing net resource flows to a particular developing country. Most notable among these have been the consortia for India and Pakistan.

The consortia, usually chaired by the IBRD, bring donors together annually for the purpose of coordinating their assistance efforts to a particular country. This coordination involves exchange of views on likely levels of total assistance, main areas of functional concentration, as well as the relationship between foreign assistance flows and the recipient's short- and long-term development policies and objectives. The meetings provide an opportunity for donors to express views of recipient policies and programs and to seek to obtain assurances for appropriate policy reforms. However, the climate is usually one of collaboration rather than confrontation; persuasion rather than strict conditionality is the main instrument used to affect policy changes.

Debt relief provided within this climate tends to be quite advantageous to the debtor. There is no strict conditionality with respect to its own policies such as is usually associated with obtaining an IMF Standby. Since there is a shared desire to increase aggregate resource transfers, there is less bargaining over the size of debt relief extended or its terms; indeed, a good deal of the bargaining tends to occur among the donors in determining their share of debt relief extended. Finally, the debt relief operations are taken in the context, not solely of short-term financial needs, but also of long-term development objectives presumably shared by donors and recipients.

There is one awkward aspect of the proceedings. The IBRD, while chairing the proceedings and often urging bilateral donors to increase their resource transfers through debt relief, does not itself reschedule its loans because of the possible adverse effect of such reschedulings on its own creditworthiness and ability to borrow in international capital markets.

From the standpoint of the creditors, the advantage of the consortium is that it permits debt relief to be considered in the context of long-term involvement and participation in the promotion of economic development objectives of the recipient and in and insuring the longer-term prospects for obtaining repayment. Against this, there is less possibility of exerting strong leverage for policy changes through strict conditionality, since the debtor is not put in a position of a supplicant for relief. In addition, of course, there is the problem that debt relief is viewed as a substitute for aid. This has posed such a serious problem for the United States that it announced at UNCTAD IV in 1976 that it would henceforth reschedule debt only in creditor clubs.[20]

VII. PROPOSALS FOR INSTITUTIONAL REFORM

GENERAL

There have been two kinds of proposals for general changes in institutions and policies affecting the debt problems of developing countries. First, there have been proposals for generalized debt relief for low-income countries. These were discussed in section IV. Agreement was reached at the UNCTAD Trade and Development Board Ministerial Meeting on the kind of action the international community is prepared to undertake. No further action is currently contemplated. Second, in the last few years the concern about the financial viability and prospects of the middle-income countries has given rise to a variety of reform proposals that would change the overall international institutional framework in order to address aspects of these countries' problems linked to private and especially to commercial bank borrowing. Most of the proposals that have received international attention aim at increasing the availability of longer-term financial capital and/or providing developing countries with more assured access to such capital. Three of these proposals are singled out for discussion here because they have received the greatest international attention and/or have been subjected to the most scrutiny: (1) the establishment of an institution to refinance developing countries' debt on softer terms; (2) the establishment of guarantees on developing countries' bond offerings; and (3) the undertaking of "massive transfers" through stepped up investment of private capital.

Refinancing. Suggestions to set up a refinancing institution to assist middle-income countries were first floated by the developing countries in the Manila Declaration in the spring of 1976. There has not been extensive discussion of this mechanism or its possible features. Nor has the developing countries' proposal been fleshed out in great detail.

In general, the proposal calls for the setting up of an international institution that would take over a significant portion of developing country outstanding debt to private entities. The institution would obtain paid in contributions in hard currency as well as subscriptions of callable capital from developed countries. It would use some of the paid-in contributions to refinance the debt obligations taken over by stretching out their maturities and lowering their interest rates. The institution could also undertake new borrowing from the private capital markets (using as backing the subscriptions of the developed countries), which it would then extend on softer terms to the developing countries. Developed countries have opposed the creation of such an institution on the following grounds: (1) it is not needed, since capital markets are functioning well and the multilateral development banks (MDBs) are providing adequate intermediation; (2) it will not work unless a great deal of funds are contributed; (3) such funding would reduce flows for other more worthwhile causes for example, assistance to the lower-income countries; and (4) it might be viewed as a means of bailing out the commercial banking system for mistakes it has made—a move quite unpopular in developed countries.

The refinancing proposal has not received a great deal of support from middle-income developing countries, in part because they tend to view it as focusing unwarranted attention on their financing difficulties, and thus imperiling their current access to private credits. It is, at the moment, unclear whether the proposal as structured will receive further international attention in UNCTAD or elsewhere.

Guarantees. Various proposals for using developed country, multilateral development bank, or other international guarantee mechanisms have been developed over the years. Guarantees are attractive instruments for promoting certain types of private capital movements. Many bilateral donors, including the United States, operate a variety of guarantee programs whose effect is to promote the movement of private capital to developing countries and/or soften the terms of borrowing. The most recent proposals for setting up guarantee mechanisms have been designed to promote the floating of developing country bond issues in developed country or international markets. This could help with current bunching problems to the extent that money raised in the short term could be used to refinance upcoming obligations. Also, over time, and depending on the terms of the bonds, guarantees may improve the overall maturity structure of developing countries' debt.

Guarantees offered by the developed countries could promote access to the longer-term bond market—where maturities may be as long as twenty years—essentially by substituting developed for developing country credit worthiness in the eyes of the investor. These markets, especially in the United States, have proved very difficult for most developing countries to enter due to competition from other borrowers. Also, the costs for arranging bond offerings are usually higher and the procedural requirements more complex than obtaining funding from commercial banks.

The Development Committee of the IBRD/IMF has provided the forum for international scrutiny and discussion of guarantees. The committee, through its Working Party on Capital Market Access has examined over the last two years a variety of guarantee issues but has focused on an international guaran-

tee proposal aimed in part on promoting access and using partial guarantees as an instrument of transition.[21] In the end it
recommended against setting up a new guarantee mechanism
and instead recommended that developing countries be extended more technical assistance in the area and utilize the
existing guarantee authority of the multilateral development
banks.

A new mechanism was not recommended in good part because a few of the developing countries, and particularly Mexico, which have been successful in entering the long-term bond
market, viewed the establishment of a new partial guarantee
instrument for developing country bond issues as undercutting
their present ability to borrow without guarantee. Also, developed countries, were not particularly enthusiastic about setting up a new guarantee mechanism.

Increased technical assistance could be useful to many developing countries.[22] But technical assistance alone is not likely
to permit developing countries to borrow the amounts of resources that would significantly affect the fundamental maturity
structure problem.

The recommendation to use the MDB guarantee authority is
also somewhat of a dead letter. The MDBs have had such
authority for a long time. They have not used it because bond
guarantees are equivalent to loans in terms of the capitalization
required to back them. To the extent that the IBRD extends
guarantee, it must reduce the amount of direct lending it does.
There is no advantage in this to the developing countries, since
the terms of the guaranteed bond offerings are not significantly
different from the terms of IBRD loans, and the total volume of
credit is not affected; that is there would be no additional lending on soft terms to substitute for harder-term credits the developing countries would have otherwise had to obtain. On the
other hand, if the charters of the MDBs could be amended so
that their guarantee extensions would be counted somewhat
fractionally in determining their liabilities, the MDBs might be
provided with more incentive to utilize this aspect of their existing authority. Even if such changes were made, however, the
result most likely would be improved maturity structure rather

than additional flows to developing countries. It is anticipated that the guarantee issue will be raised again at UNCTAD V.

Massive Transfers. The recognition that developing countries would need to borrow increasing amounts in international markets during the coming years combined with concerns about their continued access to private banking capital has led to the development of proposals within the UN, the OECD, and elsewhere for a program of "massive transfers" to these countries to be supported by actions of the various donors and the multilateral development banks. The basic notion behind this proposal, which has many variants (see, e.g., the proposals made by John Sewell of the Overseas Development Council), is that increased demand by developing countries would provide a noninflationary countercyclical stimulus to the lagging growth of developed countries' economies. It is argued that significant increases in the flow of resources to developing countries would be needed to provide such a stimulus.

In the OECD version of the proposal, the key instrument to be used for promoting the capital flow would be cofinancing of activities between private banking institutions and the multilateral development banks. It is argued that cofinancing will permit the private banking sector to increase its lending to the developing countries significantly because the MDBs will be able to pick up the long-term and perhaps riskier components of particular projects and because MDB involvement in project design and interaction with recipient governments at the policy level will assure the soundness of projects and the undertaking to broad development country policies that will enhance their positive impact on development.

The OECD proposal also calls for the investment to be directed to sectors in which, it is felt, from a global perspective there is need for additional investment: energy, raw materials, and food. From the standpoint of the developing countries, the proposal would address primarily the problem of assuring access to new capital rather than softening the terms of existing credits and indirectly, if at all, on improving the maturity structure of the overall debt outstanding.

This proposal has received favorable reaction in principle from both developed and developing countries, although many of its features have come under considerable criticism. In the first instance, the linkage of the proposal to the achievement of developed country countercyclical objectives has been questioned, since there is no assurance that the kind of activities that need to be financed by developing countries will give rise to demand for the kind of products in which there is unutilized capacity in developed countries. Second, while there is strong support for the undertaking of cofinancing by the MDBs and there has been an increasing amount of this type of MDB lending in recent years, it is questionable as to how much such cofinancing can increase over the years ahead.

Private institutions, in cofinancing operations with the World Bank, have provided resources on the order of $500 million annually in recent years. In terms of magnitude, the World Bank accounts for more than half of the cofinancing transactions with private institutions. It is unclear at this point at just what pace private lenders are prepared to expand their role, given present perceptions of prudence and the various regulations under which they operate. On the other hand, large increases proposed of approximately $10 billion a year may not be feasible simply because suitable projects may not exist. Even if private lenders should sharply step up their cofinancing in the face of an ample supply of projects, it remains uncertain that their overall exposure in developing countries would change on a relative basis. While cofinancing is a mode of financial transfer that will undoubtedly continue to increase during the years ahead, taken alone it probably can not and will not accommodate massive transfers. It is also unclear how the developing countries will react to the idea if it is divorced from increased amounts of ODA.

INSTITUTIONAL REFORMS

In the context of CIEC in June 1977 and later on at the UNCTAD Trade and Development Board meeting in March 1978, the United States, and the European Community (EC) (joined later by a number of other developed countries) tabled a proposal that outlines approaches to deal with debt problems of developing countries on a case-by-case basis. The proposal identifies two types of developing country situations: (1) debt crises involving default or imminent default; and (2) long-term financial and transfer-of-resources problems, where an "adverse structure of balance of payments hampers development." Presumably, the latter vague category means to cover all the other problems related to debt identified in section III above, which may exist prior to a debt crisis.[23]

With respect to the imminent default cases, the proposal essentially attempts to codify past practices of the creditor club mechanism. With respect to the "situation of a longer term nature," the proposal essentially attempts to spell out and codify past practices in IBRD-led consortia. According to this proposal, a developing country that "has a problem of the type described above of which debt is an element would, before the problem has reached crisis proportions request an examination of its situation by the IBRD or another multilateral development finance institution." The institution would prepare an exhaustive analysis of the situation and make recommendations for national and international action. Where there is agreement that there is a need for enhancing assistance efforts, donors would do so "to their best ability." The key action paragraph states that "Among the various measures which could be taken by a donor country for this purpose programme aid, other flexible forms of quickly disbursable aid, would be considered preferable to ODA debt reorganization."[24]

The developing countries rejected the proposal at CIEC and at various UNCTAD meetings. However, the proposal is still on the table and is undoubtedly going to receive continued attention in future negotiations, such as in UNCTAD V in the spring of 1979. Indeed, the developing countries accepted some of the fundamental principles imbedded in the proposal at the UNCTAD March Ministerial Meeting, such as the imminent-default-longer-term distinction. The proposal is not responsive to developing country demands about automaticity, assurance of equitable treatment, or the presumption of extending debt relief to achieve vaguely defined general development targets.

However, the proposal does address developing countries' concerns about dealing with debt problems in advance of crises situations.

In some respects, the distinction between imminent default and long-term structural situations is unfortunate. The situations are intimately linked, and institutional involvement by the World Bank and the IMF and bilateral creditors is appropriate in both situations. If anything, remedying long-term structural situations ought to be given priority, because to the extent that they are dealt with, the likelihood for imminent default cases would tend to diminish.

Undoubtedly, some crises will continue to arise for which debt relief is the only obvious remedy. In such situations, which could continue to be handled by the creditor club mechanism, it is essential that longer-term development concerns be given more prominence than they have been given heretofore. This could be done by a more active involvement of the IBRD and more active collaboration of the IBRD with the IMF. It could involve rescheduling of debt due over a longer period of time as well as providing systematically softer terms for the reschedulings extended to low-income countries.

In a sense, it might well be optimal that the institutional arrangements that are developed to handle longer-term situations be no different from those that deal with imminent default cases. In any case, the actors are the same in both institutional settings. The major current donors are also the major creditors. Provision would need to be made for participation of OPEC members, whose debt in some countries is mounting pari passu with their emergence since 1974 as major donors. The IMF and the IBRD should both participate, since it is inappropriate to consider short-term debt relief separately from long-term development concerns and vice versa. The setting should be one that permits an atmosphere of collaboration to emerge rather than the confrontation between debtor and creditor often present now. At the same time, stricter conditonality, not only with respect to short-term fiscal and monetary policies, but also with respect to longer-term policies and planning needs to be exercised. Whereas conditionality in creditor club arrangements may have been too strict, it may have been too lax in the context of aid consortia.

In sum, an institutional arrangement may be developed in which the developing country seeking a review of its situation notifies simultaneously both the IMF and the IBRD of the possibility that it has a problem.[25] The staff of these institutions could undertake appropriate analyses and convoke a meeting of interested parties with a view to deciding what, if anything, more needs to be done to address the problems of the particular developing country. Such a meeting could lead (though not necessarily) to a recommendation by the donors for debt relief and/or additional assistance. The course of action would depend on the circumstances faced by the developing country at each point in time. The institutional setting would combine elements of both creditor club and consortia operations. Even if a single institutional arrangement is not possible, and a dual institutional setting such as the one envisaged under the U.S./ EC proposal emerges, each institution would have to borrow some of the features of the other in order to permit the international community to deal adequately with the individual debt problems of developing countries in the years to come.

The proposal, if accepted in some form, would require some changes in donor policies. For example, the United States at the moment does not extend debt relief in nonimminent default situations, nor does it posses the aid instruments that can be used to remedy the problems the proposal identifies as likely to occur. While the United States does possess bilateral aid instruments that are both flexible and quick disbursing for example, Security Supporting Assistance and PL-480, neither instrument is intended to be used for the purposes described in the U.S./EC proposal, and their regular use for this purpose is likely to encounter congressional opposition.

VIII. SUMMARY AND CONCLUSIONS

This broad review of developing countries' debt problems and prospects does not paint a pessimistic picture of the future in terms of the likelihood for an occurrence of a generalized debt crisis in the developing countries. However, the conclusion is also inevitable that various types of debt and financing problems for individual developing countries will be with us in the years ahead.

The proposals for generalized institutional reform or policy change that have been put forth either suffer from technical drawbacks that are not likely to be overcome or are likely to run up against political constraints that may not permit their realization. On the other hand, there are a number of areas in which performance of the developing and the developed countries as well as international institutions can and should be improved within the existing institutional framework in order to permit the developing countries to manage their foreign indebtedness more effectively and efficiently without compromising their development objectives. The key to international financial reform is incremental and gradual change, not radical reform.

The changes that need to occur can be summarized as follows:

1. Developing countries' export earnings need to grow at a substantial rate—at least as high as in recent years and perhaps higher. The projections on developing countries' debt-servicing capabilities discussed earlier are predicated on an export growth of 6.1 percent over the next several years. If they fall significantly short of this growth—and many policies both on the part of developed and the developing countries have a bearing on this—a general financing problem may well develop, most likely leading to lower growth in the developing world.

2. The developing countries must improve their own policies in using private credits. Existing studies show that considerable room for improvement exists in this respect.[26] This is essential for the purpose of maintaining confidence of the private lenders. Two areas of management are of particular importance: (1) assuring that steps are taken to increase productivity of investment, thus generating the future surplus that would permit repayment; and (2) taking the proper policies to promote exports to permit the financing of the debt repayment. In either case this is not an easy task. It often requires structural changes that are difficult to accomplish. But it is *sine qua non* for continued confidence.

3. Given the nature of private credits, their maturities will continue to be too short for some developing countries. This is not a problem as long as there are opportunities to roll over past credits through the issue of new ones. But the willingness of the banking community to roll over debt and thus *de facto* to lengthen its maturity structure is critically affected by its confidence in the long-term ability of the debtor to service the debt.

4. Additional MDB lending can be an important way of lengthening the maturity structure of MICs. The MDBs' hard windows are softer than most borrowing undertaken by the MICs. Significant expansion of their activities would tend to permit the MICs to substitute MDB for harder-term private lending, if the need arose. The MDBs are thus performing an intermediation function which is over and above the contributions they are able to make in assuring the soundness of particular projects and promoting better overall LDC policy. In this connection, and in some sectors, cofinancing may be a useful way of supplementing MDB resources and leveraging additional amounts of private capital flows.

5. The scope of providing debt relief as a means of increasing net flows of resources to low-income developing countries is quite limited because of public attitudes in several important creditor developed countries such as West Germany, France, the United States, and Japan. This means that efforts to increase ODA should concentrate on other, more traditional instruments. Without such increases, however, the prospects of low-income countries will look even dimmer than they are at present. While for MICs, ODA is not an important source of finance, continued access to some concessional assistance may prove essential to permit them to continue to borrow increasing amounts on harder terms from the private market.

6. Are the existing and projected IMF facilities enough? This is a very hard question to answer. If the preceding analysis is correct and there is no general crisis of confidence in the developing countries, it would appear that the IMF could handle individual cases adequately as they arise. On the other hand, it is questionable whether the IMF alone can do a great deal if a general crisis does develop. However, it is important to note that

the mere willingness of the IMF to play an active role in individual cases through a variety of assistance instruments as well as policy involvement is very useful in strengthening private banking confidence in individual LDCs and thus averting precisely the kind of general crisis all wish to avoid.

7. It is quite clear that some combination of institutional arrangements such as those included in the U.S./EC proposal would need to emerge in the future to permit efficient and, to the extent possible, equitable treatment of individual countries' debt-servicing difficulties of a short-term or long-term nature. As they now operate, neither the creditor club system nor the aid consortia are adequate for this purpose.

8. For the United States it is probably necessary to develop more flexibility in providing debt relief than has been the practice in the recent past. This flexibility should permit rescheduling in nonimminent default situations such as those envisaged in the U.S./EC proposal but subject to congressional approval and normal budgetary processes. The alternatives for the United States are to introduce greater flexibility in existing programs or to develop a new bilateral program aimed at addressing balance-of-payments problems of developing countries. This is necessary because existing bilateral assistance instruments are not designed explicitly to address balance-of-payments problems in developing countries, including those in which debt servicing is an important component. While bilateral aid, which is usually extended on very soft terms, can assist developing countries in balance-of-payments difficulties, the purposes for which available funding through various programs can be used exclude general balance-or-payments support. This has been a problem in some cases where it may have been desirable to supplement resources provided by the IMF. While a good case for the creation of a new instrument or for the use of existing bilateral programs for this purpose can be made, at the moment there is little likelihood that either would come about because of strong congressional opposition to such use of bilateral assistance.

NOTES

1. These projections are basically derived from IBRD, *World Development Report, 1978*, August 1978.

2. ODA consists of all flows to developing countries provided by official agencies whose objective is to promote the economic development and welfare of the developing countries, and which carry financial terms that yield a grant element of at least 25 percent. Grant element is defined as the face value of loan commitments less the discounted present value of the future flow of repayments of principal and interest expressed as a percent of face value. The discount rate used is 10 percent, the conventional rate used by OECD in assessing terms. There is usually no grant element associated with private loans.

3. The IBRD estimates have been based on the SIMLINK model. In this model, foreign resource needs are ultimately derived from foreign-exchange gaps estimated by reference to projected current account receipts compared with import requirements. While this drawback is well understood, there are no readily available and practical techniques that permit alternative estimates.

4. Disbursed only.

5. UNCTAD, "Extended Indebtedness of Developing Countries: A Statistical Note," TD/B/C. 3/148, Septemeber 1978.

6. With maturities in excess of one year.

7. This excludes a small number of bilateral renegotiations involving only the United States or other major donors.

8. For description of the creditor club and consortia mechanisms, see section VI.

9. The RLDC group consists of twenty-nine countries designated by the UN on the basis of GNP, industrialization, and literacy criteria. The MSA group includes all RLDCs plus a number of additional countries judged by the UN to have been seriously adversely affected by the oil price increase. The RLDC group has received general recognition and various actions by the international community, and individual donors have focused on it. The MSA group has received less recognition and explicit attention.

10. The U.S. legislative provisions on this matter are quite complex. Separate provisions affect past AID and PL-480 loans. In both cases the recipient would be asked to expend local currencies on worthwhile development activities in lieu of repayment to the United States in dollars. Under the PL-480, only least-developed countries that are current recipients of Title III assistance are eligible. The details for implementing these provisions had not been worked out as of this writing.

11. See UNCTAD, "Report of the Intergovernmental Group of Ex-

perts on the External Indebtedness of Developing Countries," December 1977.

12. Debt rescheduling should be distinguished from RTA, for which explicit congressional appropriation approval is already needed.

13. See UNCTAD, *Eurocurrency Borrowing: A Review*, TD/B/C. 3/15, September 1978.

14. The CFF has existed for some time. However, it was substantially liberalized in 1975. Drawings under this facility are additional to those to which members are entitled under regular *tranche* policy but cannot exceed their total IMF quotas. Except for special waivers, drawings under the CFF cannot exceed 50 percent of a member's quota in any twelve month period or 75 percent in total. Repayments are usually required to be made within three to five years after the date of the drawing, at interest rates ranging between 4.735 percent and 6.375 percent, depending on the time and amount of drawing outstanding.

15. Drawings under this facility may take place over periods of up to three years. Repayments must be made within four to eight years after each drawing in equal semiannual installments; interest ranges from 4.735 to 6.375 percent.

16. Drawings may take place over a period of up to three years. Repayment in semiannual installments must begin not later than three and one-half years and must completed not more than seven years after the drawing. Charges will be equal to the cost of the borrowed funds to the fund plus a margin ranging from 0.2 to 0.375 percent, depending on length of time the drawing is outstanding.

17. For a listing of debt reorganizations in the last twenty years, see Table 9.1.

18. See statement by Richard N. Cooper, Undersecretary for Economic Affairs, before the Subcommittee on International Finance Committee on Banking, Housing and Urban Affairs, U.S. Congress, August 29, 1977.

19. See Carlos F. Diaz-Alejandro, *Foreign Trade Regimes and Economic Development: Colombia*, National Bureau of Economic Research, New York: 1976.

20. An additional factor in the U.S. decision was that India had been the main recipient of debt relief in consortia. Political relations with India in the 1974-77 period were rather cool, and U.S. assistance (except food aid) had terminated. It was viewed as politically unwise to participate in consortia reschedulings that would *de facto* result in provision of aid through the back door when there was no imminent default situation.

21. I argued for such a variant involving separate but parallel U.S. and other bilateral developed countries guarantees in *Financing Needs of Developing Countries: Proposals for International Actions*, Essays in International Finance No. 110, Princeton, 1975.

22. The United States through AID has for some time operated a small-scale technical assistance program in this area.

23. See UNCTAD, "Debt Problems of Developing Countries," TD / B/498, March 1978.

24. Ibid.

25. Developing countries have argued that such a role should be entrusted to UNCTAD. This does not constitute a viable option, because the power structure at UNCTAD favors the developing countries—not the creditor/developed countries. The latter could never agree to an institutional arrangement where their power as creditors would be diluted.

26. P. A. Wellons, *Borrowing by Developing Countries on the Eurocurrency Market* (Paris: OECD, 1977).

APPENDIX

UNA-USA Economic Policy Council Members: 1978

Chairman:

Robert O. Anderson
Chairman of the Board
Atlantic Richfield Company

Steering Committee:

Douglas A. Fraser
President
International Union—
    United Auto Workers

Peter G. Peterson
Chairman of the Board
Lehman Brothers, Kuhn
    Loeb, Inc.

Lloyd McBride
President
United Steelworkers of
    America, AFL-CIO

Robert V. Roosa
Partner
Brown Brothers, Harriman &
    Company

Council Members:

I. W. Abel
Retired President
United Steelworkers of
    America, AFL-CIO

Carolyn Shaw Bell
Katharine Coman Professor
    of Economics
Wellesley College

Charles F. Barber
Chairman
ASARCO, Inc.

Robert S. Benjamin
Co-Chairman
Orion Pictures Corporation

R. Manning Brown, Jr.
Chairman of the Board
New York Life Insurance
   Company

John R. Bunting
Chairman and Chief
   Executive Officer
First Pennsylvania
   Corporation
First Pennsylvania Bank

Lisle C. Carter, Jr.
President
University of the District of
   Columbia

Sol C. Chaikin
President
International Ladies'
   Garment Workers' Union

Jack G. Clarke
Director and Senior Vice
   President
Exxon Corporation

Jacob Clayman
President
Industrial Union
   Department, AFL-CIO

John T. Connor
Chairman of the Board
Allied Chemical
   Corporation

Jack T. Conway
Senior Vice President
Government and Labor
   Movement Relations
United Way of America

Tony T. Dechant
President
National Farmers Union

W. C. Druehl
Group Vice President
President International
Del Monte Corporation

William D. Eberle
Senior Partner
Robert A. Weaver
   Associates

Thomas Farmer
Prather, Seeger, Doolittle,
   Farmer & Ewing

Frank Fernbach
Economist
(Formerly United
   Steelworkers of America,
   AFL-CIO)

Murray H. Finley
President
Amalgamated Clothing and
   Textile Workers Union,
   AFL-CIO

Gaylord Freeman
Honorary Chairman
The First National Bank of
   Chicago

Orville I. Freeman
President
Business International
   Corporation

James P. Grant
President
Overseas Development
   Council

A. F. Grospiron
President
Oil, Chemical and Atomic
   Workers International
   Union

John D. Harper
Director
Aluminum Company of
   America
(Formerly, Chairman of the
   Board)

Walter W. Heller
Regents' Professor of
   Economics
University of Minnesota

Ruth J. Hinerfeld
President
League of Women Voters
   of the United States

Robert C. Holland
President
Committee for Economic
   Development

Robert S. Ingersoll
Deputy Chairman of the
   Board of Trustees
University of Chicago
(Formerly, Deputy
   Secretary of State)

Henry Kaufman
Partner and Member of the
   Executive Committee
Salomon Brothers

George J. Kneeland
Chairman of the Board
St. Regis Paper Company

John E. Leslie
Chairman of the Board
Bache Group, Inc.

James S. McDonnell
Chairman of the Board
McDonnell Douglas
   Corporation

Arjay Miller
Dean, Graduate School of
   Business
Stanford University

Kenneth W. Monfort
Senior Vice President
Monfort of Colorado, Inc.

John M. Musser
President
General Service
  Foundation

Robert R. Nathan
President
Robert R. Nathan
  Associates, Inc.

Russell E. Palmer
Managing Partner
Touche Ross & Company

Jack S. Parker
Vice Chairman of the
  Board
General Electric Company

Harvey Picker
Dean, School of
  International Affairs
Columbia University

Charles H. Pillard
International President
International Brotherhood
  of Electrical Workers

Abe H. Raskin
Associate Director
National News Council

Arthur Ross
Vice Chairman and
  Managing Director
Central National
  Corporation

Stanley H. Ruttenberg
President
Ruttenberg, Friedman,
  Kilgallon, Gutchess &
  Associates, Inc.

Joseph M. Segel
Chairman
Presidential Airways

Robert V. Sellers
Chairman of the Board
Cities Service Company

Jacob Sheinkman
Secretary-Treasurer
Amalgamated Clothing and
  Textile Workers Union,
  AFL-CIO

Joseph E. Slater
President
Aspen Institute for
  Humanistic Studies

O. Pendleton Thomas
Chairman of the Board
The B.F. Goodrich
  Company

J.C. Turner
General President
International Union of
  Operating Engineers

Raymond Vernon
H. F. Johnson Professor of
  International Business
  Management
Harvard University

Martin J. Ward
General President
United Association of
  Journeymen and
  Apprentices of the
  Plumbing and Pipe
  Fitting Industry of the
  United States and
  Canada

Glenn E. Watts
President
Communications Workers
  of America

Carroll L. Wilson
Director
Workshop on Alternative
  Energy Strategies
  (WAES)
Massachusetts Institute of
  Technology

Robert F. Wright
Partner
Arthur Andersen &
  Company

Since the establishment of the Economic Policy Council in 1976, the following members have entered Government service:

Cyrus R. Vance
Secretary of State

Richard Newell Cooper
Under-Secretary of State for Economic Affairs

Richard N. Gardner
Ambassador to Italy

Leonard Woodcock
Special Envoy to China

The following members have joined the Council since the adoption of the Report:

John C. Bierwirth
Chairman of the Board
Grumman Corporation

Stephen M. Boyd
Bryan, Cave, McPheeters & McRoberts

Richard W. Hanselman
Executive Vice President
Beatrice Foods Company

John R. Meyer
1907 Professor in Transportation Logistics and Distribution
Harvard Business School
Harvard University

INDEX

Dʻ

Randall Library – UNCW
HF1411 .N429   NXWW
The New international economic order : a U.S. resp

304900259253%